HISTORIC
WALKS
OF CALGARY

HISTORIC
WALKS
OF CALGARY

HARRY M. SANDERS

Red Deer PRESS

Published by
Red Deer Press
Trailer C
2500 University Drive N.W.
Calgary Alberta Canada T2N 1N4

Credits
Edited by Lee Shenkman
Cover and text design by Erin Woodward
Printed and bound in Canada by Friesens for Red Deer Press

Acknowledgments
Financial support provided by the Canada Council, the Department of
Canadian Heritage, the Alberta Foundation for the Arts, a beneficiary of the
Lottery Fund of the Government of Alberta, and the University of Calgary.

National Library of Canada Cataloguing in Publication
Sanders, Harry Max, 1966–
Historic walks of Calgary / Harry Sanders.
Includes bibliographical references.
ISBN 0-88995-297-3
1. Historic buildings—Alberta—Calgary—Guidebooks. 2. Walking—
Alberta—Calgary—Guidebooks. 3. Calgary (Alta.)—Tours. 4. Calgary
(Alta.)—History. I. Title.
FC3697.7.S24 2005   917.123'38044   C2004-903988-1

5 4 3 2 1

In memory of Diana Sim

Contents

Preface

Although I was born in nearby Drumheller, my family moved to Calgary when I was quite young, and I've long since adopted this city as my hometown. Writing this book has reminded me how strong are the ties that bind.

Both of my parents were born at the Calgary General Hospital—not the post-World War II complex that was imploded for redevelopment in 1998, but the 1910 structure that preceded it. My maternal grandparents, Moishe and Sarah Freedman, lived on the present site of the Victoria Park/Stampede Light Rail Transit station, and my grandfather taught Hebrew lessons at the House of Israel Building in Mission (now Lindsay Park Place condominiums). My mother Miriam grew up in Victoria Park and attended Victoria School, Haultain, Western Canada High, and Mount Royal College. During the 1940s, my mother's parents owned the Shamrock Grocery in the Marwood Block in Erlton. When former city parks superintendent William Reader entered the store in 1943 and suffered a fatal heart attack, it was grandmother who helped him and who called for an ambulance; my mother was present and remembers the event vividly. Like Reader, both of my mother's parents are buried on Cemetery Hill.

For their first date, in 1959, my father Morris took my mother to see *Bridge Over the River Kwai* at the Tivoli Theatre. My paternal grandfather, Harry Srolovitz, lost his leg in a railway accident in the Canadian National Railways yards, now Lindsay Park. I learned to drive on what was still left of the old Royal Canadian Air Force runway at Lincoln Park, before it was replaced by the media village for the 1988 Olympic Winter Games. I worked at the City of Calgary Archives when it was located in the Calgary Public Building, the city's Depression-era post office and federal building that now houses the lobby of the Jack Singer Concert Hall. My bachelor party was at Antonio's Garlic Clove restaurant in the Aberdeen Block in Mission. And my South Calgary home once belonged to Kay Rosettis, widow and former assistant of Joe Rosettis, a newspaper and studio photographer whose *oeuvre*—now housed at the

Glenbow Archives—forms a substantial visual document of Calgary from the 1940s to the 1960s. Decades before I worked for the Glenbow Archives, both Joe and Kay did contract work for the institution and established its first photo lab.

Some look at Calgary and see a modern city with gleaming sky-scrapers and sprawling suburbs. I am surrounded by history.

One building that falls outside this book's purview deserves mention. In the time it took me to write this volume, my friend Diana died and my daughter Anna was born—both at the Foothills Medical Centre. Built as the Foothills Provincial General Hospital in 1966, it is hardly an historic building. If it follows the pattern already set for the city's hospitals, the Foothills will be demolished before it ever becomes one. But it has a special place in my heart, as it has for so many others.

I confess that the tours that follow are closely aligned with my spheres of personal interest and research experience, and they fall within those areas of Calgary that I know best. Everyone has a tour he or she would give to visiting relatives or a newcomer to the city, one that includes the essence of Calgary as they perceive it. This book is mine.

Author's Note

Each of the entries in this book begins with a set of data elements that comprise the building's "vital statistics": original name (often followed by the current building name or primary occupant in parentheses); address; architectural style; architect; and date of construction. The information on the current name and occupant is a snapshot from the publication date and changes with time. Identifying the style of a building is often an approximation, as architects apply elements of stylistic influences but rarely limit themselves to a pure or single style. Even terminology can vary between architects or architectural historians when describing the exact same thing. Where an architect is unknown, it is often possible that the builder followed, or modified, a commercially available pattern. The date of construction is usually given as the completion date of a building, and it could appear different in other sources that supply the commencement date.

This is a book about the history of select buildings in Calgary; it is not an architectural history. Attention is paid to architectural styles and details where it enhances a building's story, provides context, or simply offers the description a reader might need to recognize a building. Serious students of architecture might find a few nuggets here, but should turn elsewhere for a serious examination of the subject.

When following these tours, the reader should be aware that many of the buildings are privately owned and ought to be viewed from a respectful distance on public space. Readers should bring sensible footwear, obey traffic regulations, and be cautious of steep hills and damaged (or in some cases, absent) sidewalks.

Author's Acknowledgements

Researching and writing this book did not begin from scratch, and my first thanks go to those who paved my way. To commemorate the seventy-fifth anniversary of Fort Calgary in 1950, longtime resident Leishmann McNeill wrote "Tales of the Old Town," a series of columns in the *Calgary Herald* that read like a walking tour of Calgary as it was in 1902. Richard Cunniffe's *Calgary in Sandstone*, published in 1969, described the city's many sandstone buildings and indicated their locations. As part of the Century Calgary series of books in 1975, published in celebration of Fort Calgary's centennial, Trudy Cowan (as Trudy Soby) wrote two walking tour books, *Be it Ever So Humble* and *A Walk Through Old Calgary*. Vicky Williams' *Calgary Then and Now*, published in 1978, compared archival photographs of streets and buildings in the city with identical contemporary views. My mother bought me a copy when I was twelve years old, and the book made a deep impression on me. Others have since written walking tour books of select Calgary neighborhoods, and, from 1997–2000, Jennifer Cook Bobrovitz—former Local History Librarian at the Calgary Public Library—contributed her "Cornerstones" column to the *Calgary Herald*. Each of these sources, and the works of other local historians and writers too numerous to mention, has been immensely helpful to me.

I am enormously grateful to architect Lorne Simpson, of Simpson Roberts Architecture Interior Design, for the many hours he spent with me describing building features and identifying building styles. If there are any errors on these pages, they are mine, not his. Since 1995, I have worked with Lorne in his capacity as the city's heritage consultant, and together we have written reports on some 100 buildings for the city's Inventory of Potential Historic Sites. I am also grateful to former heritage planner Rob Graham, current heritage planner Darryl Cariou, and planner Brenda Etherington for their assistance and for sharing their knowledge. I owe a debt of gratitude to the historians who preceded me in working on the inventory, including Sandy Aumonier, Donna Bloomfield, Marianne Fedori, Dr. Michael McMordie, and the late Elise Corbet.

As ever, special thanks go to the reference staff at the Calgary Public Library, the Canadian Architectural Archives, the City of Calgary Archives, and particularly my colleagues at the Glenbow Library and Archives: Jim Bowman, Ellen Bryant, Doug Cass, Tonia Fanella, Shona Gourlay, Jennifer Hamblin, Susan Kooyman, Pat Molseky-Brar, Lindsay Moir, Roberta Ryckman, and Lynette Walton. I also wish to thank Alex Wackett and Ji Zhao of the University of Calgary Libraries, and Ted Jeal and Ron Getty of the Calgary Exhibition & Stampede. I am grateful to Bill Yeo and to my mother, Miriam Sanders, for their careful reading of my manuscript and for their useful suggestions. Manfred Baum, Gerald Forseth, Esneva Leiser, William McLennan, and Robert Walker also provided valuable assistance, and Barry Elmer generously shared his research on Calgary architects and their commissions. Shannon Lee Rae, Lisa Thomson, Karen Olson, and Kirsten Olson spent many hours taking photographs of buildings for me. My thanks also go out to Dennis Johnson and the staff of Red Deer Press, and to my copyeditor, Lee Shenkman, for their support and their patience.

Finally, and most importantly, I wish to thank my dear wife Kirsten Olson. For too many months while I was absorbed in writing, Kirsten managed our household, raised Jonas, and gave birth to Anna. Their summer stay at the Olson farm near Cremona, where Grandma and Grandpa helped enormously, gave me much-needed time to work. For that I am deeply grateful, and now I'm ready to catch up on my chores.

Introduction

Toward the end of Booth Tarkington's 1918 novel *The Magnificent Ambersons*, best known through Orson Welles' 1942 screen adaptation, protagonist George Amberson Minafer takes a sad, slow walk homeward "through what appeared to be the strange streets of a strange city". In his absence at college and abroad—and even after his return, while he wasn't paying attention—the nameless Midland town of George's youth had changed irrevocably.

On the streets of Calgary in the 1970s, the rare person who grew up in the city—lost amid hundreds of newcomers who arrived every month, drawn by a frenzied oil boom—probably felt like George Minafer. Everywhere, landmark buildings that had stood for generations were being demolished; just as quickly, shiny office towers rose to replace them. The pace was dizzying. Between 1971 and 1981, Calgary's population increased by half (from about 400,000 to nearly 600,000), and its downtown skyline and streetscapes changed almost beyond recognition.

Many hailed the transformation as progress. Some condemned it as senseless destruction and mourned the loss of architectural jewels, ranging from the original rusticated sandstone courthouse (demolished in 1958) to the Southam Building with its hundreds of gargoyles (torn down in 1972).

It had all happened before. Nearly a decade passed between the creation of the province of Alberta in 1905 and the outbreak of World War I. Calgary underwent a phenomenal boom in that period; its population grew tenfold, from roughly 4,000 in 1901 to more than 40,000 a decade later. Municipal borders expanded massively, with new streetcar lines crisscrossing existing neighborhoods and stretching outward to distant, modern subdivisions. And old, familiar landmarks that dated back to frontier days made way for scores of new Edwardian buildings. In 1911, with the original Town Hall about to be demolished, the *Morning Albertan* (the forerunner of the *Calgary Sun*) prophesied:

> Some day in the dim and distant future Calgary
> people will seriously regret the absence of the relics of
> the days gone by, such as the old town hall and the like,
> and will marvel that the city officials in ancient days
> were so shortsighted as to dispose of them for their
> value as firewood.[1]

The *Albertan*'s warning went unheeded, and only the real estate crash of 1913 ended the city's process of destroying and renewing itself. The cycle began anew after the 1947 discovery at Leduc, Alberta, that launched the province's oil boom and made Calgary the industry's regional headquarters. It returned with a vengeance when oil prices rose sharply in the 1970s. Like those who move west to reinvent their lives, the city they come to reinvents itself.

But the past is not so easy to erase, as a stroll through many of Calgary's older districts will reveal to the keen-eyed observer. Some buildings have been preserved through serendipity or through their undiminished economic viability, others through preservation efforts. One response to the loss of built heritage came in 1964, with the creation of Heritage Park Historical Village and its transplanted architectural relics. Another was the movement to preserve historic buildings *in situ*. That cause suffered many losses before the 1970s, when provincial and municipal governments took steps to evaluate, designate, and protect historic resources. The Alberta Heritage Act, passed in 1973 and renamed the Alberta Historical Resources Act in 1975, allows the provincial and local governments to preserve heritage buildings and sites. The Calgary Heritage Authority advises City Council on heritage matters, and the city employs a full-time Heritage Planner. While the loss of historic buildings continues, government programs and incentives—combined with public awareness and initiative—ensure victories as well.

With its towering steel and glass skyscrapers, its endless modern suburbs, and its collective focus on the future, Calgary propagates its own greatest myth: that it is a city without history. But native archaeological sites, a reconstructed Mounted Police fort, and hundreds of historic homes, warehouses and commercial buildings that have escaped the wrecker's ball record the progress of a nineteenth century cowtown into a twenty-first century metropolis. Alternating boom-and-bust cycles created their own legacies, providing architectural examples of the pre-World War I real estate boom, a late-1920s economic recovery, and the petroleum wealth that flowed after Leduc. These are the hidden architectural gems that enrich the city's life.

Notes
1 "Editorial Notes," *Morning Albertan* 26 Jan. 1911: 3.

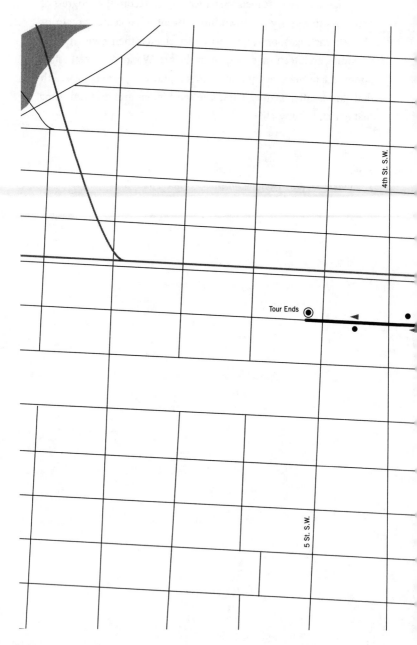

Tour Ends

4th St. S.W.

5 St. S.W.

Civic Centre and Stephen Avenue

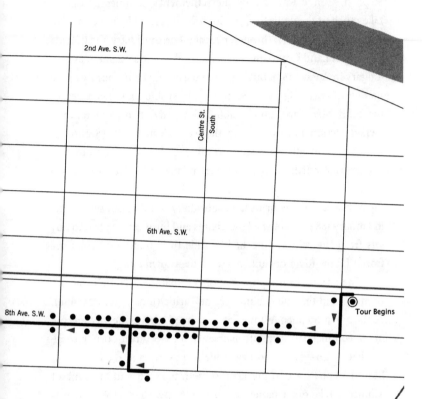

2nd Ave. S.W.

Centre St. South

6th Ave. S.W.

8th Ave. S.W.

Tour Begins

10 Ave. S.W.

1 St. S.E.

S.W.

Even before Calgary's incorporation as a town in November 1884, Stephen Avenue was already the settlement's commercial centre. Like much of the downtown, its location was fixed by the Canadian Pacific Railway (CPR) through its real estate subsidiary, the Canada Northwest Land Company. The CPR reached the settlement at Fort Calgary in August 1883, but bypassed the existing community in the shadow of Fort Calgary (in Section 14, Township 24, Range 1 west of the Fifth Meridian), and established its station on the railway-owned section immediately to the west (Section 15). (Section 15 stretches from 6th Street S.E. to 4th Street S.W., and from 17th Avenue S.W. north to the Bow River and beyond.) The corporation laid out streets and avenues—most of them named for officials of the railway company or its land subsidiary—and began selling lots in January 1884. Established merchants and businessmen had to buy lots from the railway, and had to slide their buildings across the frozen Elbow River or build anew on their town lots.

The avenue fronting the station was named Atlantic (now 9th Avenue), and the one behind became Pacific (today's 10th Avenue). To the north, Stephen Avenue (later renamed 8th Avenue) became the main commercial strip. Its namesake was Scottish-born George Stephen (1829–1921), who began life in poverty and died as Baron Mount Stephen, a past president of both the CPR and the Bank of Montreal. Like other named roads in the city, Stephen Avenue was stripped of its name in 1904, becoming simply 8th Avenue. In 1969–70, it was closed to traffic and re-invented as the Stephen Avenue Mall (later renamed Stephen Avenue Walk). Evening traffic returned after the mall received a facelift in the 1990s. However, during the day it remains a pedestrian mall, and one can freely cross from one side to the other at any point, except for the cross streets where there are traffic lights. For evening tours, one should be cautious of two-way traffic, or cross Stephen Avenue only at the crossing lights.

Through a combination of historical circumstance and deliberate city planning, Stephen Avenue has become an island of history amid a sea of land development. The best examples of local sandstone construction—largely produced between the great fire of 1886 and the economic crash of 1913—can be found here. Successive eras of development, of the boom and bust cycles of a resource-based economy, have left their imprint through the historic buildings that crowd the mall's five city blocks. Many of the façades were restored in the 1990s through a joint municipal-provincial program administered by the city on behalf of the Stephen Avenue Heritage Area Society. In 2002, the Historic Site of Monuments Board of Canada recognized a portion of the mall as the Stephen Avenue National Historic District, one of only three such designations in western Canada.

Calgary's great fire of November 7, 1886, looking north across Atlantic Avenue (now 9th Avenue) to the present site of the Glenbow Museum and TELUS Convention Centre, South Building. GLENBOW ARCHIVES NA-298-3

The tour begins at the front steps of City Hall.

City Hall
Address: 800 Macleod Trail S.E.
Style: Romanesque Revival
Architect: William M. Dodd
Date: 1911

Calgary's original Town Hall was built in 1885 at the corner of McIntyre Avenue and Drinkwater Street—where a strip of grass now separates the sandstone City Hall from Macleod Trail. Renamed City Hall when Calgary became a city in 1894, it was briefly used as a homeless shelter before being demolished in 1911. A replica has been built at Heritage Park. GLENBOW ARCHIVES NA-2861-16

As he walked up the steps of Calgary's City Hall on a June day in 1911, then turned the gold key to officially open the new sandstone edifice, federal Conservative Leader (and soon-to-be prime minister) Robert L. Borden walked right past a cornerstone that read A.D. 1907. If the inscription caught his eye, the future prime minister might have wondered why the building took so long to complete.

The sod-turning ceremony took place in 1907, and the cornerstone was laid on September 15, 1908. But problems soon developed. Building operations halted abruptly in early 1909 when the $150,000 budget was exhausted. The City Council had to pass a money by-law to authorize additional funds, and, at that time, money by-laws first had to be approved at the ballot by the ratepayers. The by-law was defeated at the polls, the contractor walked off the job, and William Dodd was fired as the supervising architect. For the better part of a year, the partly-finished municipal building remained an idle construction site.

Construction resumed in 1910 with Ernest Butler and Gilbert Hodgson as supervising architects, and City Hall was finally completed at twice the original estimate. Officials moved in at the beginning of 1911. Decorations included newly commissioned oil paintings of all of Calgary's past mayors and 210 palm trees, one of which still survived as late as 1935.

Within a year, City Hall was already too small for the expanding civic administration. Calgary had grown from a population of 4,000 in 1901 to more than 43,000 in 1911, and the city experienced a spectacular real estate boom and massive physical expansion in the years leading up to World War I. In 1913, the City Council hired English town planner Thomas Mawson to develop a long-range plan for Calgary's growth. Part of Mawson's comprehensive scheme envisioned a future civic centre south of Prince's Island, complete with a museum, exhibition hall, gardens, a boating reach—and a grand new City Hall. But the real estate bubble burst later in 1913, and the Mawson plan was shelved.

Crowded officials found some relief in 1914, when the police department moved out of the basement into its new headquarters building behind City Hall. One of the cells still remained, complete with graffiti carved by prisoners, until the building was substantially upgraded in the late 1995–97.

One major alteration took place in 1920, when the removal of the upper north side balcony fractured the building's symmetry. The south balcony, which for decades faced a back alley, was eventually closed in. With the completion of the Calgary Municipal Building in 1985 and the creation of a Municipal Plaza at that time, the south balcony again became an attractive feature of City Hall. The balcony is part of the mayor 's suite of offices.

City Hall holds many memories apart from the proceedings of City Council. The fourth floor once housed an apartment for the caretaker and his family. Generations of Calgary children came to City Hall to see the public health dentist. Visitors admired the six-foot-long scale model of the RMS *Calgaric*, a passenger liner owned by the same shipping company as the *Titanic*. (The city donated the model to the Glenbow Museum in 1962.) It was here that *Calgary Herald* reporter Chief Buffalo Child Long Lance threw a mock bomb into Mayor Samuel Adams' office in 1921—a prank that frightened one of the city commissioners into leaping out the window (he was uninjured), and also ended Long Lance's journalistic career. It was here that a mentally ill woman shot medical health officer William Hill in the back in 1937. (Dr. Hill survived, and his first request during his convalescence was for a cigarette.) It was here that elevator operators John Joseph (termed " a perfect mine of information" and "the politest elevator man in the world"[1]) and his successor, Billy Goodman, probably got to know just about everyone in town. And it was here that Jack Miller, Calgary's city clerk from 1912 to 1955, stashed away a mass of documents that now comprises much of the city's archives.

Those archives would have proved useful when the city's coat of arms was adopted in 1902. The arms are carved in relief at the top of City Hall's entrance arch, and they include a glaring error. The scroll below the shield has two dates, signifying Calgary's incorporation as a town (1882) and as a city (1894). The designers had not done their homework: Calgary had become a town in 1884, not 1882. The legal description of the coat of arms was amended in 1975, but the correction was never made to its sandstone representation over the City Hall entrance.

For years, a tall Christmas tree was placed under the central canopy, rising through the circular opening on each floor; employees from all departments could decorate the tree from their own floor. The openings were eventually closed in. However, they were re-opened when the building was extensively upgraded in 1995–97, with some of its historic architectural features restored.

City Hall was declared a Provincial Historic Resource in 1978 and a National Historic Site in 1984. In 1990 it became Calgary's first Municipal Historic Resource.

Civic Centre

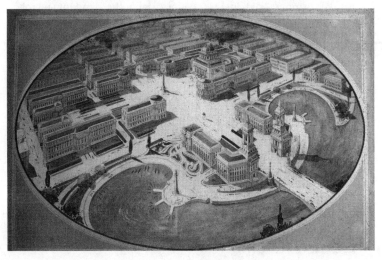

Thomas Mawson proposed a civic centre south of Prince's Island, but his plan was never realized. GLENBOW ARCHIVES

Before City Hall was built, aldermen considered locating it further west—some thought this corner too far east from the city centre. Urban renewal projects beginning in the 1960s helped remold the City Hall vicinity from an aging commercial zone into a civic centre with a concentration of public institutions. The W. R. Castell Library opened in 1963, replacing the original Carnegie Library in Memorial Park as the library system's flagship. Both publicly funded school boards—the Calgary Board of Education and the Calgary Separate School Board—constructed new headquarters buildings a block north. Mayor Ross Alger promoted a grand civic centre scheme in the late 1970s, and the discovery of Thomas Mawson's long-lost drawings at that time—they were being used as wallboard in a northwest garage—lent the proposal a sense of historical determinism. The $250-million project was defeated by plebiscite, but many of its elements—a municipal government building, performing arts centre, and public plaza—have since been realized. The construction of the Calgary Municipal Building and the Calgary

Centre for Performing Arts (later renamed the EPCOR Centre for the Performing Arts) in 1985, coupled with the development of Olympic Plaza in advance of the XV Olympic Winter Games in 1988, finally transformed a district of second-hand shops, greasy spoon restaurants, and old hotels into a public space.

Route: Cross Macleod Trail (originally known as Drinkwater Street), and enter Olympic Plaza. An east-facing interpretive panel, mounted on the Olympic arch structure, tells the history of the Olympic Plaza site. Now proceed south through Olympic Plaza to the Burns Building, the first stop on Stephen Avenue.

Burns Building

Address: 237–8th Avenue S.E.
Style: Chicago (Classical influence)
Architects: Hodgson, Bates and Beattie
Date: 1912

The rise of Patrick Burns (1855–1937) from poverty to cattle king exemplifies Calgary's early prosperity as the heart of a ranching district, and this striking six-story office tower illustrates his success. The poor Ontario farm boy moved first to Manitoba, where he started buying cattle and filling beef contracts for crews building the CPR in the 1880s. He reached Calgary in 1890, built a slaughterhouse, and established himself as a regional meat supplier. Within a few years, he expanded into ranching, meat-packing, and retailing on a large scale, and, by World War I, he had become one of Canada's most successful entrepreneurs. Burns was one of four wealthy ranchers, immortalized as the "Big Four," who offered a collective $100,000 as a financial guarantee for the original Calgary Stampede in 1912. The building remained headquarters for Burns' food empire until the building was sold in 1923.

The Burns Building is clad in terra cotta, a glazed and molded ceramic tile. The 1980s annex follows a mandatory setback from Stephen Avenue, giving it a shallower footprint than the original building. Stylized metal framing mimics the cornice of the older structure. SHANNON LEE RAE

The Burns Building's original 1911 design called for a two-story building, but, by its completion in 1913, four floors of offices had been added. Lion figures protrude from the terra cotta façade, clenching chains in their teeth to support the ground-floor canopy. Embossed letters still identify two separate front entrances as "Market" and "Offices." The large, projecting upper cornice and small cornice between the second and third floors display a typical classical feature: dentils. These tooth-like projections are strictly decorative, resembling the ends of heavy wooden beams used in building construction in past centuries. The name is derived from the obsolete French word for teeth (*dentille*).

The proposed development of a "civic centre" in the late 1970s nearly spelled the end for the Burns Building, and only a single vote in a crucial 1980 City Council decision spared it from demolition. The building was renovated and expanded in tandem with the construction of the adjacent performing arts centre between 1980 and 1983. It was designated a Provincial Historic Resource in 1987.

Route: Proceed west on Stephen Avenue, and remain on the south side of the mall.

Calgary Centre for Performing Arts (EPCOR Centre for the Performing Arts)

Address: 205–8th Avenue S.E.
Style: No particular style
Architect: Raines Finlayson Barrett & Partners
Date: 1985

The Burns Building and Calgary Public Building form historic "bookends" for the EPCOR Centre for the Performing Arts. Interpretive panels in the centre's Engineered Air Theatre recall the history of the Empress Theatre, which once stood on this block. AUTHOR PHOTO

In one of his final acts as Alberta's premier, Peter Lougheed (along with then-mayor Ralph Klein) officially opened the Calgary Centre for Performing Arts (later renamed for its corporate sponsor, an Edmonton-based power supplier) on September 14, 1985. Two historic structures—the Burns Building and the Calgary Public Building—serve as "bookends," and the varied brick and glass façade gives the impression of a streetscape rather than a monolith. The block's original streetscape, which had evolved in the course of Calgary's first century, was carefully photographed before being leveled in 1980. Longtime Calgarians recall such landmark 8th Avenue businesses as Jaffe's Book and Music Exchange (the city's largest, oldest second-hand bookstore, located here from 1927–80), the Empress Theatre (built around 1911, and reinvented in 1949 as the Hitchin' Post, which offered a program of western films), and the Modern Café, a popular greasy spoon. The 9th Avenue side was once the site of the Alexandra Hotel (built in 1911 by Albert A. Dick, who later survived the *Titanic* disaster) and the Macleod Bros. clothing store (built around 1906).

Route: Proceed west on Stephen Avenue, and cross to the north side of the mall when you see the Famous Five statues to your right.

Women are Persons! (The Famous Five statues)

In the 1920s, a petition from five Alberta women—Emily Murphy, Louise McKinney, Nellie McClung, Irene Parlby, and Henrietta Muir Edwards—resulted in the "Persons Case" that advanced women's rights in Canada. On October 18, 1929, the Judicial Committee of the Privy Council in England, the highest legal authority of the day, ruled that Canadian women are persons qualified to sit in the Senate—a far-reaching decision.

Exactly seventy years later, Governor General Adrienne Clarkson unveiled *Women are Persons!*, artist Barbara Paterson's larger-than-life bronze tableau, adjacent to the Dominion Bank Building on Stephen Avenue. (A second version was later unveiled on Parliament Hill in Ottawa. Both monuments were made possible through the Calgary-based Famous Five Foundation.)

In the 1930s, a city assessor described the buildings on the site as "several shacks used as stores, of no intrinsic value but producing some revenue."[2] They were demolished in 1946 and replaced by a single-story brick building with four storefronts, itself demolished in the early 1980s.

Barbara Patterson's Women are Persons! *(1999) commemorates the Famous Five women involved in the 1929 Persons Case. City Hall and the Calgary Municipal Building are seen in the distance.* SHANNON LEE RAE

Route: Continue west on Stephen Avenue to 1st Street S.E. (originally Osler Street).

Dominion Bank Building (Teatro Restaurant)

Address: 200–8th Avenue S.E.
Style: Edwardian Classical
Architect: G. W. Northwood, Winnipeg
Date: 1912

In 1875, Sergeant George Clift King (1848–1935) became the first officer of the North-West Mounted Police (NWMP) to set foot on the future site of Fort Calgary. Ten years later, he became Calgary's second postmaster, and, in 1886, he was elected Calgary's second mayor. King built his store and post office block on this site in 1885. He sold the store to Thomas Hatfield but remained postmaster until 1921. King was awarded the Order of the British Empire for his thirty-five years' service.

With its classical features, the Dominion Bank Building resembles an ancient Greek temple—intentionally. Architecture subliminally communicated the bank's permanence to its customers. The white terra cotta surface added drama to the design and is typical of Beaux-Arts style. Shannon Lee Rae

The Dominion Bank demolished the store in 1911 to make way for its new Calgary headquarters. Completed in 1912, the Dominion Bank Building was designed to resemble ancient Greek temples, subliminally appropriating the permanence of such structures to emphasize the bank's stability and create confidence in its future. Its terra cotta façade heralded a new, post-sandstone generation of buildings. It was declared a Provincial Historic Resource in 1979.

After its merger with the Bank of Toronto in 1955, the renamed Toronto-Dominion Bank remained in the building until 1986. Raines Finlayson Barrett & Partners, the architects who designed the performing arts centre, converted the building into their corporate offices and added a fourth floor with a glass mansard roof. Teatro Restaurant took over the main floor in 1994.

Route: Cross to the south side of the mall.

Calgary Public Building
Address: 201–8th Avenue S.E.
Style: Modern Classical
Architect: R. C. Wright, Chief Government Architect,
Department of Public Works (supervised locally by
Charles Sellens)
Date: 1931

Ionic columns form a grand entrance to the Calgary Public Building, designed by the federal Department of Public Works and built during the Great Depression. KAREN OLSON

Calgary's phenomenal growth in the years preceding World War I led the Dominion government to demolish its four-story, sandstone post office and federal government building—built on this site in 1894—and plan a massive replacement befitting the growing metropolis. In 1912, a temporary, single-story frame post office was constructed a block away, on the present site of Olympic Plaza, and demolition of the old building commenced in 1913. By the end of the year, the real estate boom had turned bust, and the outbreak of war the following year froze all government funds for the project. The site remained fenced in and vacant for the next eighteen years, and the "temporary" post office served until 1919, after which it enjoyed a long career as the City Hall Market (1920–55). The post office, meanwhile, shuttled between venues until the Calgary Public Building was finally constructed in 1930–31. An economic reversal had derailed the project, and it was finally completed during the depths of the Great Depression.

Prime Minister R. B. Bennett, the Member of Parliament for Calgary West, officially opened the eight-story Calgary Public Building on August 24, 1931. It boasted a Manitoba Tyndall limestone façade, marble floors, solid bronze radiators, and manually operated brass elevators that remain in use in the twenty-first century, the last of their kind in the city. The first three floors were dedicated to post office services, while the upper five became government and military offices. The post office moved to a new building west of the Palliser Hotel in 1961, and, in 1979, remaining federal offices were relocated to the new Harry Hays Building in Chinatown. The city purchased the federal building, which lay in the path of the civic centre that Mayor Ross Alger intended to build in the late 1970s. Despite opposition, both the Calgary Public Building and the Burns Building were spared demolition and incorporated into the new Calgary Centre for Performing Arts, with the main floor of the public building adapted as the lobby of the Jack Singer Concert Hall. The upper floors house the city parks department. It became a Municipal Historic Resource in 1996.

Route: Cross 1st Street S.E. (formerly Osler Street). The Glenbow Museum and original convention centre (South Building) are on the south side of the block, to your left. The newer North Building is on the north side, to your right. Begin on the south side.

Glenbow Museum and Calgary Convention Centre (TELUS Convention Centre South Building)

Address: 130–9th Avenue S.E.
Style: Brutalist influence
Architect: A. Dale & Associates
Date: 1975

The Glenbow Museum preserves and makes available art, artifacts, documents, photographs, and publications that record the history not only of this city and region, but of western Canada. Ironically, an historic city block had to be leveled to build the museum, hotel, and convention centre complex in the early 1970s. SHANNON LEE RAE

Former prime minister John G. Diefenbaker opened the original Calgary Convention Centre (later expanded and named for TELUS, the telephone giant that began as Alberta Government Telephones) in 1975. The sprawling concrete complex also includes the Marriott Hotel (originally the Four Seasons) and the eight-story Glenbow Museum, which, along with its library and archives, preserves and makes available the history of the city, the province, and the prairie region. It replaced nearly two dozen historic buildings, including sixteen along Stephen Avenue. One of them was the Maclean Block, where historian Grant MacEwan (1902–2000)—who also served as mayor of Calgary and as Alberta's lieutenant-governor—rented an office and wrote many of his popular local history books.

Route: Cross to the north side of the mall.

TELUS Convention Centre North Building
Address: 136–8th Avenue S.E.
Style: Post-modern
Architect: Graham Edmunds Architecture
Date: 2000

Looking west along 8th Avenue from 1st Street S.E., 1905. The south side of this block (left) was cleared in the 1970s to build the Glenbow Museum and convention centre. On the north side, the Thomson Bros. Block, centre rear, is faintly visible. The Calgary Furniture Company building, identified in the entablature by the name of its owner "F. F. Higgs," can be seen in the right foreground. Glenbow Archives NA-468-6

When the convention centre's South Building was constructed in the early 1970s, its site was leveled before construction began. But attitudes towards heritage preservation had changed by 2000, when the North Building and the contiguous Hyatt Regency Hotel were completed. Each of these complexes incorporates a handful of historic structures and historic façades.

Nonetheless, the three-story Crown Building and the former Calgary Furniture Store were demolished in 1997 to make way for the North Building. Constructed in 1911, the Crown Building (705–1st Street S.E.) briefly housed the office of the *Calgary Eye Opener*, the satirical paper published by social critic Robert Chambers Edwards. (Edwards made his longtime home and office in the Cameron Block, which also stood on the present site of the North Building until its destruction by fire in 1961.) Another Crown Building occupant was the Equine Meat Market, where horse-meat lovers of 1950s Calgary could indulge their particular cravings. For years, a large painted sign on the building's north wall proclaimed, "Give your dog and cat a treat, get them Perky, good to eat." The building's longtime owner, Jack Singer (namesake for the Jack Singer Concert Hall) was a partner in the Red Top and Perky pet food company. The Crown Building was demolished in 1998.

Built in 1903, the two-story Calgary Furniture Store building (228–8th Avenue S.E.) housed its original occupant for a decade. The next occupants were the White Lunch restaurant on the ground floor and MacLennan's Dancing Academy upstairs. Both businesses were ransacked by a mob of soldiers in February 1916, during World War I. A rumor that the restaurant manager was employing enemy aliens sparked two days of anti-German riots. Soldiers with bayonets guarded public buildings, the Palliser Hotel, and the brewery. The building later housed Cristy's Furniture and finally Western Outfitters before its demolition in 1997.

Route: Continue west on Stephen Avenue.

Neilson Block (TELUS Video Conference Centre)

Address: 118–8th Avenue S.E.

Style: Romanesque Revival (1903 building); Edwardian Classical (1910 addition)

Architect: Thomas A. Brown; Lawson & Fordyce (1910 addition)

Date: 1903 (addition 1910)

Exactly eight months after Calgary's incorporation as a city on New Year's Day 1894, furniture merchant Hugh Neilson (1849–1918) and his family arrived from their native Chatham, Ontario. Neilson quickly incorporated the Neilson Furniture Company, whose objects included "the manufacturing and dealing in furniture, upholstery, musical instruments, sewing machines and general household goods, and to deal in carpets and undertakers' supplies, and to carry on the business of undertakers."[3] As he had done in Chatham, Neilson won election to Calgary's city council in 1899, and he also became president of the local Liberal Association.

Neilson built a three-story sandstone shop on Stephen Avenue in 1903, and in 1910 he added two more floors. The contrast in appearance illustrates changes in architectural preferences and stone-cutting technology. The rough-hewn stones of the 1903 building are consistent with its contemporaries, and the rounded windows reflect a preference for Romanesque Revival style. The smooth-dressed stones of the 1910 addition, and its rectangular windows, illustrate the use of advanced stone-cutting machinery and a shifting preference to Classical Revival style. The building suffered fire damage in 1937 and 1987. Neilson's Furniture remained at this address until 1968, and, by the 1980s, it provided low-cost studio and gallery space for local artists. The façade was incorporated into the new convention centre in 2000, but the rest of the structure was demolished. Its recessed storefronts, typical of Edwardian Commercial buildings, were designed to give shopkeepers space for outdoor displays or merchandise stands.

The original 1903 Neilson Block was built of rusticated sandstone with a rubble foundation. The smooth-cut two-story stone addition built in 1910 reflects changing architectural tastes and the arrival of stone-cutting technology. SHANNON LEE RAE

Route: Continue west on Stephen Avenue.

Doll Block (Kanata Trading Post)

Address: 116–8th Avenue S.E.
Style: Richardson Romanesque
Architects: John A. Maycock, completed by Dowler and Michie
Date: 1907

Since it was built in 1907, the building once known as "Doll's Diamond Palace" has borne the name "L. H. Doll" in its parapet. Ontario-born Louis Henry Doll (1867–1961) arrived in Calgary in 1889 and, for the next twenty years, operated a well-known business as a jeweler, watch-maker, and optician. Only a year after he built this ornately decorated building—described as "the largest and most handsome jewelry house west of Toronto"—tragedy struck. Doll's ten-year-old daughter Florence died of scarlet fever, plunging the pioneer businessman into depression. He lost interest in his jewelry business and in 1921 was committed to the mental institution at Ponoka, Alberta.

After his brief apprenticeship to Doll, David E. Black (1880–1972) established his own 8th Avenue jewelry shop, which has since been re-created at Heritage Park. Black relocated his business to the Doll Block in 1910, where it fell victim that Christmas to what was then Calgary's largest ever jewelry heist. Pretending to deliver a package to Black's office, the noon-hour thief—who was never caught—made off with some $10,000 worth of gems. By the time Black sold out to Henry Birks & Sons in 1920, he employed sixty-five people and operated the largest watch repair shop in western Canada. He headed the Chamber of Commerce in 1923 and became a lifetime director of the Calgary Exhibition & Stampede, for which he manufactured souvenir pins. As alderman from 1918–21, Black served under the City Hall clock his firm had installed in 1911.

Appropriately for a watchmaker, Black was a frequent time-keeper for foot races, chuckwagon races, wrestling bouts, and box-ing matches in the city. His wife Mae Lillian (1882–1955) was a founder and president of the Alberta Tuberculosis Association.

Restored in 1994, the Doll Block was one of five historic buildings incorporated into the TELUS Convention Centre and Hyatt Hotel in 2000. To the west, simplified interpretations of the Doll Block fill in two gaps in the historic streetscape on either side of the Thomson Bros. Block. SHANNON LEE RAE

The next jeweler to occupy the Doll Block was Hedley R. Chauncey, a former business associate of Black's. Chauncey bought the building, renamed it the Chauncey Block, and operated his business here until 1946. A longtime alderman and chairman of the parks and playgrounds committee, Chauncey contested the mayoralty in 1945 and lost.

Sandstone arches and bands punctuate the Doll Block's red brick façade, creating a polychromatic effect. Seashell patterns adorn the third-floor oriel window, and, at the top, two small bartisan turrets flank the detailed brick and stone parapet. The Doll Block was restored in 1994 to house offices for the Calgary International Organ Festival and the Esther Honens International Piano Competition. It was incorporated into the new TELUS Convention Centre in 2000.

Route: Continue west on Stephen Avenue.

Thomson Bros. Block (Thomsons Restaurant)

Address: 112–8th Avenue S.E.
Style: Romanesque Revival
Architect: H. D. Johnson
Date: 1893

After apprenticing in a bookshop in their native province, Ontario-born brothers James Arthur and Melville Patrick Thomson moved to Portage la Prairie, Manitoba, in 1881 and established themselves as booksellers, stationers, and "fancy goods dealers". Melville moved to Calgary in 1884 to open a second store, and James followed in 1887. The brothers expanded their business to include a printing service and lending library, and for a time they published a monthly literary and humor journal. They built this three-story sandstone block to house their business in 1893. Its curved parapet coping and central pediment resemble the false fronts typically seen on wooden buildings of that era, which, with its rounded windows, charac-

Round-headed windows on the third floor are typical of Romanesque Revival style. A checkerboard pattern on the third story adds variety to the sandstone façade. The curved parapet coping and central pediment resemble false fronts typically seen on wooden buildings of the Thomson Bros. Block's era. SHANNON LEE RAE

terizes the Thomson Bros. Block with the hybrid "Boomtown Romanesque" style. The brothers later settled in Vancouver; they sold their bookstore to future mayor James S. Mackie in 1900 but remained absentee landlords of the building until 1916. It became a Provincial Historic Resource in 1981 and was incorporated into the Hyatt Regency Hotel in 2000. The ground floor houses the hotel's Thomsons Restaurant.

An 1899 love triangle in the apartments upstairs nearly led to murder. A year earlier, twenty-five year old Edward Harris and his wife had moved to Calgary from New Brunswick. Edward went into business with George Gouin, an auctioneer and commission agent who lived in a bachelor suite in the Thomson block, and, before long, the Harrises moved into an apartment across the hall. Edward eventually became suspicious of the relationship between his friend and his wife. The drama unfolded on Saturday, November 4, 1899. Edward returned early from a day at the Calgary Gun Club, and checked on friends his wife was to visit. They had not seen her. Edward returned to the Thomson block and saw Gouin's blinds lowered. Edward's wife was not home. He took a gun from his drawer and hurled himself against Gouin's door, broke it down, and saw Gouin and Mrs. Harris. As the two men wrestled, Edward's gun was fired into Gouin's abdomen. While his wife hailed a doctor from down the hall, Edward fled in his horse and buggy. He got as far as Midnapore before deciding to turn back and give himself up.

Gouin survived his injury and Edward was charged with attempted murder. Crown prosecutor Arthur L. Sifton, the city solicitor and future Liberal premier of Alberta, considered it an easy case. Edward's lawyer was a relative newcomer to Calgary—R. B. Bennett, who later became provincial Conservative leader and served as prime minister of Canada from 1930–35. This was the case that made Bennett's legal reputation in Calgary. The young defense lawyer exposed Gouin's prolific love life and characterized him as a homewrecker. Public sympathy sided with Harris, and the jury deliberated only ten minutes before acquitting him.

Route: Continue west on Stephen Avenue. The next two
buildings are treated as one stop.

Lineham Block (Hyatt Regency Hotel lobby)

Address: 104–8th Avenue S.E.

Style: Victorian-influenced Gothic (originally); Classically-
influenced (after modifications)

Architect: Edward McCoskrie (1907 addition designed by
William M. Dodd)

Date: 1886 (addition 1907)

The I.G. Baker Block, left, and Dunn and Lineham Block, right, appeared identical when this photograph was taken in 1888. Both were later remodeled. GLENBOW ARCHIVES NA-115-11

Imperial Bank of Canada (Catch Restaurant)

Address: 102–8th Avenue S.E.

Style: Victorian-influenced Gothic (originally); Edwardian Classical (after 1909 modifications)

Architect: Edward McCoskrie (1892 alteration designed by Child and Wilson; 1909 alterations by Darling and Pearson, Toronto)

Date: 1886 (later additions)

The same view in 2004 shows the Catch Restaurant (left), restored to its appearance as the Imperial Bank of Canada, and the Lineham Block (right). The stone balustrade above the bank building's dentilled cornice was a 1909 modification.
SHANNON LEE RAE

Calgary's great fire of November 1886 is generally viewed as the dividing point between the wooden frontier town that preceded it and the sandstone city that followed. Local deposits meant quarried stone was readily available, and, after the blaze that destroyed some eighteen buildings, both fire safety and fire insurance rates encouraged its use.

At the time of the conflagration, the Lineham Block and the neighboring Imperial Bank of Canada Building were well under construction or already completed. They were constructed in tandem, shared a common wall, and were originally identical in appearance. Butchers Matthew Dunn (dates unknown) and John Lineham (1858–1913) built the eastern block, which in 1886 housed the first two chartered bank branches in Calgary—the Bank of Montreal and the Imperial Bank of Canada. Lineham became sole owner in 1890, and his estate finally sold the building in 1926. The Ontario-born entrepreneur engaged in farming, ranching, timber, oil, and real estate; he founded the town of Okotoks and served as its first mayor; and he spent three terms in the legislature as a Conservative MLA. He built a two-story brick addition atop the original building in 1907. The Parisian, a locally owned clothing store, occupied the Lineham Block from 1926–88. Modern black glass covered the façade until 2000, when the building was restored to its 1912 appearance and incorporated into the new Hyatt Regency Hotel as the Lineham Lobby, the hotel's Stephen Avenue entrance.

The Imperial Bank of Canada Building was originally constructed to house I. G. Baker and Company, a mercantile firm based in Fort Benton, Montana. Before the CPR arrived in 1883, Fort Benton was a major supply house for southern Alberta, and I. G. Baker held lucrative contracts with the NWMP, including the construction contract for Fort Calgary itself. But the Montana-based company eventually lost its competitive advantage and sold its local interests to the rival Hudson's Bay Company (HBC) in 1891. The Imperial Bank of Canada bought this building in 1892, and it remained a bank branch until the 1960s. The rival Canadian Bank of Commerce kept its branch in the old Burns Block on the opposite corner, and when the two institutions merged in 1961—forming the Canadian Imperial Bank of Commerce—only one would remain. The new CIBC operated from this building while the Burns Block was replaced by a new, purpose-built banking facility. The Imperial Bank Building was designated a Provincial Historic Resource in 1977, and in the 1980s it housed the Alberta Historical Resources Foundation, a provincial body that assists in the interpretation and preservation of Alberta's historical resources.

If for no other reason, the Imperial Bank building would be notable for the law firm of Sifton, Short and Stuart that opened its offices over the bank in 1901. Arthur L. Sifton was the city solicitor who had drafted the city charter in 1893. He went on to become Alberta's first chief justice (1907–10), its second premier (1910–17), and a federal cabinet minister in the Union government during World War I. Sifton attended the Paris Peace Conference in 1919 and was one of two Canadians to sign the Treaty of Versailles. James Short was a high school principal and crown prosecutor, and the namesake for James Short Park. Charles Stuart was a Liberal politician, provincial supreme court justice, and founding chancellor of the University of Alberta.

Route: Cross Centre Street (originally McTavish Street) to the northwest corner on your right. As you cross, observe the Calgary Tower to your left, at the T-intersection formed by Centre Street and 9th Avenue. Calgary's historic Canadian Pacific Railway Station was demolished in 1966 to make way for the Husky Tower, completed in 1968 and later renamed the Calgary Tower.

Another lost landmark is the Burns Block, built at the southwest corner of Stephen Avenue and Centre Street in 1902. Its clock tower, which could be seen from the concourse in front of the railway station, was a landmark until the building was demolished in the early 1960s. The clock mechanism was saved and is now housed in the cupola at the James Short Parkade. Glenbow Archives NA-1437-3

The Canadian Pacific Railway Station was demolished in 1966 to make way for the Calgary Tower. GLENBOW ARCHIVES NA-1451-36

Hudson's Bay Company (Royal Bank of Canada)

Address: 102–8th Avenue S.W.

Style: Italian Renaissance

Architect: C. Osborne Wickenden, Vancouver (1895 addition designed by George Brown; 1905 addition designed by John Woodman)

Date: 1890 (additions 1895, 1905)

When the Calgary settlement moved from its original location around Fort Calgary in 1884, the Hudson's Bay Company acquired this site and built a wood frame store that remained in use until 1890. That year, the HBC built the eastern portion of this rusticated sandstone building, and, in 1895, it was doubled in size. A further addition in 1905 took over the site of a home once occupied by Senator James A. Lougheed (grandfather of Premier Peter Lougheed) and his family.

Calgary's phenomenal growth prior to World War I led the Bay to construct a massive new department store a block west. When it opened in 1913, the Bay sold its old premises to the Royal Bank of Canada for a record-setting fee at the peak of the real estate boom. The building was repaired after a devastating fire in 1921. While the original, modified Italian Renaissance exterior remains, the rear cinderblock wall reveals a complete interior reconstruction that took place in 1977. The Royal Bank brought stonemasons from Britain to work on the façade, including one who had worked on St. Paul's Cathedral, Windsor Castle, and Notre Dame Cathedral in Paris. The building was designated a Registered Historic Resource (a provincial designation, lesser in status than Provincial Historic Resource) in 1982.

The Hudson's Bay Company built the present Royal Bank building in 1890 and moved into its present department store a block west in 1913. GLENBOW ARCHIVES ND-8-277

Route: Cross to the south side of the mall, and proceed a short distance west.

Lougheed Block (Abelia Floral Gallery/Avenue Diner/The Belvedere)

Address: 105, 107–8th Avenue S.W.
Style: Romanesque Revival
Architects: Child and Wilson
Date: 1899

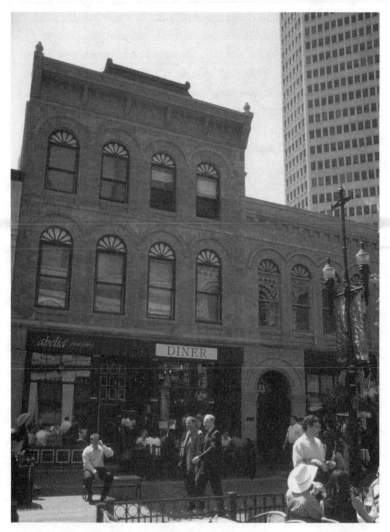

Two buildings comprise the Lougheed Block/Ward Block: the three-story former Great Western Saddlery building and the two-story former Union Bank. The prominent arched entrance to the Union Bank side was restored in the mid-1990s. Banks favored Romanesque Revival style for their branches, and Senator Lougheed evidently built to suit his tenant.

While apparently a single sandstone building, this is actually two separate structures, both built in 1899 as revenue property for Senator James A. Lougheed.

The three-story eastern building originally housed Winnipeg-based Great Western Saddlery, managed by pioneer Calgary saddler Robert John Hutchings. The next tenant, dry goods merchant Glanville's Ltd., gave the building its identification as the Glanville Block during its 1904–12 occupancy. Tom Campbell—who by royal warrant was a hatter for the Prince of Wales—operated his "Smile" Hat Shops here from 1912–32. Campbell's billboard on a barren northeast hill gave that feature its familiar name: Tom Campbell's Hill. Laura Salverson, an Icelandic writer who twice won the Governor General's Award for Literature, kept a studio in the building in the 1930s.

The two-story western building was built to house the Union Bank of Canada, and the branch manager lived in an apartment upstairs. The branch relocated in 1904, and, from 1904–11, the Dominion Bank (a forerunner of TD Canada Trust) maintained a branch here. The building later housed a series of businesses, but the most lasting in memory was one of the shortest-lived occupants: the People's Lunch, which operated briefly in 1919 but whose painted sign is still visible over the rear entrance. (The upscale Belvedere restaurant has occupied the space since 1999.)

In 1911, Lougheed sold both buildings to the Right Honourable William Humble Dudley Ward (1877–1946), and, for many years, both buildings were collectively known as the Ward Block. Ward once held high office in Britain as government whip in the House of Commons and Vice Chamberlain of His Majesty's Household. He was involved in counter-espionage as a commander in the Royal Navy during World War I.

In 1918, the Prince of Wales—the future King Edward VIII, who once bought a hat from Tom Campbell—met and fell in love with Ward's wife Freda. Later dubbed "the first Wallis Simpson," Freda carried on a long-lasting affair with the Prince that shattered her husband's political aspirations. Ward settled in Calgary, where he nobly oversaw the Prince's Canadian business interests.

Both buildings were renovated in 1929 and restored to their historic appearance in 1996–97.

Route: Continue west on Stephen Avenue.

Macnaghten Block (Conga Room/Boodlum Boutiques)

Address: 109–8th Avenue S.W.
Style: Italianate
Architects: Child and Wilson
Date: 1889

This photograph was titled "A Typical Business Block" when it appeared in the Dominion Illustrated *on June 28, 1890—a special edition featuring Calgary. From left to right: the Macnaghten Block; Hutchings and Riley (the future Club Café); and the Calgary Herald Block, with signage in the upper windows for the I.O.O.F. (Independent Order of Odd Fellows), which had its headquarters in the building.*
Courtesy of the Calgary Herald

Frances Alexander Macnaghten (1863–1951), a wealthy Irishman and future son-in-law of the chief justice of the Supreme Court of Canada, took up ranching in what is now the Bowness district in the 1880s. Like his fellow members of the Ranchmen's Club, Macnaghten had strong ties in town: he joined the Calgary Polo Club, invested in the Calgary Brewing & Malting Company, and built the two-story, cream-colored brick Macnaghten Block in 1888–89. (He built a second Macnaghten Block in 1907, which still stands at 207–8th Avenue S.W.) After his titled nephew died without an heir in 1916, Macnaghten returned to Ireland as the Eighth Baronet of County Antrim.

By 1900, the building was known as the Ellis & Grogan Block, for the longtime real estate, insurance, and commercial agency that occupied it. Anthony Grogan was also treasurer of the local Liberal party, and, in 1900, the Liberal committee rooms were housed upstairs. When their Clarence Block office across the street was destroyed by fire on Christmas Day, 1900, lawyers James A. Lougheed and R. B. Bennett—both staunch Conservatives—relocated to the former Liberal rooms.

In 1916, Russian Jewish immigrant Harry Smith (originally Shumiatcher, circa 1894–1979) opened the Boston Hat Works and News Company here. At first there was little space for the few periodicals the store carried. Crowded in the small store were shoe repair, shoeshine, hat cleaning, and news departments. But Harry soon discovered the profit potential of news sales, got out of the shoe business, and renamed the store Harry's News. He found his niche as the city's largest importer of British magazines and newspapers, and before long was known as the "British Mail King of the City." Others called him "the Mayor of 8th Avenue." Harry kept track of his patrons' reading habits. He maintained hundreds of individual mail slots in the store, in each of which he placed a regular customer's favorite publications. Customers could pick up all their reading material in the slot; they could also be sure the store had not sold out their favorite titles.

His growing business gave Harry the opportunity to open a second store, World News and Tobacco, which his younger brother Billy operated for a time. Harry later helped Billy establish his own store, Billy's News, which became a landmark business in its own right. Harry moved to Vancouver in 1934. Harry's News relocated in 1967 and remained in business until the 1990s. The building's façade was restored in 2000.

Route: Continue west on Stephen Avenue.

Club Café (Ha Long Bay II Restaurant)
Address: 111–8th Avenue S.W.
Style: Italianate
Architects: Child and Wilson
Date: 1889

Cowboy Eddie King rode his horse through the Club Café in July 1923. GLENBOW ARCHIVES NA-2768-4

Most fables have a kernel of truth, and the legend that cowboys ride their horses through restaurants during Stampede week began here in 1923. That year marked the first for the annual Calgary Exhibition and Stampede; the big rodeo had been held twice previously, in 1912 and 1919, but only as a special event and not as part of the long-established annual Exhibition. Many now-familiar Stampede traditions, like pancake breakfasts and frontier-style storefront decorations, got their start in 1923. And that July, cowboy Eddie King rode his horse through the Club Café.

The café was the creation of Roy H. Beavers (1885–1968), a Kansas-born restaurateur and sports enthusiast who had first come to Calgary on the carnival circuit and decided to stay. Beavers and his family eventually owned several restaurants, a bakery, and—beginning in 1948—catering services for the Stampede. Beavers was also a Stampede associate director and helped draft a local code of business ethics. He helped form the Calgary Booster Club, which promoted local sports, and served as president of the Calgary Bronks, a precursor to the Calgary Stampeders football club.

Businessman John Lineham (1858–1913), a stockman who later became the first mayor of Okotoks, built this two-story brick and sandstone building in 1889. The first major occupant (from 1889–99) was Hutchings & Riley, the pioneer saddlery firm that succeeded the business of Calgary's first mayor, harnessmaker George Murdoch. When Great West Saddlery took over the business in 1899, partner William J. Riley formed a new association with Eneas McCormick, a future alderman and longtime Stampede associate director. Riley & McCormick, a landmark business still extant in the twenty-first century, occupied this storefront until 1910. It was then transformed into the Globe Theatre—a cinema, live stage and lecture hall that had its own house orchestra—before the Club Café moved in four years later.

The most notable upstairs tenant was photographer Edward Blake "Curly" Curlette, whose work documented Calgary's growth during the first half of the twentieth century. His studio was destroyed in the 1946 blaze that damaged the building.

The façade was reconstructed to its 1889 appearance in 2000 and is largely composed of original salvaged bricks.

Route: Proceed west on Stephen Avenue.

Calgary Herald Block (Divino Wine & Cheese Bistro)

Address: 113–8th Avenue S.W.

Style: Early Commercial

Architect: Unknown (1905 addition designed by Lawson and O'Gara)

Date: 1887 (rear addition 1905)

Arnold Cohen had this sign for Reliable Clothing and Boys' Town painted at the rear of the Arnold Block in 1960. The sign was visible from the 9th Avenue parkade that had been built across the lane in 1958, and an arrow on the sign showed customers who had parked there where to find the store. The parkade has been demolished, the store is gone, but the sign remains. Shannon Lee Rae

Four years after the first issue of the *Calgary Herald, Mining and Ranche Advocate and General Advertiser* was printed from a tent in 1883, the pioneer newspaper moved into this purpose-built two-story sandstone block on Stephen Avenue. Alexander Lucas (1852–1942) and George Eastman (dates unknown) purchased the Herald Printing and Publishing Company in 1886, and, when they built this new headquarters the following year, they reportedly incorporated the canvas tent that had been the paper's original home into the ceiling. Lucas soon bought out Eastman's interest in the paper, but it plunged into financial difficulties and moved to more spartan quarters by the time he sold it in 1894. Lucas has the distinction of being the last mayor of the town of Calgary. On January 1, 1894—only days before Lucas resigned and new elections were held—Calgary became the first city incorporated in the North-West Territories. History also recalls Lucas as the first mayor of the city of Calgary; his successor, Wesley Fletcher Orr (1831–1898), who worked for Lucas as the *Herald*'s editor, was the first person *elected* as mayor of the city of Calgary.

From 1900–15, the building housed the Calgary Wine and Spirit Company, a liquor vendor owned by Quebec-born brothers Athanase, Simeon, and Phileas Laurendeau (who also owned the Edmonton Wine and Spirit Company). Albertans voted the province dry in a 1915 referendum that led to eight years of prohibition (1916–24). The Laurendeaus shifted their business interest to coal mining, and the storefront became a boot and shoe shop until the 1930s. Upstairs occupants included professional offices, club rooms, an art gallery, a dancing academy, and the First Calgary Spiritualist Church, whose members believe it is possible to communicate with the dead.

Clothier Edward Cohen bought the building in 1940 to house his Reliable Clothing Company. He renamed it the Arnold Building (for his son Arnold, who eventually took over the business as Arnold's of Calgary) and covered it with a chrome and vitrolite façade in Moderne style (a contemporary of Art Deco style, less ornamental, and influenced by industrial design). Arnold's moved to the suburbs in the 1970s; the original façade was restored in 2003, when the entire building became the Divino Wine & Cheese Bistro.

Route: Cross to the north side of the mall, and return a
short distance east.

Ashdown's Hardware Block (Micah Gallery & Gifts / Bear & Kilt Pub)

Address: 110–8th Avenue S.W.
Style: Romanesque Revival
Architect: Child and Wilson
Date: 1891

In 1889, Winnipeg-based J. H. Ashdown Hardware acquired the
Calgary Hardware Company, founded in 1885 as Rogers and Grant
Hardware, and retained former owner Archibald Grant as its local
manager. The company demolished the original 1885 store in 1891
and replaced it with this three-story sandstone edifice. The *Herald*
observed that it "presents a noble appearance, suggesting massive-
ness and strength."[4] The year of construction stands in relief on the
sandstone façade.

The company's founder, James Henry Ashdown (1844–1924),
had left his native England and settled at Red River, Manitoba,
where he was held prisoner by Louis Riel's provisional government
during the Manitoba Insurrection of 1870. Ashdown later won a
contract to make stovepipes for the garrison at Fort Garry, and, in
1907–08, he served as mayor of Winnipeg.

As an early remaining example of sandstone construction,
Ashdown's Hardware has rusticated sandstone and the rounded
windows typical of Romanesque Revival style. Generations of
Calgarians knew Ashdown's through this store, which remained in
business until 1971, or through the company's catalog order service.
Local historian Jack Peach once wrote of the elevator at Ashdown's,
a creaky grill-enclosed cage that offered a lofty perspective of the
entire store. "If you couldn't find what you wanted along the many
aisles," he wrote, "you boarded the lift for a bird's eye view, at a
snail's pace, and from up near the ceiling you could spot exactly
what you sought."[5] The building was heavily renovated during

World War I and again in 1949. It housed Kelly's Stereo Mart (1972–87) and was restored in the 1990s. It has housed the Micah Gallery since 2001, and the basement Bear and Kilt Pub since 1993.

This rusticated sandstone building housed a hardware business from 1891–1971.
SHANNON LEE RAE

Route: Proceed west on Stephen Avenue.

Molson's Bank Building (James Joyce Pub)

Address: 114–8th Avenue S.W.
Style: Edwardian Classical
Architect: Unknown
Date: 1912

Calgarians are familiar with the Lougheed Building, a monumental 1912 structure a few blocks from here. Few know that it was the second building by that name. Senator James A. Lougheed—a well-connected Calgary lawyer, socialite, Conservative politician, real estate developer, and grandfather of Premier Peter Lougheed—built his original eponymous block on this site in 1892. The sandstone building collapsed in flames in 1911, just as the senator was building his modern structure on 1st Street S.W.

The present building was completed the following year and originally housed Molson's Bank. Most Canadians recall John Molson (1763–1836) for the brewery he founded, but, like his son, John Jr. (1787–1860), he was both brewer and banker. The younger Molson established Molson's Bank in 1855, and its Calgary branch operated at this location until it was absorbed by the Bank of Montreal in 1925. The next occupant was the Bank of Toronto; after its 1955 amalgamation with the Dominion Bank of Canada, this became a branch of the new Toronto-Dominion Bank until it closed in 1967.

The Indiana limestone façade, with its classical features and lions' heads, reflected a new, post-sandstone era of commercial construction on Stephen Avenue. Engraved dates on the façade indicate the founding date of Molson's Bank and the year of the building's construction; "B of T," engraved on a shield above the main entrance, reflects the Bank of Toronto's occupancy. The James Joyce Pub opened in the building in 1997, and, as an "authentic Irish pub," it does not serve Molson's. The building was designated a Provincial Historic Resource in 1979, and its façade was restored in 2003.

This classical bank building, with its Indiana limestone façade, reflected a new, post-sandstone era of commercial construction on Stephen Avenue. SHANNON LEE RAE

Route: Continue west on Stephen Avenue.

Tribune Block

Address: 118–8th Avenue S.W.
Style: Romanesque Revival
Architect: Child and Wilson
Date: 1892

Long-time Calgarians can hardly forget the *Albertan*, once the only morning newspaper in the province. But few remember that the *Albertan*, like its successor, the *Calgary Sun*, also succeeded an earlier publication—the *Calgary Tribune.*

The *Tribune*'s first editorial, published in 1885, was frank. "We have begun the publication of The *Tribune* mainly for the purpose of earning a livelihood for ourselves," it read.[6] But the *Tribune* was also dedicated to promoting the interests of western Canada. In 1899 it amalgamated with Charles B. Halpin's newly established *Albertan*, and for the next two years it was published under the awkward name *The Albertan and The Alberta Tribune.*

The little paper went through a series of owners and editors until 1902, when William McCartney Davidson took over as "sole owner, sole editor, sole reporter and sole mortgager".[7] Having worked at papers like the *Toronto Star*, Davidson must have been astonished at what he had acquired: a semi-weekly published out of a tiny loft, on a press that was "as contrary an old brute as ever did service in a newspaper office."[8]

That office was the Tribune Block, built by *Tribune* founder Thomas B. Braden (1851–1904) in 1892 and the home of Calgary's morning newspaper until 1907. Braden, a Liberal from Coburg, Ontario, had founded the *Calgary Herald* in 1883 but quickly sold it to Conservative editor Hugh St. Quentin Cayley (for whom Cayley, Alberta, was named). Braden then established the *Tribune*, which he published out of a frame building on this site from 1889–92. The present structure was built with financial backing from Senator James A. Lougheed, who built the adjacent

The façade of this two-story sandstone building was obscured by an Art Moderne treatment in 1938. It was restored in 1976 and again in the 1990s. The title block in the stepped parapet is now a replica of the original and is part of the 1990s restoration. GLENBOW ARCHIVES PA-3527-1

Lougheed Building at the same time. (That original Lougheed Building was destroyed by fire in 1911 and replaced with the present Molson's Bank Building.)

Businessman and hotelier Charles Traunweiser (1873–1954) owned the Tribune Block from 1907–19, and made it the home of his popular Hub Cigar Store and Billiard Hall. Photographer Harry Pollard (1880–1968) lived in the building during Traunweiser's ownership, and Pollard's studio and gallery occupied seven rooms.

Pollard came to Calgary in 1899 at the age of seventeen and quickly set up a portrait studio. In time he became one of Calgary's two pre-eminent photographers. He eventually became nationally famous as the press photographer for the CPR. Collectively, his images of Calgary and southern Alberta are a priceless visual document of our history.

Part of that visual document was forever lost on the afternoon of Sunday, January 25, 1914. A fire broke out in his studio, which was completely destroyed. New technology probably added to the destruction: by 1914, photographers had abandoned glass plates in favor of nitrate plastic film, which was highly flammable.

Pollard understood the historical value of the photographs, some of which he had acquired from another studio that dated back to the 1880s. "The loss is irreparable," he said. "They were photographs of early life and scenes in Calgary when this city was in its frontier days."[9]

Not everyone considered the loss of historic photographs to be the greatest disaster of the fire. Winners of a curling bonspiel had brought their trophy cups to be photographed at Pollard's studio and had left them for the weekend. One newspaper headline said it all: "Three Curling Cups Are Lost in Fire."[10]

The remainder of Pollard's massive collection is now housed at the Provincial Archives of Alberta in Edmonton. Ironically, after retiring in the 1950s, he allegedly considered destroying his 10,000 negatives unless he could find the right home for them. Eventually, the provincial government bought the collection, and it is available for all Albertans to see.

The building later became Binning's Ltd., a clothing store, and Binning's Batchelor Apartments. In 1938, its rough sandstone façade was covered by a white stucco Art Moderne exterior. It later housed Cole's The Book People (1972–86). The Tribune Block was restored in 1976 and again in the 1990s. It was declared a Municipal Historic Resource in 1998. The Tribune Restaurant opened in 2005..

Route: Cross to the south side of the mall.

Art Gallery of Calgary
Address: 117, 119–8th Avenue S.W.
Style (both buildings): Edwardian Commercial
Architects: William M. Dodd
Date: 1903

The Art Gallery of Calgary comprises two historic 1903 buildings, the brick Calgary Cattle Company building and the sandstone Calgary Milling Company building.
SHANNON LEE RAE

These two adjacent buildings, both constructed in 1903, were restored in 1998 and converted into the new home of the Art Gallery of Calgary, an institution previously known as the Muttart Art

Gallery and located above the Memorial Park Library. Both buildings became Provincial Historic Resources in 1998, and Municipal Historic Resources in 1999.

The Calgary Cattle Company built the eastern, two-story brick structure as its office and retail meat market. Incorporated in 1902, the firm boasted Senator James A. Lougheed and future prime minister R. B. Bennett among its directors, and future Calgary mayor and provincial Liberal leader George H. Webster as manager.

Rancher Patrick Burns (1856–1937) bought the company and the building in 1905, and, by 1908, it was the home of his Pioneer Meat Market (which he had earlier acquired from rancher and businessman William Roper Hull). A self-made millionaire, Burns was one of the Big Four ranchers who backed the first Calgary Stampede in 1912. He was appointed to the Senate in 1931.

The Pioneer Meat Market occupied the main floor of 117 from 1908 until 1920. Existing "Pioneer Market" signage at the rear of the building dates from this period. Upstairs tenants included doctors, lawyers, brokers, real estate offices, a photography studio, a fire insurance company, and the Christian Science Hall. The owners of neighboring Silk-O-Lina bought this building in 1967 and expanded their clothing and fabric store, which remained in business until 1991. It was restored in 1998 as part of the new Art Gallery of Calgary.

The building stands alone as the sole remaining home of the *Calgary Eye Opener*, which legendary editor Robert Chambers Edwards (1864–1922) briefly published from this building when he moved his High River newspaper to Calgary in 1904. For two decades, Edwards pounded out his one-man journal on a "semi-irregular" basis—that is, when he wasn't on a bender. Eschewing employees, a printing press, or even a typewriter, the cigar-smoking editor wrote copy on a roll-top desk in his Cameron Block rooms (now the site of the TELUS Convention Centre North Building), or else down the street in his favorite haunt, the Alberta Hotel.

In an era when newspapers reeked of political partisanship, the *Eye Opener* stood independent. Edwards pulled no punches, and he didn't care whom he offended. He stood for honest government, women's rights, and justice for common folk; he was the avowed opponent of heartless corporate interests, hypocrisy, and self-proclaimed moral guardians. Edwards' reforming zeal eventually led him to politics, and, in 1921, he was elected to the Alberta legislature as an independent. "His candidature was as original as his newspaper," noted the Calgary *Albertan*. "He made only one speech and that lasted just one minute."[11] When he died at age 58, Edwards was mourned across the country. He lies buried in Union Cemetery, along with copies of the *Eye Opener* and a flask full of whiskey.

The western, sandstone building was constructed by the Calgary Milling Company as a grocery store and retail outlet for the mill's products. Incorporated in 1898, the company was the successor to the city's original flour milling operation, founded by Donald McLean in 1892. The company's shareholders included Isaac Kendall Kerr and Peter A. Prince, industrialists who helped found the Eau Claire and Bow River Lumber Company in 1886 and the Calgary Water Power Company in 1889.

In 1912, Robin Hood Mills acquired the Calgary Milling Company but declined to buy its downtown store. The store was sold to its manager, former alderman (and future Conservative MLA) John Irwin, who was once considered a possible candidate for lieutenant-governor of Alberta.

Nippon Silks & Products Co. moved into this building in 1930. In 1941, against the backdrop of World War II and anti-Japanese sentiment, the business changed its name to Silk-O-Lina Ltd. and eventually became a regional chain. This store expanded into the former Calgary Cattle Company building in 1967, but closed its doors for good in 1991.

Route: Continue west on Stephen Avenue.

Criterion Restaurant/Merchants Bank of Canada (Vacant)

Address: 121–8th Avenue S.W.
Style: Edwardian Classical
Archictect: Unknown (1903 alteration designed by Taylor, Hogle and Davis of Montreal, with Wilson and Wetenhall as associate architects)
Date: 1889 (enlarged 1903)

This building's sandstone façade dates from 1903, and its classically influenced appearance was designed to convey permanence—a perfect message for the Merchants Bank of Canada, its occupant from 1903–14. The building has long outlasted the bank, which was taken over in 1921 by the Bank of Montreal.

But the building itself is older still. Rather than build a new structure, the bank renovated an earlier edifice, built by an English émigré named Thomas Oxendale Critchley in 1889. That year, Critchley opened the Criterion English Club, where the criterion for admission was a $10 membership fee. As Calgary's first exclusive gentlemen's club, it did not catch on. But two years later, Critchley and his crowd of hard-drinking, polo-playing remittance men—the younger sons of titled English families, sent to the "colonies" and supported by a remittance from home—helped found a much more enduring institution: the Ranchmen's Club.

The Criterion remained a fine restaurant nonetheless, where a full breakfast, lunch, or dinner cost twenty-five cents. And on December 4, 1901, it hosted the most exclusive event on Calgary's social calendar: the founding banquet of the Calgary Old Timers' Association, open to those who had established residence prior to 1883, the year the railway arrived. The *Herald* termed the dinner as a "gathering of those who metaphorically came over on the Mayflower."[12] The association founded that night was later reorganized as the Southern Alberta Pioneers and Their Descendants, a co-ed group open to anyone whose family was here by 1890.

After its stint as the Merchants Bank, the Criterion building served as a recruiting office during World War I and home to the

The sandstone façade of the Criterion Restaurant / Merchants Bank of Canada building features a central arched window and two smaller windows known as oculi. SHANNON LEE RAE

82nd Battalion and the Canadian Patriotic Fund. It later housed federal government offices, and, from 1935 until 1970, the Bank of Canada. During Calgary's first centennial—the 100th anniversary of Fort Calgary in 1975—this building was headquarters for the Century Calgary organization and its comic cowboy mascot, "Centenny Al." After a long turn as the Calgary Parking Authority, in 1998 the building was converted briefly into the hip restaurant Criterion, which revived the old name (and created Calgary's first *Ally McBeal*-style co-ed washroom). It became a Municipal Historic Resource in 1993.

Route: Continue west on Stephen Avenue.

Jacques Jewellery (Tropicana Gifts & Novelties)
Address: 123–8th Avenue S.W.
Style: Edwardian Classical
Architect: Unknown
Date: 1893

In the 1980s, in an apparent statement of independence, this historic rusticated sandstone building was painted red, white, and blue. The paint was removed and the historic façade restored in 2004.

George Jacques (1855–1926), Calgary's original jeweler and watchmaker, arrived in the city in 1881 from his native Ontario. He built this two-story building with its distinctive oriel window in 1893, and it housed his business until he retired in 1906. The Calgary Normal School—a precursor to the later teacher training institute by the same name, which eventually became the nucleus of the future University of Calgary—operated here in 1894. From about 1909–74, the building housed the Calgary Shoe Hospital, a landmark city business.

Route: Cross to the north side of the mall. The next two buildings are treated as one stop.

After years as the mall's painted "red, white and blue" building, the former Jacques' Jewellery building again became a Stephen Avenue jewel when it was restored in 2004. SHANNON LEE RAE

Clarence Block (McNally Robinson Booksellers)

Address: 120–8th Avenue S.W.
Style: Classically influenced
Architect: William M. Dodd
Date: 1901

Shallow columns known as engaged pilasters, each topped by an Ionic capital, provide a vertical element to the Clarence Block's façade. A strong cornice and alternating curved and triangular pediments over the second floor windows (an Italianate detail) add a horizontal quality. The balustrade above the roofline is interrupted by a central triangular pediment with a relief lion's head in its apex.
SHANNON LEE RAE

Norman Block (Winners Apparel)

Address: 128–8th Avenue S.W.
Style: Classically influenced
Architect: William M. Dodd; Fordyce and Stevenson
 (reconstruction after 1933 fire)
Date: 1901

Senator James A. Lougheed had four sons, and he named a building on 8th Avenue for each of them: Clarence, Norman, Douglas, and Edgar. Only two remain. The Edgar Block (210–8th Avenue S.W.)

was demolished in 1929 to build an extension to the Hudson's Bay Company store, and the Douglas Block (337–8th Avenue S.W.) was demolished in the 1960s to make way for the Royal Bank Building, now incorporated into the Bankers Hall complex.

The Norman and Clarence blocks form part of a busy street scene in this early 1930s photograph of Stephen Avenue. GLENBOW ARCHIVES NA-899-3 (DETAIL.)

Lougheed built the original, three-story sandstone Clarence Block in 1892, and for many years it housed the law offices of Lougheed and Bennett. He built the adjacent Norman Block, also of sandstone, in 1900. On Christmas day that year, Clarence Block residents returned from midnight mass to find smoke issuing from the building. The fire alarm, according to the *Albertan*, "broke down after a clatter or two, and it was good luck that any firemen turned up at all.[13] Many firemen slept through the blaze.

Firefighters were hampered by low water pressure; flames spread west to the Norman Block, which had been completed only weeks earlier, and east to the Tribune Block, home to the *Albertan* offices and printing plant. The Tribune Block was damaged, the

Norman Block gutted, and the Clarence Block completely destroyed. Along with his buildings, Lougheed lost his entire law library. Fire Chief James " Cappy" Smart was injured in the blaze. The *Albertan* published a sardonic poem about the fire:

> Tinkle, tinkle, little bell,
> Ring the city's funeral knell;
> Up above the ground so high,
> You can't hear it, nor can I.
>
> Ring out, ring out its faint alarms,
> Ring it till you tire your arms;
> Ring yet again, without a fear
> Not a soul in town can hear.
>
> Patter, patter, the brigade
> Runs to render all their aid;
> 'Helen Blazes!' hear them shout
> To see the tiny waterspout.
>
> E're that bell rings any more,
> We hope the council will get sore;
> But if they don't we'll use our wit,
> And quench all future fires with spit.[14]

Lougheed rebuilt both buildings, although the new sandstone Clarence Block, designed in Classical Revival style, was constructed on a smaller scale. Fire broke out again in 1904, this time in the Norman Block. Again, water pressure failed, Chief Smart was injured, and the Norman Block was gutted. This time, the Senator had his law library hastily removed. It wasn't necessary; the Clarence Block was undamaged. Lougheed rebuilt the Norman Block, which was again damaged by fire in 1908 and again gutted in 1933. It was rebuilt the same year within the existing walls. The Clarence Block survived minor blazes in 1908, 1913, and 1930.

Besides Lougheed and Bennett, notable tenants of the Clarence Block included the offices of Max Aitken (who, as Lord Beaverbrook, later became a British press baron), and future Alberta premier John E. Brownlee, who articled with Lougheed and Bennett in 1905. Architect Harold Hanen renovated the building in the early 1970s, and, a decade later, he proposed building Stephen Square, a 7th Avenue tower that would have incorporated the Clarence Block as its southern entrance. (The project was stillborn with the onset of the recession in the early 1980s.) Restaurateur Vitold Twardowski spearheaded a mid-1970s transformation of the Clarence and Tribune blocks into a small-scale mall, and he made it the home of his Ambrosia Restaurant. In 2002, Winnipeg-based McNally Robinson Booksellers entered a long-term lease on the Clarence Block and converted the entire building into a bookshop and restaurant.

Besides its offices and shops, the Norman Block housed the Lyric Theatre, later renamed the Pantages and incorporated into the Pantages entertainment circuit. In 1922, the theatre was replaced by the Arcade, a shopping centre that was connected to a 7th Avenue produce market by a second-floor back-alley walkway—an early antecedent to Calgary's Plus-15 walkway system inaugurated in the 1970s. Traces of the walkway can still be seen in the lane.

Tommy Burns, the only Canadian ever to win boxing's world heavyweight championship, operated a clothing store in the Norman Block from 1911–13. An interpretive sign placed on the building in the 1970s suggests it was built on the site of an early Lougheed family residence. But Norman himself believed the house had been further east, on the present site of the Ashdown's Hardware Block. Later alterations made the façade unrecognizable, but it was restored to its early appearance in 1997 and became Winners Apparel.

Route: Cross to the south side of the mall.

Bank of Nova Scotia (Rococo Restaurant)

Address: 125–8th Avenue S.W.
Style: Art Deco
Architect: John McIntosh Lyle of Toronto (Fordyce & Stevenson, local supervisors)
Date: 1930

Just days before Christmas 1926, a devastating fire wrecked three wooden buildings that dated back to the 1880s and cleared the site for the present structure. One of the ruined buildings was Nolan's Hall, built in 1886 and onetime local headquarters of the One Big Union, a radical national labor organization founded in Calgary in 1919. Lost with Nolan's Hall were all the regalia of the Royal and Antediluvian Order of Buffalos, which made its headquarters there. The adjacent building housed Taylor's Toy and China Shop, where the entire stock of Christmas toys was destroyed. The third, easternmost structure was only 12.5 feet wide.

The Bank of Nova Scotia built this Art Deco structure in 1929–30 and occupied it until nearby Scotia Centre was completed in 1976. It was the only prairie commission for Toronto architect John M. Lyle, who designed that city's Royal Alexandra Theatre and the interior of Union Station. The building's flattened, stylized classical details evoke Greek temples, but with an Art Deco flair. Western motifs stand in hand-carved relief on the stone façade: bows and arrows, bison and horses, natives and Mounties, a saddle on a fence, a wheat sheaf, and a gushing oil derrick. The metal window frames bear traditional images representing Canada's colonial origins: the lily (France), thistle (Scotland), shamrock (Ireland), rose (England), and leek (Wales). Interior details included marble floors, counters, and main staircase, as well as extensive use of bronze work and wood paneling.

After the bank's departure, one suggested use for the vacant, stately building was as the Alberta Stock Exchange. Instead, it became the Cha Cha Palace dance hall in 1980 and by the 1990s had become The Banke nightclub, where the former safety deposit vault served as the coat check. The building became a Provincial Historic Resource in 1981. It was restored in 1998–2000 and revamped as the Rococo Restaurant.

Stylized relief carvings on this former Bank of Nova Scotia make this façade one of the mall's most fascinating. SHANNON LEE RAE

Route: Continue west on Stephen Avenue.

T. C. Power & Bro. Block (Canadian Impressions)

Address: 131–8th Avenue S.W.
Style: Victorian
Architect: Unknown
Date: 1885

In the summer of 1887—two years after this two-story frame building was constructed—someone pasted a handbill on its east wall, announcing a public vote to approve By-law No. 61. The shopping list in this $30,000 measure included a fire hall, steam fire engine, and a hook-and-ladder wagon.

The emphasis was understandable. On November 7, 1886, a fire that broke out behind S. Parrish & Son's store (at the northwest corner of what is now Centre Street and 9th Avenue S.W.) spread quickly, destroying some eighteen buildings in the town centre. This building was spared and has lasted to become the only remaining downtown building that survived that great fire. The by-law handbill was exposed in 1969 when the neighboring building was demolished. The by-law, and the section of wall on which it had been pasted, was cut out and placed in the Glenbow Museum. (Three decades later, the vacant lot was filled when Bang & Olufsen built the present stone structure at 129–8th Avenue S.W. The building won a city heritage award in 2003 for "Compatible New Design in a Heritage Context.")

T. C. Power & Bro., a mercantile firm based in Fort Benton, Montana, built this Victorian commercial structure in 1885. Its local manager was Daniel Webster Marsh (1838–1916), a U.S. Civil War veteran who, like his famous namesake Daniel Webster, hailed from New Hampshire. Marsh served as Calgary's fourth mayor in 1889–90, and, from 1893–1901, he owned and operated the general store at this address under his own name. During Alberta's first provincial election campaign in 1905, Conservative leader (and

Built in 1885, the former T. C. Power & Bro. store survived Calgary's great fire in 1886 and is now the oldest remaining building in downtown Calgary. SHANNON LEE RAE

future prime minister) R. B. Bennett established his committee rooms here.

Most Calgarians remember this building as the Pain Block, named for Thomas Pain Furriers, the chief occupant from 1933–78. Other occupants included the *Market Examiner*, a weekly agricultural newspaper, and Adam's Radio Parlors, which sold radios and eventually television sets. The false-fronted façade, covered in 1959 with green vitrolite in Art Moderne styling, was restored in 1996.

Route: Continue west on Stephen Avenue.

Alberta Hotel Building

Address: 808–1st Street S.W.
Style: Romanesque Revival
Architect: Wilcox and Johnson of St. Paul, Minnesota (supervised locally by McVittie, Child and Wilson) (Child and Wilson, 1891 rear addition; Wilson and Lang, 1906 addition)
Date: 1890 (additions 1891, 1906)

Calgary's original grand hotel was built in the wake of the great fire that devastated the young town in 1886. Since the day it opened in January 1890, the Alberta Hotel has remained a downtown landmark and a focal point of the city's storied past.

The Alberta Hotel was a godsend to frontier Calgary. Before it opened, rustic accommodations had improved little in the seven years since the CPR arrived. "The importance of good hotels in such towns as Calgary can scarcely be over-estimated," editorialized the *Calgary Herald* when the Alberta opened. "Many a capitalist has been induced to invest in places where the thriving, well managed hotel was found to be the index of the enterprise and thrift and prosperity of the people."[16] Two such capitalists were the hotel's builders, T. S. C. Lee (dates unknown) and Alfred Brealey, (1861–90) whose names still grace the building's keystone. Like so many during ranching's golden age, these two men invested both in Calgary real estate and on the open range.

This east-looking view of Stephen Avenue was taken in October 1889. A cow cross-es the road as the Alberta Hotel, right, is being prepared for its grand opening in two months' time. To the left, the Bank of Montreal has just built its sandstone edi-fice with a distinctive turret, later demolished to build the present 1930 structure. The arch in the distance is on McTavish Street (now Centre Street), and welcomes the visit of Lord Stanley, the governor general. Stanley donated a championship cup for hockey in 1893. GLENBOW ARCHIVES NA-2864-1323

Calgary was the capital of southern Alberta's ranching king-dom, and in the Alberta Hotel wealthy ranchers found a home away from home. Such guests included George Lane, owner of the famous Bar U Ranch; Fred Stimson, its manager; and cattleman and meatpacking king Pat Burns. It was in Lane's room in 1912 that American promoter Guy Weadick tapped a group of ranchers—since immortalized as the Big Four—to finance his idea for a "Frontier Week" celebration. It was staged that year as the original Calgary Stampede.

Ted Shelly, who started as a twelve-year-old bellboy and retired twenty-six years later as manager, recalled seeing cattlemen make enormous deals in the hotel, sealed only by a handshake. "No lawyers were required," he remembered; "their word was as good as any bond."[17]

Located at Calgary's busiest intersection—the corner of Scarth Street and Stephen Avenue, renamed 1st Street W. and 8th Avenue in 1904—the Alberta became the city's social hub. Notable visitors or pillars of society could be seen at any time in the smoke-filled lobby, dining room, or the famous long bar (at 125 feet, described variously as the longest in Calgary, in Alberta, or in all of western Canada). It was the crossroads where tobacco-spitting cowboys and clueless remittance men rubbed shoulders with politicians, literati, and captains of industry. Itinerant professionals, entertainers, and traveling salesmen stayed at the hotel and offered their services within its walls—everything from specialty medicine and prosthetic outfitting to palm reading and pastoral services. It was not unusual for cowboys to ride a horse up to the bar—except for the one who drew his pistol and shot every bottle, glass, and mirror in sight, then wrote a $2800 check to cover the damage.

Evenings saw the "armchair brigade" fill the lobby's overstuffed horsehair chairs, and their easy conversation lasted to the wee hours. Members included editor Bob Edwards, whose gleanings at the Alberta Hotel inspired much of his wit in the *Calgary Eye Opener*; Paddy Nolan, star defense lawyer and Edwards' drinking companion; legendary fire chief James "Cappy" Smart; rancher William Roper Hull; and architect J. J. "Deafie" Wilson, who mistook every remark as an invitation to have a drink. On summer nights, guests took the chairs out to the setback along the avenue, where they smoked, gossiped, and watched the world go by. As years passed and the city grew, the setback was needed for sidewalk space and the chairs remained indoors.

Future prime minister R. B. Bennett, who lived on the third floor and took his meals at the dining room's "Bennett table," eschewed the lobby revelry. A teetotaler, Bennett spent the evenings in his Clarence Block law office or reading the Bible up in his room.

Prohibition, which in Alberta lasted from 1916 to 1924, spelled the end of the Alberta Hotel. Its final owner, Charles Dangerfield Tapprell, held a farewell dinner and closed the doors forever. The building became Alberta Corner, a retail and office complex that became a landmark in its own right, with such notable tenants as the French consulate (1930–32). By the 1970s, it had deteriorated, but new owners spared it from demolition and renovated the building inside and out. Rough-finished concrete replaced deteriorated sandstone blocks, and gargoyles from the demolished Southam Building were mounted in the façade.[18]

In 1997, family-owned Encorp Inc. added the building to its vintage downtown properties, which also included the nearby Alberta & Hull Blocks and the sandstone Clarence Block. Former guest room floors became character office space with bare rough-finished stone walls and ten-foot high ceilings. The open courtyard, formed by the original U-shaped structure and a 1906 annex, was glassed in as Murrieta's West Coast Bar and Grill.

Route: Cross to the north side of the mall.

Bank of Montreal (vacant)

Address: 140–8th Avenue S.W.
Style: Modern Classical
Architect: Kenneth G. Rae
Date: 1930

On the granite base of this Classical Revival building, near the eastern edge of the south elevation, is an architectural detail unique in Calgary: the architect's signature. Kenneth G. Rae designed more than sixty buildings for the Bank of Montreal, as well as the Montreal Stock Exchange. Designed to evoke a Greek temple, the building was constructed in two phases to ensure uninterrupted service as this new building replaced the bank's earlier structure on the site. The façade is Manitoba Tyndall limestone, and the relief carving in its central pediment depicts two native men carrying the bank's crest, with tipis and woods in the background. The building has been declared a Provincial Historic Resource.

After a ninety-nine year presence on the site, the Bank of Montreal closed this branch in 1988. The building's 1993 restoration was the first of many such efforts on Stephen Avenue in the 1990s. It housed A&B Sound from 1993–2005.

Bank of Montreal, circa 1931–35. Employees enjoyed the use of a rooftop garden until it was removed in 1940. The Norman Block and Clarence Block can be seen to the right. GLENBOW ARCHIVES NA-899-3

Route: Cross 1st Street S.W. (formerly Scarth Street) to the northwest corner of the intersection.

Hudson's Bay Company

Address: 200–8th Avenue S.W.
Style: Chicago
Architects: Burke, Horwood and White of Toronto (original store); Horwood and White (1930 addition)
Date: 1913 (additions 1930, 1958)

When it opened on August 18, 1913—the same day that the Marx Brothers started a week-long engagement on the stage of the nearby Empire Theatre—Calgary's fourth Hudson's Bay Company store was only about half of its present size, and was situated at the corner of 7th Avenue and 1st Street S.W. The six-story building contained forty departments, a circulating library, first aid facilities, and a mezzanine-floor "Rendezvous" where patrons could sit and read, write letters, or wait to meet up with friends. The store even had a rooftop playground, where shoppers could leave their children to play on the seesaws and swings under the supervision of a "governess." The *Albertan* compared the store with Harrod's in London.

The familiar sidewalk colonnade was part of a 1930 addition that extended the store to 8th Avenue. The Calgary Municipal Airport was developed in Renfrew at the same time, and a three-million-candle power aeronautical beacon mounted on the roof of the Bay was visible 150 miles away.

A final addition in 1958 extended the building further west along 8th Avenue and brought the store to its current dimensions. It also meant demolition for the Empire Theatre, where the Marx Brothers had performed so many years earlier. Both the 1930 and 1958 additions duplicated the terra cotta façade of the original building, but with minor differences. The rhythm of upper-floor windows changes from the 1913 phase to the additions, and textured details in the 1913 and 1930 wings are simplified in the 1958 extension.

Photographed in October 1929 while still under construction, this addition extended the Hudson's Bay Company store, at 7th Avenue and 1st Street S.W., all the way south to 8th Avenue. Minor differences distinguish the original store from its later additions. GLENBOW ARCHIVES NA-2037-21

Route: Cross to the south side of the mall.

Alberta Block

Address: 805–1st Street S.W.
Style: Edwardian Classical
Architect: William M. Dodd
Date: 1903

Alberta Block, 2004. Jimmie Condon's well-known restaurant has been replaced by a Subway sandwich shop. SHANNON LEE RAE

Anyone familiar with heritage preservation in Alberta will recognize the central pediment on the west side of the Alberta Block, which inspired the logo of the Alberta Main Street Programme, a government organization that assists in the revitalization of aging historic commercial districts.

William Roper Hull (1856–1925) built this brick and sandstone block in 1903, both as a revenue property and as offices for his own business interests, which included ranching, meatpacking, and real estate development. Hull had settled in Calgary in the 1880s, and, in 1893, he built the Hull Opera House. He sold his pioneer meat business to Patrick Burns in 1905 and shifted his interests to real estate development. Hull purchased the adjacent Hodder Block at 205–8th

Avenue S.W. in 1905 and renamed it the Hull Block. His estate retained these properties until 1950.

The Alberta Block's tenants read like a who's who of early twentieth-century Calgary. Frederick C. Lowes—a flamboyant real estate developer, speculator, and financial broker—made millions of dollars during the city's pre-World War I boom and dramatically lost his fortune in the bust that followed. The building's architect, William Dodd (who later designed City Hall), kept his offices here. Moose Baxter's Turkish baths occupied the basement. The building also housed the Calgary Board of Trade (1903–04) and the Co-operative Commonwealth Federation, precursor to the New Democratic Party (1944–48). And the corner storefront, once the home of the Trader's Bank of Canada, housed Jimmie's Café—originally known as the Palace of Eats—from 1934–48.[19] Owner Jimmie Condon (1889–1981), a Greek immigrant from Turkey, settled in Calgary in 1911 and became a well-known confectioner, restaurateur, and sports promoter. Jimmie's became a landmark business on Calgary's busiest corner, and it was here, legend has it, that Calgary's first milkshakes were served. For years Condon sponsored amateur teams in a variety of sports, each known as the "Jimmies." The Booster Club named him Calgary's "Sportsman of the Year" in 1963, and the Jimmie Condon Arena in suburban Kingsland was named for him in 1981. University of Calgary students will know him as the donor of the Greek philosophers statues in the campus administration building's courtyard "jungle" and the health sciences centre.

Route: Proceed south on 1st Street S.W. to 9th Avenue (originally Pacific Avenue).

Grain Exchange Building
Address: 815–1st Street S.W.
Style: Edwardian Classical
Architects: Hodgson and Bates
Date: 1909

Relief lettering over the main entrance still announces the original anchor tenant of Calgary's first skyscraper. The Grain Exchange Building was the only structure of this scale in the city to use rusticated sandstone rather than smooth-dressed stone. Interlocking letters next to the main entrance form Wlliam Roper Hull's monogram. KAREN OLSON

With its rusticated sandstone façade, the city's original sky-scraper—at six stories, a technological marvel when it was built—paradoxically evokes Calgary's 1880s frontier period. It was the first in the city built using reinforced concrete construction, which allowed for its unprecedented height. Interlocking letters in stone relief on a pillar next to the main entrance form the initials of William Roper Hull, the rancher-turned-developer who acquired this property in 1902 and was already planning to build an office tower when the nascent Calgary Grain Exchange approached him for space. By 1919, the exchange had outgrown its space and moved to the Lancaster Building, but it closed permanently during the Great Depression. Until Hull's estate sold the Grain Exchange Building in 1951, it was heated by the boiler in the Alberta Block, which Hull also owned, through heating pipes that passed between the buildings under the back lane.

Route: Cross both roads to the southeast corner of the intersection.

Palliser Hotel (Fairmont Palliser Hotel)

Address: 133–9th Avenue S.W.
Style: Edwardian Classical (influenced by Chicago style)
Architects: Edward and W. S. Maxwell
Date: 1914 (addition 1929)

Calgary's railway hotel was conceived in an era of spectacular
growth in the city, and its corporate masters at the Canadian Pacific
Railway judged it an "almost essential" link in its continent-wide
hotel chain. "Calgary itself will continue to grow," observed CPR
President Sir Thomas Shaughnessy in 1907, "and a building which
at this time would appear almost extravagant will in the not remote
future be quite warranted by the traffic."[20] It took three years, a mil-
lion-and-a-half dollars, and the work of five hundred men (including at least two construction fatalities) to build the eight-and-a-half
story Palliser, named for Capt. John Palliser (1817–1887), who headed a British scientific expedition to the prairies in 1857–60. But by
the time it opened on June 1, 1914, the boom had turned bust, ren-
dering Shaughnessy's prediction premature. "The only thing in
Calgary worth looking at or being interested in is the hotel,"
observed a travel writer from Utica, New York, the following year.
"[Its] ten [sic] magnificent stories rise above the surrounding hov-
els and shacks and homely frontier town like a Grecian statue on a
clam flat."[21]

One optimistic note when the hotel opened was the Turner
Valley oil boom of 1914, which filled the Palliser with hastily formed
oil company offices and brokers conducting loud transactions on
the café's tableside telephones (which finally had to be removed to
maintain decorum). Victory loans, fundraisers, and meatless menus
dominated the World War I years, but by the 1920s the Palliser's
character of elegant hospitality emerged. The fashionable set
danced to the Palliser Hotel Trio or Ma Trainor's Calgary Hillbillies;

Two window wells on the guest room floors give the Palliser an E-shape, which the Morning Albertan *commented upon in its January 19, 1914 issue, while the hotel was under construction: "To a man flying far above it in an aeroplane, as will be common someday, it will look like a giant letter 'E' with the flanges of the letter without which the word 'energy' could not be spelled."* SHANNON LEE RAE

obliging waiters poured ginger ale for guests who had cached hip flasks and liquor bottles behind tablecloths or evening gowns, until the charade ended with the 1924 repeal of Prohibition.

A 1929 expansion added three floors and a new penthouse, but, as with the original building, the addition was ready just as economic conditions declined. According to legend, a broker ruined by the stock market crash that heralded the Great Depression leapt from the hotel's new parapet to his death on the tracks below. For years, the buff-colored bricks of the addition glistened long after those of the lower floor had discolored with age. R. B. Bennett, the Calgarian who served as prime minister from 1930–35, lived in rooms 759 and 760.

The Palliser had found its place as the city's social heartbeat. Service clubs made it their headquarters, as did the new Calgary Petroleum Club in 1928. The Palliser's annual Cowboy Ball became a longtime feature of Stampede Week, and every year at that time, the free-flowing liquor at the hotel gave it a new nickname: the Paralyzer. During World War II, servicemen and air cadets filled the hotel's halls and rooms while attending functions or on leave. After the Leduc oil discovery of 1947, American oilmen made the Palliser their office and residential address. Bell captain Cecil Heath made a fortune from guests' stock tips, and at least once he attended an oil company board meeting wearing his bellman's uniform. Calgary's first cocktail lounge opened in the penthouse in 1959.

The hotel was modernized in the 1960s to compete with newer competitors, but, by the late 1970s, CP Hotels recognized history as a strong selling feature for its chain. The Palliser was restored to its original beauty in the 1980s. It was renamed the Fairmont Palliser when CP Hotels became Fairmont Hotels in 2001.

Route: Cross both roads again, proceed north on 1st Street S.W. to Stephen Avenue Walk, and turn left. Remain on the left (south) side.

Leeson-Lineham Block

Address: 209–8th Avenue S.W.
Architect: Unknown
Architectural style: Edwardian Classical
Date: 1910

Horizontal sandstone bands offer contrast to the Leeson-Lineham Block's red brick façade, creating a polychromatic effect. The original cornice has been replaced, and the storefront and entrance canopy restored to their original appearance in 1998.
SHANNON LEE RAE

When Mayor Reuben Rupert Jamieson officially opened the Grosvenor Café in the new Leeson-Lineham Block on December 6, 1910, restaurant-goers and 8th Avenue pedestrians were treated to a new sound: the city's first Auxetophone, an early sound amplifier that provided ambient music without the musicians. Its chief failings were its extremely high price ($500) and even higher, unchangeable decibel level. Before long, the Grosvenor went the same way as the now-forgotten Auxetophone.

Like many of southern Alberta's ranchers, George K. Leeson (1843–1910) and John Lineham (1858–1913) also invested in city properties, and when the two men built this six-story commercial block in 1910, it was one of the city's tallest buildings. Of its long list of tenants, colorful examples include the United Farmers of Alberta, the Canadian Official War Photographs office, the Cunard Steamship Company, the Nu-Bone Corset Company, Department of Labour Prisoners of War, the Royal Canadian Legion, the Salvation Army public relations office, a Christian Science Reading Room, the Scientology Centre, Cult Information Services, and a psychic ministry. From 1948–49, it housed Calgary's newest prestigious organization—the Calgary Petroleum Club.

Route: Continue west on Stephen Avenue.

Palace Theatre

Address: 219–8th Avenue S.W.
Style: Modern Classical, with restrained detailing
Architect: C. Howard Crane of Toronto
Date: 1921

Allen's Palace Theatre, as it was called when it opened on October 25, 1921, was appropriately named. This was the age of movie palaces, when a night at the movies was a grand affair in an elaborate setting. It was the latest in a nationwide chain of theatres owned by a transplanted Jewish-American family who had moved to Calgary in 1909 and made the city their headquarters for over a decade. They built the "deluxe" Allen Theatre in 1913, and, eight years later, replaced it with the much larger Allen's Palace a block to the west. Based on the design of the Allen Theatre in Toronto, the Calgary version boasted 1,951 seats, a ladies' retiring room, and a men's smoking room. It also had a stage and orchestra pit, and its program included vaudeville and symphony performances. The *Calgary Herald* launched its radio station, the future CFAC, from the Palace in 1922, and, from 1925–27, future Alberta premier William Aberhart broadcast his weekly "Back to the Bible Hour" radio show from the Palace.

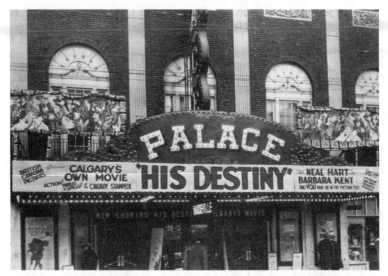

The two-story Palace Theatre features Corinthian pilasters that support a horizontal entablature and separate the red tapestry brick façade into seven bays, each with a stylized window. Storefronts originally flanked the main entrance. In 1925, the Palace showed the world premier of His Destiny, *filmed in part at the Calgary Stampede.* GLENBOW ARCHIVES NA-446-132

Jules, Jay, and Barney Allen had left Calgary by the time the Palace opened, while cousin H. J. Allen remained to supervise its construction. Within months of its opening, Toronto-based rival Famous Players opened the Capitol Theatre across the street (on the present site of Scotia Centre). The Allens were unable to compete successfully, and, in 1929, Famous Players acquired the Allen chain, including the Palace in Calgary. For more than forty years, two of Calgary's grandest theatres remained under common ownership and stood nearly opposite one another. The Capitol was demolished in 1972, and the Palace closed its doors in 1990. It remained vacant over the next eight years, although it provided a set for *Legends of the Fall*, a 1993 film shot partly in Calgary and starring Brad Pitt, Aidan Quinn, and Anthony Hopkins. It reopened as the Palace Nightclub in 1998 following a four million-dollar renovation, but the club remained in business only five years. In 1996, the building was designated both a Provincial Historic Resource and a National Historic Site.

Route: Cross to the north side of the mall.

Mackay and Dippie Block (Dairy Queen)

Address: 218–8th Avenue S.W.
Style: Edwardian Commercial
Architect: Unknown
Date: 1909 (1910 addition)

In 1888, Scottish-born taxidermist Walter James Grant Mackay (1871–1966) and future Calgary mayor James S. Mackie (1861–1949) opened a gunsmith and taxidermy shop under the name Mackie and Mackay. Mackie sold his share a dozen years later to George Frederick Dippie (1873–1935), a taxidermist from Yorkshire, and the business became Mackay and Dippie. The two partners built this eponymous two-story brick building in 1909, expanded it the following year, and remained at this address until 1928. Dippie was a pioneer natural history collector and a bird specialist, and he served the Calgary Natural History Society as its longtime secretary. "Gramps" Mackay lived to ninety-five, long enough for his memory to be regarded as a living record of local pioneer life. He donated his fine collection of natural history specimens and native artifacts to the Luxton Museum in Banff.

Sandstone keystones are centred at the top of both arched windows on the top floor of the Mackay and Dippie Block. The names of the two taxidermists appear in the entablature below the cornice, as well as the year the business was founded and the year of the building's construction. Shannon Lee Rae

Longtime Calgarians remember this building as D'Allairds, a popular clothing store, from the 1940s to the 1970s. Between 1914 and 1946, it also housed the ticket, telegraph and freight office of Canadian National Railways and its predecessor, the Canadian Northern Railway. The building was incorporated into Scotia Centre in the mid-1970s and became a Dairy Queen. The original façade was reconstructed in 1998.

Route: Continue west along Stephen Avenue.

Turner-Hicks Block (Riley and McCormick)
Address: 220–8th Avenue S.W.
Style: Edwardian Commercial
Architect: Unknown
Date: 1907

Merchant Joseph C. McFarlane built this two-story brick building in 1907 to house his business, McFarlane & Northcott Hardware, quickly followed by the Turner-Hicks Hardware Company, which remained until 1909. Most Calgarians remember this building as People's Jewellers, which operated here from 1947–82. But its history derives as much from a much newer occupant that is older than the building itself: Riley & McCormick, the pioneer saddlery established in 1901. The building is also home to what has been called "the oldest horse in Calgary." Riley & McCormick had a wooden horse built as a mascot, and staff placed it outside the store each day as a sidewalk advertisement. The original horse was later donated to the Glenbow Museum; the one that today's staff members wheel out every business day is its 1930 replacement. During World War II, Australian airmen training in Calgary under the British Commonwealth Air Training Plan "kidnapped" the horse and tied it to a streetcar. Store manager Ernie Astell chased the streetcar, shouting "Bring him back, bring him back," and succeeded in recovering the horse—sans ears. At the McCormick family's request, the Australian high commissioner to Canada saw to it the ears were repaired.

This two-story brick building was restored to its original appearance in 1998. It is home to Riley and McCormick's wooden mascot, termed "the oldest horse in Calgary." Shannon Lee Rae

Past generations of children climbed on the horse, and both prime ministers and ordinary citizens have been photographed with it. A sign at its base now asks visitors to look, but not touch.

The building was incorporated into Scotia Centre in the mid-1970s. The historic Riley and McCormick western wear moved its downtown store here in 2000, and, in 2001, the store became the Calgary Convention and Visitor Bureau's tourist information centre.

Route: Continue west along Stephen Avenue.

Kraft Block (Limited Edition McDonald's)

Address: 222–8th Avenue S.W.
Style: Edwardian Commercial
Architect: Unknown
Date: 1907

Captain Tompkins built the Western Block in 1907, and its early occupants included the Calgary Drafting Company, the Calgary Conservatory of Music, and Heintzman's Pianos. In 1928 it was renamed the Kraft Block for its new owner and occupant—Kraft the Furrier, a retail fur business established by August Kraft in 1908, and which remained at this location until 1953. When the building was incorporated into Scotia Centre in the mid-1970s, its upper floors were re-aligned with the shopping centre, which explains the back-painted upper windows. The façade was restored in the mid-1990s when the main floor was converted into the "Limited Edition" McDonald's restaurant. Damaged bricks from the façade were taken down, reversed, and put back up.

Route: Cross to the south side of the mall, and continue west.

When the Kraft Block was restored in the mid-1990s, damaged bricks from the façade were taken down, turned around, and replaced in the wall. SHANNON LEE RAE

This Edwardian building was remodeled in Art Deco styling in 1929 after it became a branch of the Trusts and Guarantee Company. Its stylized classical features are typical architecture for a financial institution, but with an Art Deco twist. SHANNON LEE RAE

McPherson Fruit Company (Arnold Churgin Shoes)

Address: 227–8th Avenue S.W.

Style: Art Deco

Architect: G. M. Lang (1929 alteration designed by D.S. McIlory)

Date: Circa 1905 (altered 1912, 1929)

At the beginning of the twentieth century, the 200 west block of 8th Avenue developed as part of Calgary's early warehouse district and was serviced by a railway spur line between 8th and 9th avenues. The Winnipeg-based Macpherson Fruit Company built this brick structure around 1905 and used it as its local warehouse until 1912. The building was then renovated to become the Northern Crown Bank, which was absorbed into the Royal Bank of Canada in 1918. The jet-black Art Deco façade dates from 1929, when the Trusts and Guarantee Company (later renamed Crown Trust) renovated the building as its local branch, which it remained until 1968. Shoe merchant Arnold Churgin (1927–1987), who introduced European designer shoes to the city in the 1960s, opened his eponymous store here in 1968.

Route: Continue west to 2nd Street S.W. (formerly Hamilton Street) and cross to the northwest corner.

Lancaster Building

Address: 304–8th Avenue S.W.

Style: Chicago

Architect: James Teague, Victoria (completed by William Stanley Bates)

Date: 1912–19

Although its construction began in 1912, the outbreak of World War I delayed the project, and the Lancaster Building was not completed until 1919. It was built for owner James S. Mackie (1861–1949), an English-born gunsmith who settled permanently in Calgary in 1886, served as mayor in 1900–01, and bought and operated the Thomson

Brothers' book and stationery shop in the Thomson Bros. Block before shifting his attention to real estate development. Mackie's interest in history led to the building's name, after England's House of Lancaster.

The nine-story brick building is clad in terra cotta on its two lower floors and its eighth. Its many prominent occupants included the Calgary Grain Exchange, which relocated here from the Grain Exchange Building when the Lancaster opened, and the main post office, located here from 1919–31. The Mackie family continued to own the building into the 1980s, when it was sold to Oxford Developments, which had built the adjoining Toronto-Dominion Square in 1977. In a project recognized by the Heritage Canada Foundation, the Mackies restored the facade in 1978-79 and renovated the interior, linking the building at Plus-15 level to TD Square and its Devonian Gardens. Like the Hollinsworth Building, the Lancaster forms the cornerstone of a block-sized office and retail complex. Buildings demolished to make way for TD Square included the Wales Hotel, which stood directly north of the Lancaster Building, and the lavish Birks' Jewellery store (312, 314–8th Avenue S.W.).

The nine-story Lancaster Building forms the cornerstone of the block-sized TD Square, to which it is attached at the Plus-15/food court level. Shannon Lee Rae

Route: Cross to the south side of the mall.

Canada Life Assurance (Hollinsworth) Building

Address: 301–8th Avenue S.W.
Style: Edwardian Classical
Architects: Brown and Vallance of Montreal
Date: 1913

With its rounded corner, the Canada Life Assurance (Hollinsworth) Building forms the cornerstone of the block-sized Bankers Hall complex. The historic building's design is repeated in additions to the west and south. SHANNON LEE RAE

Although the cornerstone outside its Stephen Avenue Walk entrance identifies this as the Canada Life Assurance Building, the ground-floor retail tenant gave the edifice its more commonly used name: the Hollinsworth Building. Hollinsworth & Company Ltd., a ladies' ready-to-wear store, occupied the main floor from 1926–74, and, in the 1930s, store manager Kenneth Lancaster could look out the window to the building across the street that shared his last name.

The Canada Life Assurance Company built this early sky-scraper in 1912–13, the height of Calgary's pre-World War I boom, which had slumped by the time the building opened on January 1, 1914. The terra cotta façade, one of very few remaining in the city, emphasized height through its five-story rounded arches that separate the windows into columns. It is an early example of the use of structural steel and reinforced concrete foundations. Interlocking letters (CL) form a corporate monogram over the rounded corner entrance. Canada Life's historic logo, showing a pelican feeding its young, appears in relief over the main Stephen Avenue entrance and in inlaid tile on the lobby floor.

The Hollinsworth Building was saved from threat of demolition in the 1970s. It was designated a Provincial Historic Resource in 1979. Most of this block was cleared in the 1980s—including the 9th Avenue "Petroleum Row" of Modern 1950s buildings, among them the Pacific Building and the Petroleum Building, with its Pump Room lounge—for the development of Bankers Hall. (In the 1950s and 1960s, Modern style—with its rectangular massing, metal and glass "curtain walls," expressed structure, and absence of historical references—became widely popular.) The Hollinsworth became the cornerstone of the complex, its interior reconstructed, and its façade restored and reconstructed at ground level. A wealth of archival documents discovered in its offices reflecting the work of law firms, oil and coal mining companies, and other businesses were salvaged and transferred to the Glenbow Archives.

Route: Continue west along Stephen Avenue to 3rd Street S.W. (originally called Barclay Street, and now known as Barclay Mall). Stephen Avenue Walk ends here, and 8th Avenue becomes a traffic-bearing road. Cross 3rd Street S.W. on the north side of 8th Avenue S.W.

Calgary Eaton Centre

Address: 400–8th Avenue S.W.

Style: Classically influenced (with Romanesque Revival detailing)

Architect: Ross and Macdonald of Montreal (supervised by Calgary architect George Fordyce) (1929 store); WZMH Group Architects Ltd. (Calgary Eaton Centre)

Date: 1929 (Eaton's Department Store; addition 1950s); 1990 (Calgary Eaton Centre)

Portions of the façade were saved from the demolished Eaton's store and placed on the new Calgary Eaton's Centre. AUTHOR PHOTO

When the new Calgary Eaton Centre opened in 1990, it seemed like a ghost to Calgarians who remembered the old Eaton's Department Store, built in 1929 and demolished in 1988. The new retail complex occupied the same site and incorporated seven bays from the original store's four-story Tyndall limestone façade.

Eaton's was built during a late-1920s building boom in the city and was located to the west of the main shopping district. It was officially opened by Lady Flora McCrae Eaton, daughter-in-law of company founder Timothy Eaton. In addition to its filigreed, brass elevators—with uniformed operators who called out the departments on each floor, the building boasted a wooden-treaded escalator, the first in the province. The Tyndall limestone façade featured a large arcade entrance and spiral wound pilasters framing the second-story arched windows. A 1950s addition to the north lacked the window displays of the original 8th Avenue portion. A new Eaton's store, opposite 2nd Street S.W. from the original, was built in 1986 in advance of the Calgary Eaton Centre development. (That store was built on what was once the site of William Aberhart's Calgary Prophetic Bible Institute, built in 1927 and demolished in 1968. A south-facing display window along the 8th Avenue side of the 1986 store tells the story.) Sears took over the store after Eaton's went bankrupt in 2000.

A display window at the southwest corner of the Calgary Eaton Centre, facing 2nd Street S.W., tells the history of Eaton's in Calgary. But the timeline ends before the Eaton's bankruptcy.

Route: Cross to the south side of 8th Avenue, continue west to the corner of 4th Street S.W. (originally called Ross Street), and cross 4th Street. Proceed west on 8th Avenue.

Penny Lane

Address: 513–8th Avenue S.W.
Style: Edwardian Commercial buildings
Architects: Unknown
Date: Several buildings, ranging from 1908 to the 1940s

In 1972, a collection of nine former warehouses and office buildings on this block, built between 1908 and the 1940s, were completely remade into a single indoor shopping mall. They have all been connected at the ground and second levels, and represent an early example of adaptive reuse for heritage buildings in Calgary. Among them are the Mason and Risch Block (507–8th Avenue S.W.), built in 1912 for the Mason and Risch Piano Company; the Blow Building (513-515–8th Avenue S.W.), built for Dr. Thomas Henry Blow in

Nine historic buildings were interconnected to create Penny Lane mall in 1972. Exterior paint gives the appearance of a unified structure. SHANNON LEE RAE

1908; and the Canadian Fairbanks Merchandise Co. Ltd. Warehouse, built for A. L. Langman in 1908. In 1919, the Canadian Fairbanks building became the original home of the Colonel

Belcher Hospital, Calgary's veterans' hospital created in the wake of World War I. The hospital moved west into the Blow Building in 1926 and was relocated to the Connaught district in the 1940s. Other notable occupants of the present Penny Lane were the Commercial High School (1920–25), Garbutt's Business College (1920–40) and its successor, Henderson's Business School (1940–55), and a variety of federal government offices.

Exterior paint gives the varied façades the appearance of a unified structure. Ghost signage from Canadian Fairbanks and the Calgary Cartage Company is still visible on the west and east faces of the buildings. A twin-tower proposal in 2002 appeared to threaten Penny Lane's future, but the project has not been realized.

Route: Proceed west to 5th Street S.W. Cross both roads, and proceed west.

Barron Building

Address: 610–8th Avenue SW
Style: Modern, with Art Deco influence
Architect: John A. Cawson
Date: 1951

This site lay far to the west of the downtown core when businessman Jacob Bell Barron (1888–1965) started building this eponymous tower in 1949. The Great Depression and World War II had interrupted large-scale building construction in Calgary, as it also did in Edmonton. J. B. Barron's project addressed a dearth of modern office space in the city, and it did so at a spectacular moment. Since 1914, the Turner Valley oil field had made Calgary the centre of Alberta's petroleum industry. A major discovery at Leduc in 1947 could have shifted that locus to nearby Edmonton. But the Barron Building, completed in 1951, offered desperately needed office space and quickly attracted three major oil companies—Mobil, Shell, and Sun Oil—as tenants. The Barron Building helped anchor the oil industry in Calgary, and shifted the centre of business westward within the city.

With its façade of yellow brick, aluminum detailing, and Tyndall limestone, the Barron Building combines elements of Art Deco and Modern styles. SHANNON LEE RAE

The building is transitional in design. Its vertical central bay, stepped-back form, and molded aluminum detailing references pre-World War II Art Deco styling. The horizontal window bands that flank the central bay reflect post-war Modern design.

Although trained as a lawyer, Barron became a theatre manager; he operated the Palace Theatre in the 1920s and bought the Grand Theatre in the Lougheed Building in 1937. Barron incorporated the new Uptown Theatre into the Barron Building, and he lived in the penthouse suite, which included a rooftop lawn and garden. The complex remained under Barron family ownership until 1981. By the time local businessman Blake O'Brien bought the building in 1992, it had become (in the words of *Calgary Herald* business reporter Deborah Yedlin) a "fixer-upper."[22] O'Brien moved into the penthouse and began removing asbestos and slowly developing the Barron as character office space. It remains home to the Uptown Theatre, closed by owner Cineplex-Odeon in the late 1980s, and re-opened in the 1990s as an independent cinema and live theatre venue. Another notable tenant is the Historical Society of Alberta, which moved its office here in 2002.

Tour ends.

Notes

1 "The Politest Elevator Man in the World," *Calgary News-Telegram* 28 Sept. 1912: 21.

2 City of Calgary, Corporate Records, Archives, Assessment and Tax Records, Assessment History Cards.

3 *North-West Territories Gazette* 15 Oct. 1894: 4.

4 "The Buildings of 1891," *Calgary Weekly Herald* 6 Jan. 1892: 2.

5 Jack Peach, "1920 elevator still giving Calgarians a lift," *Calgary Herald* 27 June 1981: F4.

6 "The Tribune," *Calgary Tribune* 16 Sept. 1885: 2.

7 "Albertan Licked Hardships To Flourish As Daily Paper," *Albertan* (Anniversary supplement) 23 Apr. 1942: 2.

8 *Ibid.*

9 "Tribune Block Fire Does Damage to the Extent of $25,000," *Morning Albertan* 26 Jan. 1914: 8.

10 "Three Curling Cups Are Lost in Fire," *Calgary Daily Herald* 26 Jan. 1914: 9.

11 "R. C. Edwards, M. L. A., Editor Eye Opener, Dead," *Morning Albertan* 15 Nov. 1922: 2.

12 "The Old Timers Hold Their First Great Banquet in Calgary," *Daily Herald* 5 Dec. 1901: 1.

13 "Fire! Fire! Calgary Meets the Inevitable Scourge," *Albertan and the Alberta Tribune* 29 Dec. 1900: 1.

14 *Ibid.*

15 "Great Crowd Applauds as Arthur Pelkey is Set Free by Jury Monday Afternoon," *Calgary Daily Herald* 24 June 1913: 16.

16 "The Value of Hotels," *Calgary Daily Herald* 20 Jan. 1890: 2.

17 "Made More As Bellhop Than As Manager," *Calgary Herald* 9 May 1946: 9.

18 The smaller gargoyles over the building's main floor arches are original and still bear alpha-numeric designations inscribed at the time they were cut down from the Southam Building, indicating their original positions on that building's façade. The larger figures, depicting arche-typical characters from a newspaper office, are replicas.

19 Years after Condon's death, Calgary restaurateur Brad Myhre acquired the restaurant's mahogany wall-mounted booths and diner counter from Condon's niece, who was storing them in her Lower Mount Royal garage. Myhre installed them in his Belmont Diner (2008–33rd Avenue S.W.), which he opened in the Marda Loop district in 2002. The following year, Myhre opened the Palace of Eats (1411–11th Street S.W.), a smoked meat deli in the Connaught district that perpetuates the original name of Jimmie's Café.

20 John A. Eagle, "Shaughnessy and Prairie Development, 1889-1914," in *The CPR West: The Iron Road and the Making of a Nation*, ed. Hugh A. Dempsey (Vancouver: Douglas & McIntyre Ltd., 1984) 142.

21 "A Vision of Calgary By Tourist Who Looped North America Recently," *Calgary Daily Herald* 8 Oct. 1915: 5.

22 Deborah Yedlin, "Barron Building Stands Firm in City's Downtown Core," *Calgary Herald* 5 Aug. 2001: B10.

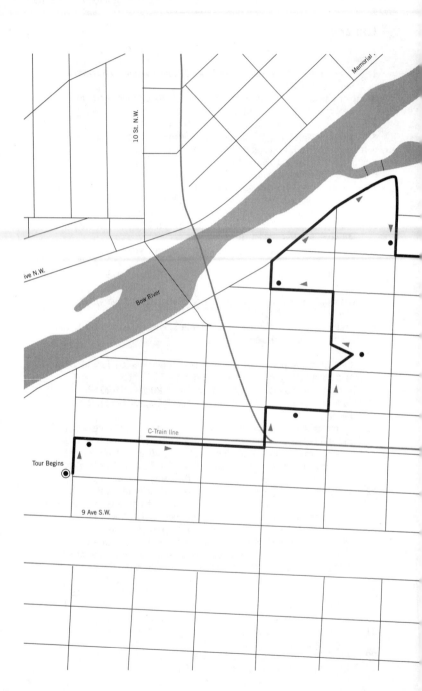

Memorial ·

10 St. N.W.

ive N.W.

Bow River

C-Train line

Tour Begins

9 Ave S.W.

Downtown, Eau Claire, and Chinatown

e's Island Park

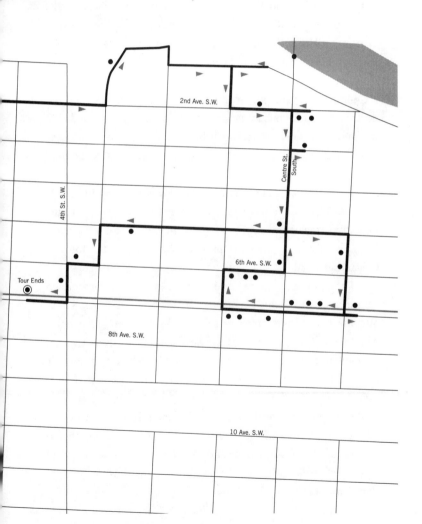

2nd Ave. S.W.

Centre St. South

4th St. S.W.

6th Ave. S.W.

Tour Ends

8th Ave. S.W.

10 Ave. S.W.

Although Calgary's greatest concentration of downtown historic buildings lies along Stephen Avenue, many significant older structures stand isolated amidst modern office towers, or form small clusters wherever a group of them have escaped the wrecker's ball.

This tour comprises portions of four different downtown districts, as the city defines them for planning purposes. It begins in the Downtown West End, which lies between 9th Street S.W. and 14th Street S.W., and from the Canadian Pacific Railway (CPR) tracks to the Bow River. The area lay outside the central business district until after World War II, but includes Mewata Armouries and the original Mount Royal College campus.

Next is Eau Claire, which lies between 2nd Street (originally Hamilton Street) and 9th Street S.W. (originally Egan Avenue), and north from 3rd Avenue to the Bow River. It was originally settled in the late nineteenth century, largely by Scandinavians who had come from Wisconsin to work for the Eau Claire and Bow River Lumber Company.

To the east of Eau Claire lies Chinatown, between 2nd Street S.W. and Macleod Trail S.E., and generally from 3rd Avenue to the Bow River (the boundary jogs south to 4th Avenue east of 1st Street S.E). Established in 1910, the present Chinatown is the third in Calgary's history.

The tour also skirts, and concludes in, the Downtown Commercial Core, which generally extends from 3rd Street S.E. to 9th Street S.W., and from the CPR tracks north to 3rd Avenue. Although this zone was part of the earliest built-up area in Calgary, the city's resource-based prosperity has not been kind to its historic preservation. Apart from the civic centre and Stephen Avenue (which lie within the Downtown Commercial Core, and are covered in Tour 1), historic buildings are few and exist in the shadow of skyscrapers. The greatest concentrations can be found on 6th and 7th avenues (originally Angus and McIntyre avenues, respectively) and 1st Street S.W. Seventh Avenue became the downtown Light Rail Transit (LRT) corridor in 1981.

Start: Mewata Armouries, 801–11th Street S.W.

Mewata Armouries

Address: 801–11th Street S.W.
Style: Tudor/Gothic Revival
Architect: T. W. Fuller, Department of Public Works
Architect; local supervision by Leo Dowler, Dominion
Government Architect in Calgary
Date: 1918

Mewata Armouries, 2003. With its crenelated, or notched, roofline, its corner towers, and buttresses with turrets, the armory evokes the fortress-like qualities of the castles it is meant to resemble. SHANNON LEE RAE

Militia units—in later parlance, the reserves—had a thirty-year history in Calgary by 1913, when citizens voted by plebiscite to donate part of Mewata Park to build an armory that would serve as militia headquarters. The park, one of Calgary's first, had been set aside in 1885 at the urging of William Pearce, Dominion Superintendent of Lands and Mines. The name Mewata is believed to derive from the Cree ("O be joyful"). Construction of the fortress-like brick and sandstone building began in 1915, but World War I delayed completion until 1917. It was dedicated on Armistice Day, November 11, 1918. The basement once housed a bowling alley and shooting galleries. With its crenelated, or notched, roofline, its corner towers, and buttresses with turrets, the armory evokes the fortress-like qualities of the castles it is meant to resemble. Steel trusses support the roof over a massive interior drill hall.

Mewata Armouries was meant to consolidate city militia units into a single headquarters, but the 1919 transfer of the Lord Strathcona's Horse cavalry regiment to Calgary resulted in the building's use by the permanent army for the next fifteen years, until the development of Currie Barracks.

Notable events at the armory have included: a military ball held for the Prince of Wales (the future King Edward VIII, later to become the Duke of Windsor) in 1919; a heated argument between Social Credit party leader (and future Alberta premier) William Aberhart and the intellectual father of the Socred movement, Major C. H. Douglas, in 1934; and the sudden death of City Solicitor T. W. Collinge of a cerebral hemorrhage in the Garrison officers' mess in 1944. In the 1950s, the city contemplated demolishing the armory and building a new City Hall on the site. Mewata Armouries was designated a Provincial Historic Resource in 1979 and a National Historic Site in 1991.

Route: Proceed north to 7th Avenue S.W., turn right (east), and cross 11th Street S.W. to the southeast corner of the intersection.

Kerby Memorial Building (Kerby Centre)

Address: 1133–7th Avenue S.W.
Style: International
Architect: J. M. Stevenson
Year: 1948

Generations of Calgarians remember the original Mount Royal College building, which from 1911–72 stood at 1128–7th Avenue S.W., directly across 11th Avenue from what is now the Kerby Centre. Rev. George W. Kerby (1860–1944), the minister of Central

Methodist Church (now Central United Church), founded the Methodist college in 1910 on a campus near Mewata Park and the Bow River. Kerby wanted it to be Calgary College, but the name had already been taken by a short-lived institution that aspired to become the University of Calgary. According to lore, Premier Alexander Rutherford telephoned Kerby at home to inform him a new name would be needed; Kerby reportedly looked out his window, saw the Mount Royal district, and suggested the name.

The original brick Mount Royal College building opened in 1911 and was demolished in 1972. It was built by contractor James H. Garden, who later served on the Board of Governors, and whose brother John succeeded Rev. George W. Kerby as principal. After the Kerby Memorial Building opened, the original building remained the residence building and Conservatory of Music. GLENBOW ARCHIVES NA-2448-1

Kerby established an institution that prepared students for university entry, and presided over its 1931 upgrade into a junior college affiliated with the University of Alberta, with the capacity to offer university-level courses. Kerby retired in 1942 and died two years later.

In 1949, the college expanded into a modern building across 11th Avenue, built partly through funds donated by former prime minister (and local member of Parliament) R. B. Bennett. The Kerby Memorial Building was named for Mount Royal's late founding principal; its gymnasium was named for Dr. George D. Stanley, the college's longtime chairman and a member of Bennett's federal Conservative caucus.

Mount Royal eventually became an interdenominational college and moved to its present Lincoln Park campus in 1972. The original 1911 building was demolished, and its site remains a parking lot. In 1973, the Kerby Memorial Building became the Kerby Centre, an educational and activity centre for senior citizens.

Route: Proceed east along 7th Avenue to 8th Street S.W. Cross both roads, and proceed north on 8th Street to 6th Avenue S.W. Turn right (east) on 6th Avenue, and proceed east.

Brinkhaus Jewellers (former Diamond residence)

Address: 823–6th Avenue S.W.
Style: American Foursquare
Architect: Unknown
Year: 1911

Diamond family residence, n.d. COURTESY OF JAY JOFFE

In 1911, contractor Frederick Howes built this brick dwelling—the only house remaining in what was once an overwhelmingly residential district—for himself and his family. According to lore, his wife died suddenly and he no longer wanted to live here. Within a year it became the home of Jacob and Rachel Diamond, Calgary's first permanent Jewish residents.

Jacob Diamond (born Tabarisky, 1859–1929) came from Lithuania, then part of the Russian Empire, and emigrated to Canada around 1879. He married Maria Stoodley (1872–1944) of Pembroke, Ontario, who converted to Judaism and changed her name to Rachel. The Diamonds reached Calgary in 1889, and Jacob later established a liquor store on the present site of Olympic Plaza. An active member of the local Masonic and Odd Fellows lodges, Jacob was also a pillar of the Jewish community. Religious services were held in the Diamonds' home (at that time in Victoria Park). When Alberta's first synagogue was established in the city in 1909, it was named in Jacob's honour—the House of Jacob. He served as its president for many years and helped purchase land for the Jewish burial society on Cemetery Hill. Like many other families, the Diamonds kept a horse in a stable behind their home.

After Jacob's death, the house was divided between multiple tenants. His daughter Hattie Joffe and her family took up residence during World War II, but owing to wartime conditions they could not ask their tenants to leave. The house became apartments in the 1950s and an art gallery in the 1970s. Jeweler Karl Brinkhaus bought the building in 1974 and transformed it into Brinkhaus Jewellers, a landmark family business later operated by his son Norbert. Where Diamonds once lived, diamonds are now sold.

Route: Continue east along 6th Avenue to 7th Street S.W. Cross both roads, proceed north on 7th Street, and cross 5th Avenue S.W.

McDougall Centre

Address: 455–6th Street S.W.
Style: Edwardian Classical (influenced by Beaux-Arts)
Architect: Allan Merrick Jeffers
Year: 1908

McDougall Centre, 2004. Five circular attic windows once looked out from the caretaker's apartment. SHANNON LEE RAE

Appropriately, the Alberta government's southern headquarters was designed by the same architect who conceived the Alberta legislature in Edmonton. However, it took eight decades before both buildings served similar purposes.

The sandstone McDougall Centre was originally built in 1906–08 to house the Calgary Normal School, one of three teacher training colleges that served the province until the University of Alberta took them over in 1946. It was built partly in compensation for the city not getting the provincial university. Premier Alexander Rutherford laid the cornerstone in June 1907, and the sandstone building was officially opened in September 1908. Giant columns, a triple-arched entrance, and overall symmetry define the appearance of this imposing structure, the largest educational building in the province in its day. A 1907 construction accident claimed the life of Sidney Cornford, who is buried in Union Cemetery.

When the normal school moved to the present Southern Alberta Institute of Technology (SAIT) campus in 1922, the Calgary School Board took over the building for use as McDougall Elementary School (named for Methodist missionary John McDougall) and as school board offices. Declining enrolment led to its closure in 1981, and the provincial government purchased the building, demolished its unsympathetic additions, and reopened it in 1987 as Government House South. It was declared a Provincial Historic Resource in 1982.

Route: Continue north on 7th Street to 3rd Avenue S.W. Cross both roads, and proceed west on 3rd Avenue to 8th Street S.W.

Norwegian Lutheran Church (Trinity Lutheran Church)

Address: 840–3rd Avenue S.W.
Style: Gothic Revival
Architect: Unknown
Date: 1910 (basement); 1924 (superstructure)

When industrialists Peter A. Prince and Isaac K. Kerr moved their lumber company from Eau Claire, Wisconsin, to Calgary in 1886, they also brought a group of Scandinavian lumbermen, most of them Norwegian. Like the mill itself, the district these workers built and then inhabited took the name of their former American home—Eau Claire. In 1899, they established a local congregation of the United Norwegian Lutheran Church of America. Members built a concrete basement church in 1910 and dedicated it as the Norwegian Lutheran Church. The Homestead-style parsonage at the rear was built in 1914, and, on its twenty-fifth anniversary in 1924, the congregation completed and dedicated the church's super-structure. But the Norwegian character of the Eau Claire district eventually eroded; beginning in 1927, morning services were held in English instead of Norwegian, and within a decade the evening Norwegian services were discontinued. The church was renamed Trinity Lutheran in 1941. Its local parish all but vanished as inner city decline and urban renewal transformed Eau Claire in the decades following World War II. But Trinity continues to draw parishioners from across the city spectrum and remains a vital inner-city congregation.

Trinity Lutheran Church, 2003. Shannon Lee Rae

Route: Proceed north on 8th Street S.W. to the sandstone arch visible from the rear of the parsonage.

Peace Park Memorial Arch

A plaque in the small riverside park behind this sandstone arch identifies Peace Grove, a group of twelve elm trees planted in 1992 to recognize Canada's international peacekeeping role. But there is no explanation of the sandstone arch or why it stands there.

This is the third location of the five-meter-high arch. It originally formed the main entrance of the Rohl Block (later renamed the Strathcona Block), a three-story residential/commercial block at 707–3rd Street S.E. built by businessman Conrad Rohl in 1909. Located directly east of police headquarters, the building housed the Calgary Turkish Baths for many years. It was demolished in the early 1980s to make way for the Calgary Municipal Building, but the arch was salvaged and placed in storage.

Its next incarnation came in 1985, when the stones were reassembled on the south side of Memorial Drive, opposite the Bridgeland-Memorial LRT station. The arch was dedicated as a new monument to replace cottonwood trees that had been planted along Memorial Drive in 1922 to commemorate fallen soldiers of World War I. The trees were cut down in the early 1980s for LRT construction and street widening.

In 1992, the arch was relocated to Peace Park, where it serves as a memorial to soldiers who died in both world wars and Korea. In one of history's coincidences, returning soldiers from World War I passed within sight of the arch when they paraded along 7th Avenue in 1919. Architect Leo Dowler designed the building.

The arch originally formed the main entrance to the Strathcona Block at 707–3 Street S.E. GLENBOW ARCHIVES PA-2807-4183

Route: Follow the Bow River pathway east from the Peace Park memorial arch. You will reach a point where you can turn left (north) to a bridge that leads to Prince's

Island. Do not take the bridge. Instead, turn right at this point, and follow the path south to 6th Street S.W. (which is not marked). Continue south, and cross 1st Avenue S.W.

Graphic Arts Building (Joseph Phillips Building)

Address: 101–6th Street S.W.
Style: Industrial (classically influenced)
Architect: Unknown
Year: 1911

The industrial design of the former Graphic Arts Building reflects its original use as a print shop. Though undistinguished architecturally, the building is notable through its longtime association with the influential Farm and Ranch Review. SHANNON LEE RAE

For more than sixty years after its construction in 1911, this building housed the offices of the influential *Farm and Ranch Review*, founded in Calgary in 1905 by Charles W. Peterson, Malcolm D. Geddes, and Ernest L. Richardson.

Among his other accomplishments, the Danish-born Peterson (1868–1944) served as deputy commissioner of agriculture for the North-West Territories (NWT) from 1897–1902. He later worked for the CPR as general manager of its Irrigation and Colonization

Company and as superintendent for irrigation. During World War I, Peterson served as secretary of the National Service Board and then as the nation's deputy fuel controller. Geddes had edited the *Farmer's Advocate* before moving to Calgary and entering the real estate business. He was killed in a tragic mountain climbing accident on Mount LeFroy in 1927. Richardson (1876–1940) was the longtime manager of the Calgary Exhibition and its successor, the Calgary Exhibition and Stampede.

Although the building's occupants included agriculture-related businesses, its publishing and printing tenants have supplied its public identity and its name. They have included the Herald-Western Company Ltd. and Burroughs & Co. Ltd., a publisher of law books. Phillips Bros. & Associates renovated the building as a modern office block between 1999 and 2004 and named it the Joseph Phillips Building for the company's late founder.

Route: Cross 6th Street S.W., proceed east on 2nd Avenue to 3rd Street S.W. (originally Barclay Street), and cross. To the left (north), 3rd Street becomes Barclay Parade. Proceed north on Barclay Parade, past the smokestack that once formed part of the industrial operations in Eau Claire. Keep to the right, and cross Barclay Parade when you see the 1886 Café to your left.

1886 Café (former Eau Claire and Bow River Lumber Company office)

Address: 187 Barclay Parade S.W.
Style: Utilitarian, reminiscent of a worker's cottage
Architect: Pattern book design
Year: 1911

This café's name refers to the founding date of the Eau Claire and Bow River Lumber Company, once the Northwest Territories' largest lumber supplier. The original Eau Claire office no longer exists; the restaurant building was constructed in 1911 as the company's second office. It was also headquarters for the Calgary Water Power Company, an electrical company owned by Peter Prince and Isaac K. Kerr—the same industrialists who owned the Eau Claire firm. Prince's Island to the north was named for Peter Prince. It was originally a point bar (a sediment deposit where the river curves) but was separated from the bank by a man-made logging channel. Industrial operations continued on this site until 1945, and Prince's Island was donated to the city as a park in 1946. The city's bus barns took over the lumber company's site. (As a corporate entity, Eau Claire survived until 1992 as Northern Eau Claire Construction Materials until its parent company finally closed it.)

The site was completely remade in the early 1990s with the construction of the Eau Claire Market and its surrounding restaurants, bars, and condominiums. The 1886 Café is the only historic building remaining.

The 1886 Café, 2004. Constructed in 1911 as the Eau Claire and Bow River Lumber Company's office, it is the company's only remaining building. Owner Peter Prince lived in a nearby mansion on 4th Avenue, now preserved at Heritage Park where it was moved in 1967. Shannon Lee Rae

Route: Cross Barclay Parade again, and follow it to the north
and east as it curves around the north side of the Eau
Claire Market. Turn right on 2nd Street S.W., and proceed south along the east side of the market until you
reach the T-intersection of 2nd Street and Riverfront
Avenue, where a set of stairs leads down to street level.
Be extremely cautious—you are walking by the market's
loading docks. Note the Greyhound complex to your left,
east of the market.

Once you have descended the stairs, cross 2nd
Street S.W. Turn left (north), cross Riverfront Avenue,
and then turn right (east), proceeding east along
Riverfront Avenue. Be cautious, as the sidewalk
becomes a dirt path. Continue east to Sien Lok Park,
and enter between the two Chinese lions. An historical
interpretive panel tells the story of Chinese immigrants.
Find a spot in the park to view the Centre Street Bridge.

Centre Street Bridge

Address: 118 Riverfront Avenue S.E.
Designer: John F. Green
Year: 1916

Between Calgary's incorporation in 1884 and a massive annexation in
1907, the Bow River formed the community's northern boundary.
Fogg's Ferry, established in 1882, provided a river crossing at this point.
A. J. McArthur, a businessman and politician who was trying to develop Crescent Heights, recruited investors into building a privately
owned Centre Street Bridge in 1906. The city purchased the already-
decaying bridge in 1912 with the intention of replacing it; it was condemned in 1915 and part of it collapsed into the swollen river that
spring. City Engineer George W. Craig, City Commissioner John W.
Garden, and a third man named Edwin Tambling were on the bridge
at the time; Craig grabbed one of the bridge's timbers, Garden fell into
the river and had to be rescued, and Tambling drowned.

North span of the original Centre Street Bridge collapses into the Bow River, June 1915. GLENBOW ARCHIVES NA-671-8

Craig had designed a replacement bridge in 1912, but construction was delayed. Thomas Mawson, a English town planner who was consulting for the city in 1913–1914, suggested a level bridge with an enormous elevator that would carry vehicles up and down the height at the bridge's north side. The present design was the work of John F. Green and the bridge was completed by the end of 1916 at a cost of $400,000. The bridge was extensively rehabilitated in 1974 and 2000.

The concrete decorative elements on the bridge's four kiosks—each topped by a stately lion and decorated with bison heads—were originally designed by city employee James Langlands Thompson, a Scottish stonemason, who patterned the lions on those on Nelson's Column in London's Trafalgar Square. The finishing work was done by "Cement Joe" and "Cement Bill," as the bridge-building crew called brothers Dymtro and William Stogryn. The decaying lions and bison heads were replaced with replicas in 2002. One of the restored original lions now rests in front of the Calgary Municipal Building. The bridge became a Municipal Historic Resource in 1992.

Route: Return west to the park's entrance, and cross
Riverfront Avenue at the east side of 1st Street S.W.
(originally Scarth Street). Continue south on 1st Street to
2nd Avenue (originally Abbot Avenue), also known as
Daqing Avenue (pronounced "da-ching," named in 1985
for Calgary's twin city in the People's Republic of China).
Turn left (east) on Daqing Avenue, and proceed east.

Chinese United Church

Address: 124–2nd Avenue S.W.
Style: Modern Gothic
Architect: Maxwell Bates
Year: 1954

The Chinese United Church originated as the Chinese Mission,
which was established in 1901 and affiliated with the Baptist
Church. Former mayor Thomas Underwood built the original
Chinese Mission on 10th Avenue S.W. and provided land for a new
building near the Canton Block in 1910. The two-story brick building served as a church, English-language classroom, gymnasium (in
its function as the Chinese YMCA) and as the venue for Cantonese
operas. One of its most influential members was Ho Lem
(1870–1960), a prominent businessman and pillar of the Chinese
community. Ho Lem raised substantial funds for the new Chinese
United Church—one of the Chinatown's first buildings constructed after World War II—and he unveiled its cornerstone on
November 19, 1954. The Mission building to the east became a
rooming house, and was demolished in the 1970s to make way for
Oi Kwan Place, a towering senior citizens' residence.

Route: Continue east on Daqing Avenue to Centre Street
(originally McTavish Street). Cross both roads to the
southeast corner of the intersection.

Chinese United Church, 2004. Its architect, Maxwell Bates, also designed St. Mary's Cathedral in the Mission district. He is also remembered as an artist and poet.
SHANNON LEE RAE

Canton Block

Address: 202-210 Centre Street S.E.
Style: Edwardian Commercial
Architect: J. B. Henderson
Year: 1910

Canton Block, 2003. Chinatown's only remaining original 1910 building is a typical Edwardian Commercial building and has no Chinese motifs. SHANNON LEE RAE

Built in 1910, the Canton Block and its now-demolished contemporary, the Chinese Mission at 120–2nd Avenue S.W. (the site of Oi Kwan Place), anchored Calgary's third Chinatown permanently at the southern end of the Centre Street Bridge. The first Chinatown developed near the CPR station (present site of the Calgary Tower) in the 1890s; the second was located at 10th Avenue and 1st Street S.W. When the second Chinatown was threatened by proposed railway development, a small group of Chinese businessmen sought permanency by becoming their own landlords. Among them was Luey Kheong, one of the city's first Chinese merchants, the first to bring his wife from China, and father of Calgary's first Chinese-Canadian baby. A racist citizen movement opposed to the project failed, and the Canton Block, with its eight storefronts and second-floor residences, formed the nucleus of today's Chinatown. Unlike more recent structures, the Canton Block bears no Chinese motifs; stylistically, it is indistinguishable from its Edwardian counterparts throughout the city. The building was subject to police gambling raids in its early years.

In 1911, Chinese revolutionary leader Dr. Sun Yat-Sen visited Calgary on a North American fundraising tour in support of his cause; he spoke in Kheong's Canton Block store and was feted in the Kwong Wing Kee Restaurant, also in the building. Within a year, China's emperor was deposed and Dr. Sun had become the first provisional president of the Chinese republic.

Noted restaurateurs M. C. Wong and C. H. Poon—both of whom were known unofficially as the "mayor of Chinatown"—successively operated a Canton Block restaurant from the 1920s to the 1960s. Upstairs, clan associations known as tongs offered housing, reading rooms, and recreation for their members.

As with the whole of Chinatown, the Canton Block was threatened in the late 1960s by a proposed Bow River Expressway, which would have hugged the south bank of the Bow River and displaced everything in its path.

Route: Proceed east on 2nd Avenue S.E. (as Daqing Avenue becomes east of Centre Street).

Ho Lem Block (Shon Yee Benevolent Association, Calgary Branch)

Address: 109–2nd Avenue S.E.
Style: Edwardian Commercial
Architect: Unknown
Year: 1911

In 1901, Canton-born Ho Lem (1870–1960) left his homeland—and, temporarily, his wife and son—for Canada. He learned English (with a Scottish accent) at the Chinese Mission, and worked as a dishwasher and then as a cook before sending for his family in 1907 and establishing his own restaurant and boarding house on 9th

Avenue S.E. One of his boarders, Dr. Michael C. Costello, served as mayor during World War I. Ho Lem was one of the first Chinese Calgarians to convert to Christianity, and he eventually served as an elder at Knox United Church.

Around 1917 Ho Lem bought this two-story commercial block, and here he operated his Calgary Knitting Mills until World War II. He became president of the Chinese National League, a social and political organization affiliated with the republican politics of Dr. Sun Yat-Sen and Generalissimo Chiang Kai-Shek, and now embodied in the government of Taiwan. Ho Lem sold the western half of this building to the League in 1919 to serve as its headquarters, which included a reading room and boarding house. For many years the League's rival organization, the Chinese Masons, made their headquarters in the next building to the west, at 107–2 Avenue S.E. (now the Golden Inn Restaurant). The Chinese National League moved into new quarters a block south in 1954.

Ho Lem died as a pillar of Calgary's Chinese community. His son, George Ho Lem, served as an alderman (1959–65) and in 1971 became Alberta's first Chinese-Canadian member of the Alberta legislature.

Centre: this typical Edwardian Commercial building housed a restaurant and grocery business before Ho Lem bought it in 1917. Right: the Golden Inn Restaurant at 107a–2nd Avenue S.E. once housed the Chinese Masons. SHANNON LEE RAE

Route: Return west along 2nd Avenue to Centre Street, and
turn left (south). Proceed south on Centre Street to 3rd
Avenue S.E. (originally Egan Avenue), and turn left
(east). Continue east on 3rd Avenue.

Chinese National League

Address: 110–3rd Avenue S.E.
Style: Modern Classical, with some Moderne influence
Architect: Unknown
Year: 1954

Chinese National League, 2003. SHANNON LEE RAE

This building, with its aluminum signage and abstracted classical
details in its Tyndall stone façade, forms a delightful 1950s period
piece in the heart of Chinatown. It was built to replace the League's
former hall in the Ho Lem Block to the north, opening in April 1954
with four days of banquets. The building has served as meeting
space, offices, housing, and recreation for League members as well
as for the new immigrants it served. The stylized sun at the base of
the flagpole is emblematic of the nationalist government of Taiwan.

Route: Return west on 3rd Avenue, and cross Centre Street. Turn left (south), and proceed to 5th Avenue S.W. (originally Northcote Avenue). Go to the base of the cupola at the corner. Interpretive panels on the north side tell the story of the cupola and the clock.

James Short Park
Address: 112–5th Avenue S.W.

Cupola in James Short Park, 2004. SHANNON LEE RAE

James Short Park was once the site of the sandstone James Short School, built as Central School in 1905 to supplement the original wooden school on the same property, and later renamed for its early principal. James Short (1862–1942) moved to Calgary in 1889 and served as Central's principal until he took up the law in 1892. When a group of local Chinese businessmen first bought development land in the present Chinatown in 1910, citizens who opposed the creation of Chinatown hired Short as their lawyer. Ironically, the parkade under James Short Park serves the very Chinatown his clients tried to stop. The Chinese Cultural Centre stands partly on land Short once owned.

When James Short School was demolished in 1969, the Local Council of Women appealed successfully for the cupola to be saved. For years, it stood on Prince's Island and was finally returned to its place of origin when James Short Park was developed in 1995. Although it had space for a clock, in all its years atop the school the cupola never contained one. The mechanism inside it was originally housed in the clock tower above the Burns Block (101–8th Avenue S.W.), demolished in the early 1960s.

Route: Cross both Centre Street and 5th Avenue S.E., and proceed east along 5th Avenue to 1st Street S.E. Turn right, and proceed south along 1st Street.

North-West Travellers Building

Address: 515–1st Street S.E.
Style: Edwardian Classical
Architect: Richards and Burroughs
Year: 1913–14

Early in the twentieth century, Calgary was the home base for hundreds of commercial travelers and manufacturers' agents, who showed samples and took orders on behalf of a vast array of manufacturers, wholesalers, and jobbing houses. The Northwest Commercial Travellers Association of Canada, a Winnipeg-based organization, sought personal benefits and improved conditions for its members. In 1913–14, the association built this complex for members' professional and social use. Here, traveling salesmen could rent offices, sample rooms, and residential suites, and find refreshment at the Commercial Club, a licensed establishment for members. The provincial government also rented space in the building for the Attorney General's Detective Department and Liquor License Branch. The advent of prohibition in 1916 spelled the end of the Commercial Club, and before long the building proved to be a white elephant. The association moved to the nearby Odd Fellows Hall and rented its own building from 1926–33 to the Calgary School Board for use as the Commercial High School.

The North-West Travellers Building was originally designed as a five-storey struc-ture, but only four floors were built. Its notable features include its central pediment and flagpole, entablature with original lettering, stone shields, and a limestone ground-level façade with accurate reconstructed storefronts. SHANNON LEE RAE

From 1928–35, part of the building housed the Calgary Public Museum. Hailed as one of only five municipally owned museums in the country, the museum boasted art displays and historical and natural history exhibits (including Oliver Cromwell's glasses and a sectioned, working beehive). The museum operated through the worst years of the Great Depression and never charged admission. But, by 1935, its private and government grants evaporated and the museum closed its doors. Its collections were dispersed; some artifacts were returned to donors, others destroyed, and others still were passed on to the Calgary Brewing and Malting Company's Horseman's Hall of Fame. Those in the latter group eventually made their way to the Glenbow Museum.

In its next incarnation, much of the building served as the YWCA Blue Triangle Service Women's Leave Centre during World War II. The North-West Commercial Travellers Association finally sold the property around 1945, and in 1948 it was converted into the Salvation Army's men's social service centre and hostel. Neil Richardson's Heritage Properties Corporation acquired and restored the building in 2003 and converted it into character office space. The building was designated a Provincial Historic Resource in 2003.

Route: Continue south along 1st Street S.E. to 6th Avenue (originally Angus Avenue).

Fire Hall No. 1 (Budget Rent-a-Car)

Address: 140–6th Avenue S.E.

Style: Classical

Architects: Lang and Major (Hodgson, Bates and Butler, associate architects)

Year: 1911

This classically detailed brick structure was Calgary's second fire headquarters, built in 1911 to replace the original central fire station at 122–7th Avenue S.E. (now the site of Royal Canadian Legion No. 1). It was built during the tenure of Fire Chief James "Cappy" Smart (1865–1939), who held the post for thirty-five years. The five arched bays with their swinging doors were designed for both horse-drawn vehicles and the motorized equipment that was beginning to replace them. The building's corner position provided rapid access both to 6th Avenue and 1st Street S.E. Before a 1920 addition extended the second floor to the west, firefighters had to use the outdoor fire escape to access their upstairs dormitory.

The former Fire Hall No. 1 was adaptively reused as Budget Rent-a-Car in 1989.
SHANNON LEE RAE

By 1945, larger fire engines could no longer fit through the bay doors; the swinging doors and etched glass windows above them were removed and replaced by larger overhead doors. At the same time, the copper dome and stone detailing were removed, both as a safety precaution for the aging tower and to install an air-raid siren. The station was finally replaced in 1973. It was designated a Registered Historic Resource in 1975, but remained vacant for years while proposals for its use were debated. In an example of creative re-use, the building became Budget Rent-a-Car in 1989, and the company spent over a million dollars restoring it. The copper cupola was re-created in 1991, but designers misread historic photographs, and it contains one more pillar than the original had.

Route: Cross both 1st Street and 6th Avenue S.E., and proceed south along 1st Street to 7th Avenue S.E. (originally McIntyre Avenue).

Cathedral Church of the Redeemer

Address: 218–7th Avenue S.E.
Style: Gothic Revival
Architect: John Charles Malcolm Keith of Victoria, B.C.
Year: 1904

The Cathedral Church of the Redeemer is the second-oldest existing church in downtown Calgary. Its façade is built of rusticated Paskapoo sandstone. SHANNON LEE RAE

The cornerstone of Calgary's Anglican cathedral (designated until 1949 as the Pro-Cathedral, or temporary cathedral, until plans for a larger, permanent cathedral were finally abandoned) indicates that it was laid September 8, 1904, by the governor general, the Earl of Minto. It was indeed laid by Minto, but not until September 13; his arrival was delayed but the stone had already been carved. The first service in the new building was held July 30, 1905, but it was not consecrated until May 22, 1910. Columns on the carved oak altar, manufactured by Calgary's Cushing Brothers mills, were patterned after a pillar in Westminster Abbey. It became a Provincial Historic Resource in 1977.

The Anglican Pro-Cathedral was built just west of Calgary's original wooden Anglican church, built in 1884 and demolished in 1907 to build Paget Hall (218–7th Avenue S.E.), the parish hall. (Paget Hall, in turn, was demolished in the 1970s.)

Route: Cross 1st Street, and proceed west along 7th Avenue
S.E.

St. Regis Hotel (Regis Plaza Hotel)
Address: 124–7th Avenue S.E.
Style: Edwardian Commercial
Architect: Alexander Pirie
Year: 1913

Businessman Albert C. Johnson built this terra cotta-clad hotel in 1913 and leased it to Carl Grunwald, who operated it as the Grunwald Hotel. At a time when most of Calgary's hotels lined 9th Avenue near the railway station, forming the city's "whisky row," the Grunwald stood apart. It had no bar or liquor license and originally appealed to business travelers. Johnson cancelled Grunwald's lease in 1917 over rent arrears and operated the hotel himself as the St. Regis. Zurich-born Jacob A. Knoepfli, a carpenter and home builder, bought the hotel in 1924 and opened a beer room when prohibition was repealed that year. Knoepfli built the nearby Hotel York in 1929 and owned both hostelries until 1946. The St. Regis was damaged by fire in 1958 and 1990, and it was extensively renovated in the 1970s. In 1997 it was renamed the Regis Plaza.

Route: Continue west on 7th Avenue S.E.

Regis Plaza Hotel, 2004. Originally operated as the Grunwald Hotel and later as the St. Regis, it is one of the city's few remaining buildings clad in terra cotta and the only remaining example of a one-time temperance hotel. It was damaged by fire in 1958 and 1990. SHANNON LEE RAE

Great War Veterans Association (Royal Canadian Legion #1)

Address: 116–7th Avenue S.E.
Style: Classically influenced
Architects: J. E. Burrell and James Basevi
Year: 1922

Royal Canadian Legion, 2004. The original second-floor balcony has been removed, and the brick and sandstone façade was sandblasted in 1981. Shannon Lee Rae

When he visited Calgary in September 1919, as part of a goodwill Canadian tour, the Prince of Wales—the future King Edward VIII—turned the sod for the Great War Veterans' Association clubhouse. He promised to return some day and see the fine edifice that would be built on the site. Once he had left, the crowd lunged toward the spot where he stood, hoping to bag some some soil that had touched the royal spade. (One wonders how many such bags of dirt still remain in attic chests or basement storerooms.) Everyone knew he would return; on the same trip, the heir apparent to the British throne bought a spread south of the city and named it the EP Ranch.

The moment came eight years later, when the prince returned and was expected to motor through the city, waving to the crowds that already awaited him when the train arrived. The proposed route would have taken him right past the building he promised to see. However, reported the *Albertan*, the prince "lived up to his reputation for making a quick getaway from the crowds by fleeing to the Country Club for lunch and golf accompanied by his brother."[1] By the time he next returned to the city, it was as the Duke of Windsor, as the former king was styled following his 1936 abdication.

Initially, only the basement was completed, and construction resumed in 1922 when government funds and public contributions reached the required sum. On September 6, 1922, Lieutenant-Governor R. G. Brett officially opened what was originally known as the Memorial Hall. The main floor included a large meeting hall, and the use of large steel trusses allowed the room to be free of pillars.

In 1925, the Great War Veterans Association merged with other like groups to form the Royal Canadian Legion, and this building became its No. 1 branch. Conservative leader (and future prime minister) R. B. Bennett paid off the mortgage in 1927. The Legion building became Provincial Historic Resource in 1981.

The original building on the property was Calgary's first Fire Hall No. 1, a brick building constructed in 1887 and demolished in 1911. James "Cappy" Smart, Calgary's fire chief from 1898–1933, lived immediately west of the fire hall, on the present site of the parking lot between the Legion and the old Hotel York.

Route: Continue west on 7th Avenue S.E.

Hotel York

Address: 102–7th Avenue S.E.
Style: Edwardian Commercial, with Art Deco motifs
Architect: Unknown
Year: 1929

Art Deco motifs decorate the former Hotel York, built in 1929–30. SHANNON LEE RAE

Between 1887 and 1910, this corner was the site of the Knox Presbyterian Church, one of the first substantial sandstone buildings constructed in the city. Dr. Neville James Lindsay, a physician, businessman, and one-time alderman, bought the property in 1910, and the Knox congregation built a new edifice, now known as Knox United Church, nearby. Lindsay proposed building a ten-story office complex on the site; he demolished the church and began using the stones to build a mansion along the Elbow River south of the city (later known as Lindsay's Folly). But Calgary's real estate boom collapsed in 1913, and Lindsay's wealth vanished. His unfinished mansion collapsed into ruin, and the former church property remained undeveloped.

Building prospects looked better by 1928, when builder Jacob A. Knoepfli, owner of the nearby St. Regis Hotel, bought the corner and started building the new Hotel York in June 1929. The first class, 187-room hotel was lavishly finished in a combination of Egyptian and Spanish styles, and the brick and Tyndall stone exterior sported Art Deco motifs. The hotel housed a billiard parlor, bowling alley, and the radio broadcasting studios of CFCN. By the time

Mayor Andrew Davison officially opened the hotel in 1930, the Great Depression had begun.

The York maintained its high-class trade for many years, but its status ultimately declined. It was repaired after small fires in 1970 and 1990, and in 1993 it was acquired by the city's non-profit housing agency, Calhome Properties, and converted into a low-income housing project. The hotel's strip bar continued to operate for a short time after its sale, distinguishing it as the only city-owned establishment of its kind in Calgary.

The parking lot behind the hotel was the site of Hull's Opera House, built by William Roper Hull in 1893 and demolished in 1963. When it opened, the opera house could seat one-quarter of Calgary's 4,000 residents. After its initial glory years, the building was converted into residential and commercial space and renamed the Albion Block.

Route: Cross both Centre Street and 7th Avenue S.E., and proceed west along 7th Avenue.

Tyndale Memorial Bible House (Inn From the Cold Society)

Address: 117–7th Avenue S.W.
Style: Edwardian Commercial; 1926 modification includes a Gothic-style arch
Architect: Unknown
Year: 1910

In its original incarnation, this small commercial building housed the Calgary Plumbing and Heating Company. It was purchased by the Canadian Bible Society in 1926 and rededicated as the Tyndale Memorial Bible House, named for William Tyndale, the sixteenth-century scholar who translated the New Testament into English. Former mayor Thomas Underwood, a dedicated Baptist whose eponymous business block had previously housed the society, laid the cornerstone on May 26, 1926. The sandstone façade—with its

Gothic Revival arch, its relief figure of a Bible, and its prominent identification block (which includes the initials BFBS, for British and Foreign Bible Society)—dates from that time. The building remained a Bible bookstore until 1989, when the Canadian Bible Society moved to the warehouse district. It housed the Calgary Urban Project Society from 1989–97, and since 1997 has been the headquarters of the Inn From the Cold Society, where homeless people register for emergency overnight shelter in participating city churches.

The modified 1926 façade of the former Tyndale Bible House was a very late use of Calgary sandstone. Most of the city's sandstone buildings predate World War I.
SHANNON LEE RAE

Route: Continue west along 7th Avenue S.W.

Calgary Stock Exchange Building (Southern Fun Arcade)

Address: 129–7th Avenue S.W.
Style: Edwardian Commercial
Architect: Unknown
Year: 1913

This building's diminutive scale contrasts with the grand designs that lay behind it. The Calgary Stock Exchange (CSE) was incorporated October 25, 1913, just as the city's phenomenal pre-World War I real estate boom turned bust. At first, the CSE existed in name only. But rumors of "black gold" in the vicinity—later substantiated by the discovery of oil in Turner Valley in May 1914—fueled the city's first, brief oil boom. Within days of the discovery, Calgary was gripped by what one journalist termed "petroleumania ragiensis." Citizens dropped everything to line up and buy stocks; hundreds of oil companies were set up in the space of weeks, many of them flim-flam operations. Curbside brokers flogged stock certificates with evangelical zeal.

With more or less success, the CSE promised to regulate trading and to establish market prices. When it opened in temporary quarters in June 1914, the CSE was only one of several new exchanges in the city. It emerged from the pack as the most reputable and, in the end, as the only one that endured. The CSE built its headquarters on a 7th Avenue lot owned by Senator James A. Lougheed, whose business partner, Edmund Taylor, was also the CSE's president. Construction stopped temporarily, only days after it began, with the outbreak of World War I. Finally, on October 26, 1914, U.S. Consul Samuel C. Reat officially opened the building. Calgary's social élite gathered on the trading floor to hear speeches, songs, and orchestral music. "The occasion was one which will long be remembered," predicted the *Calgary Herald*.[2]

Within a year, however, the $11,000 facility had become a white elephant. The oil boom fizzled, stock trading plummeted, and the

A video arcade now occupies the original home of the Calgary Stock Exchange. On the old trading floor, the only exchanges these days are banknotes for quarters.
SHANNON LEE RAE

nation was at war. In 1915, Senator Lougheed evidently bailed the CSE out of debt and assumed ownership of the building. By the end of the year, the exchange moved to less expensive digs; in 1917, the once-proud institution became dormant. It took another major oil discovery to revive the exchange permanently in 1926. (The CSE became the Alberta Stock Exchange in 1974, and in 1998 it merged with its Vancouver counterpart to become a junior venture exchange.) The original building became part of the New Calgary Market, a grocery and meat market largely operated by Chinese-Canadians, in 1916. A corridor over the back alley connected the building to shops in the Lougheed-owned Norman Block on 8th Avenue S.W., and traces of the walkway can still be seen in the lane. From 1930 to 1971, the building housed Wilkinson Electric. The main floor became a games arcade in the early 1970s.

Route: Continue west on 7th Avenue to 1st Street S.W.

Central Methodist Church (Central United Church)

Address: 131–7th Avenue S.W.
Style: Romanesque, with Gothic Revival features
Architects: Badgely & Nicklas of Cleveland, Ohio; J.F.
    Burrell and R.E. McDonnell (reconstruction after fire)
Year: 1904–05; rebuilt 1916–17; additions 1948, 1952,
    1955–56

When the Central Methodist Church was gutted by fire on February 29, 1916, *Calgary Herald* photographer William J. Oliver did not have to step outside to take a spectacular photograph of the blaze. The Southam Building, which stood directly north of the church from 1913 until it was demolished in 1972, housed the *Herald* offices from 1913–32, and Oliver had only to open the window to get his shot.

The "mother church" of Calgary's Methodist congregations originated in 1875 as Reverend John McDougall's Calgary Methodist Church, and its congregants eventually included Senator James A.

Lougheed, Prime Minister R. B. Bennett, and mayors W. H. Cushing and Fred E. Osborne. Rev. George W. Kerby served as its minister from 1902–10, when he resigned to become principal of the new Mount Royal College. Lady Belle Lougheed laid the cornerstone for this Gothic-influenced building in May 1904, and the rusticated sandstone church was dedicated in February 1905. After the fire, it re-opened in April 1917 with a new Casavant organ installed. It joined the United Church of Canada in 1925 as Central United Church.

Additions built in 1948 and 1952 did not compromise its historic appearance, but two Modern entrances built in the mid-1950s did. Before the incongruous corner entrance was removed in 1996, it covered half of the cornerstone.

Calgary Daily Herald *photographer William J. Oliver had only to aim his photograph from an office window to take this picture of Central Methodist Church burning on February 29, 1916.* Glenbow Archives NB-16-428

Route: Cross 7th Avenue S.W., and proceed north on 1st Street S.W. to 6th Avenue.

Lougheed Building

Address: 604–1st Street S.W.
Style: Chicago
Architect: Len Wardrop of Dart and Wardrop, Salt Lake City, Utah
Year: 1912

Lougheed Building, 2003. KAREN OLSON

When it opened in 1912, Sir James A. Lougheed's eponymous new block epitomized Calgary's expansive mood at the height of its phenomenal pre-World War I boom. The L-shaped building contained five floors of offices, sixteen storefronts, basement restaurants and shops, and a rooftop penthouse suite. It wrapped around the Sherman Grand Theatre, a separate structure whose lobby and main entrance were housed in the Lougheed, making the two buildings inseparable for the generations of Calgarians who came here for vaudeville, symphony, "talkies," and public meetings and lectures. Office tenants have included the most powerful players in the city's economic and political realms, including the United Farmers of Alberta, the United Grain Growers, the Alberta Wheat Pool,

Home Oil, and—in the 1960s and 1970s, when Lougheed's grandson Peter was shaping his provincial party for government—the Progressive Conservative Association. Don's Hobby Shop was located here from 1959–2004. The theatre was twinned in 1972, and a decade later it became the Showcase Grand under the ownership of the Cineplex Odeon chain. It closed in the late 1990s and operated for a few years as an indoor golf driving range.

Both the building and the theatre survived early twenty-first century threats of demolition. Neil Richardson's Heritage Properties Corporation bought the Lougheed in 2003, and the city approved a tax-relief scheme to support the building's restoration on the same spring morning in 2004 that the Lougheed was damaged by fire. Theatre Junction, a local dramatic company of players, bought the Grand Theatre the same year and announced plans to restore it for live theatre.

The narrow gap between the AGT Building and the Lougheed Building forms a snicket, a type of established footpath rare in Calgary but a common feature in English towns and cities, providing alternative pedestrian pathways. This one provided egress from the Grand Theatre, but it has been closed off by a chain link fence.

Route: Continue east on 6th Avenue S.W.

Alberta Government Telephones Building

Address: 119–6th Avenue S.W.
Style: Art Deco-influenced
Architect: Peter Rule; Fordyce & Stevenson, consulting
    architects
Date: 1930

Vernor Winfield Smith, Alberta's minister of Railways and Telephones (and namesake for the town of Winfield, Alberta) laid the cornerstone for Calgary's new Alberta Government Telephones (AGT) headquarters only days after the stock market crash that heralded the Great

Depression. AGT staff architect Peter Rule (his actual job title was Building Inspector) designed an impressive monumental structure, the first public building of its scale built in the city in a decade. Its strong vertical façade comprises brick, glass, steel and Tyndall stone, and evokes both the Modern movement (with its expressed structure and lack of detail) and the Gothic-style skyscrapers then popular in Chicago and New York. Among other innovations, the AGT Building contained the first automatic elevators in the province. AGT (renamed and privatized as TELUS in the 1990s) later expanded its operation into the adjacent, extant Utilities Building (a 1939 Moderne building with Art Deco detailing); in the 1950s, it constructed a massive new communications centre across the back lane from both buildings, fronting 7th Avenue S.W. Both historic buildings on 6th Avenue were made available for Calgary's proposed Institute for Modern and Contemporary Art in the 1990s, but the project was eventually shelved and the buildings remain vacant. The AGT Building's cornerstone was removed at an unknown date.

The Alberta Government Telephones Building was conceived as a six-story building, but only four floors were built. It evokes the Gothic skyscrapers that towered over Chicago and New York at the time it was built. SHANNON LEE RAE

Route: Continue east on 6th Avenue S.W. to Centre Street,
turn left (north), and cross 6th Avenue.

Odd Fellows Temple (Calgary Chamber of Commerce)

Address: 517 Centre Street S.W.
Style: Edwardian Classical
Architect: D. S. McIlroy
Date: 1913

Red brick and locally quarried sandstone, a common configuration of materials in pre-World War I Calgary buildings, contrast nicely in this façade. Like the Odd Fellows before it, the Chamber of Commerce makes its headquarters on the top floor, with rental offices below. The elaborate details around the fourth-floor windows, compared with simpler shapes and designs on the lower floors, reflect this arrangement. The building now forms the cornerstone of Petro-Canada Centre, which towers above it. SHANNON LEE RAE

In 1884 harness maker George Murdoch (1850–1910) assumed office as Calgary's first mayor, and that same year he founded the first lodge of the Independent Order of Odd Fellows (IOOF) in what is now Alberta. The benevolent fraternal society built this impressive headquarters in 1913, but one of its design elements was never completed. Stone capitals decorate the tops of the pilasters (shallow pillars) that are spaced along the south and east façades, but only two of the capitals—those furthest to the west along the south side—are decoratively carved. The mason hired for the job found it a more difficult task than he expected, and after he quit the remaining roughed-in capitals remained untouched. For decades, the Odd Fellows Temple remained the meeting place for several lodges, including three lodges of the Rebekahs, the parallel women's organization. It was also a revenue property that housed office and commercial tenants. The IOOF sold the building in 1971, and the Calgary Chamber of Commerce bought it in 1978 and converted it into the Chamber's headquarters. The sale of high-rise-density rights on this property—transferred to the neighboring Petro-Canada Centre, built in 1983–84—compensated the Chamber for loss of development potential. The building became a Provincial Historic Resource in 1987.

Route: Proceed north on Centre Street to 5th Avenue S.W., and turn left (west). Proceed west on 5th Avenue to 2nd Street S.W. Cross 2nd Street, and continue west.

Calgary Petroleum Club

Address: 319–5th Avenue S.W.
Style: International
Architect: Rule Wynn Rule
Year: 1958

In 1950, the prestigious Renfrew Club merged with the Calgary Petroleum Club, and the amalgamated organization boasted the largest membership of any men's association in western Canada. This angular Modern clubhouse, complete with a MEMBERS ONLY plaque at the entrance, was built in 1957–58. This powerful organization had a men-only policy for decades, and the folly became apparent when federal Energy Minister Patricia Carney had to use a side entrance to address the group in the 1980s. A giant mural at the rear of the building depicts scenes from Alberta's petroleum history.

Wealth and power converge at the prestigious Calgary Petroleum Club. SHANNON LEE RAE

Route: Continue west on 5th Avenue to 3rd Street S.W. (originally Barclay Street, and now Barclay Mall). Cross 3rd Street, turn left (south), and proceed south to 6th Avenue S.W. Turn right (west), and proceed west on 6th Avenue to 4th Street S.W.

Knox United Church

Address: 506–4th Street S.W.
Style: Gothic Revival
Architect: Francis James Lawson
Year: 1913

Calgary's oldest Protestant congregation originated in 1883 as Knox Presbyterian Church, and before long its original wooden edifice was relocated from Inglewood to the northeast corner of what is now 7th Avenue and Centre Street. In an early use of sandstone, the church was rebuilt on that site in 1886. Dr. Neville J. Lindsay bought that building in 1910 as development property. He demolished the church and saved the sandstone to build a mansion on the Elbow River. Lindsay lost a fortune when the real estate boom ended in 1913; his unfinished mansion collapsed into ruin and the church site remained vacant until the York Hotel was built in 1929–30.

Knox held services at the Sherman Grand Theatre in the Lougheed Building until the present sandstone church was dedicated in 1913. It boasted 1200 seats and a Casavant organ. But its massive $184,610 cost resulted in long-term debt that was not retired until 1954. The congregation joined the church union in 1925 as Knox United Church, but dissenting parishioners formed their own splinter congregation, Knox Presbyterian. The adjoining Christian Education Wing was constructed in 1960. The sandstone church became a Provincial Historic Resource in 1980 and a Municipal Historic Resource in 1999.

A massive square bell tower and arched doorways emphasize the Gothic appearance of Knox United Church. Its façade comprises smooth-dressed sandstone blocks cut into polygonal shapes. GLENBOW ARCHIVES NA-2442-1

Route: Cross both 6th Avenue and 4th Street S.W.

Court of Queen's Bench

Address: 609–4th Street S.W.
Style: Modern
Architect: Alberta Public Works Department (Ron Clarke,
Chief Architect)
Date: 1962 (addition 1976)

The east-facing gold doors of the Court of Queen's Bench, a frequent backdrop when television reporters file courthouse stories, are familiar to anyone who watches local news. Keen observers will note that the large bronze Canadian coat of arms over the doors lacks the modifications made by the Chrétien government in the 1990s. SHANNON LEE RAE

A large sandstone block inscribed "1888" forms part of the interior lobby wall, of the Court of Queen's Bench contrasting the surrounding 1960s public works architecture. The stone was part of Calgary's original courthouse, which stood on this site from 1888–1958. Many Calgarians opposed the demolition of their historic courthouse.

Premier Ernest C. Manning laid the cornerstone of the present building in 1960, but a steel strike in the United States and other complications delayed its completion until 1962. Its façade is faced in granite, marble and Tyndall stone. The courthouse was originally five stories tall, and a four-story addition was built in 1974–76.

Route: Proceed south on 4th Street to 7th Avenue S.W., and turn right (west). Proceed west along 7th Avenue.

Alberta Court of Appeal (Court House #2)

Address: 530–7th Avenue S.W.
Style: Classical Revival
Architect: A. M. Jeffers, provincial architect; modified by Richard P. Blakey
Date: 1914

The austere appearance of Calgary's second courthouse reflects both its somber function and the diminished economic circumstances during its construction. The only adornments are in the central bay, with its arched entrance, Tuscan columns, and carved shields and provincial emblem. SHANNON LEE RAE

Calgary's second courthouse was the final piece in what became a block of three sandstone institutional buildings, which also included the original 1888 courthouse (demolished in 1958) and the Land Titles Building, built in 1908 and demolished in 1970. The new courthouse was one of the last major sandstone buildings constructed in the city. Besides its main function, the building also housed the Calgary Natural History Society museum from 1914–27. After the new Court of Queen's Bench was completed, this building became the Glenbow Museum from 1964 until the present museum opened in 1975. This building was designated a Provincial Historic Resource in 1977. It became the Alberta Court of Appeal in 1986, but toxic mold forced its closure in the 1990s. It remains vacant but will be incorporated into a new courthouse complex begun in 2004.

Tour ends.

Notes

1 "Prince Stays in City All Day for Golf," *Calgary Albertan* 11 Aug. 1927: 1.
2 "New Calgary Stock Exchange Formally Opened Last Night," *Calgary Daily Herald* 27 Oct. 1914.

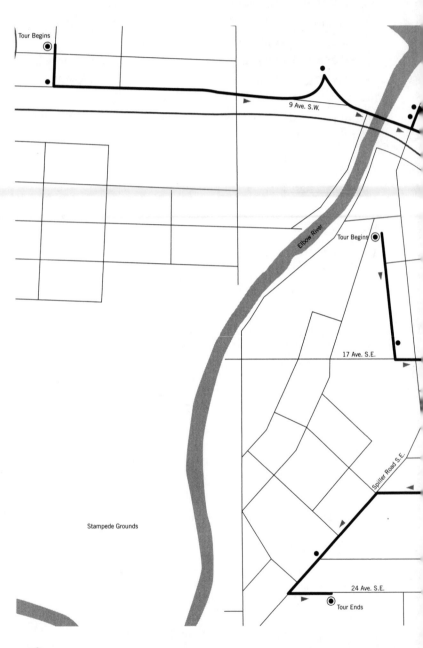

Tour Begins

9 Ave. S.W.

Elbow River

Tour Begins

17 Ave. S.E.

Spiller Road S.E.

Stampede Grounds

24 Ave. S.E.

Tour Ends

East Village, Fort Calgary, Inglewood, and Ramsay

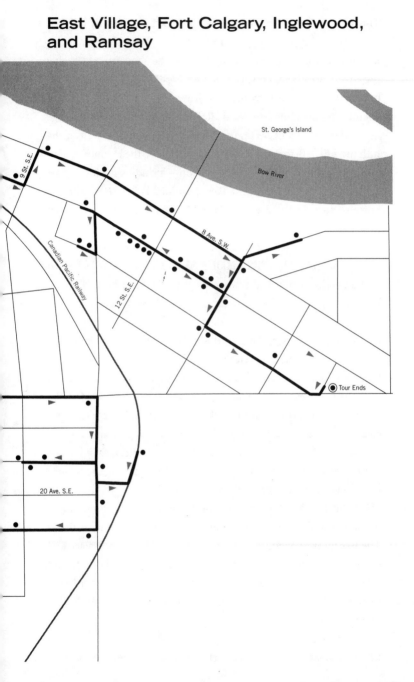

St. George's Island

Bow River

9 St. S.E.

Canadian Pacific Railway

8 Ave. S.W.

12 St. S.E.

Tour Ends

20 Ave. S.E.

This tour includes some of the oldest settled portions of Calgary, some pre-dating its incorporation as a town in 1884. The tour begins in East Village, a designation applied in the 1990s to a decaying mixed-use area between City Hall and Fort Calgary Historic Park, bounded on the north by the Bow River, and on the south by 9th Avenue and the Canadian Pacific Railway (CPR) tracks. East Village lies at the east end of Section 15, Township 24, Range 1, west of the fifth meridian. Before the railway arrived in 1883, the Dominion government had reserved land in this section—including the future East Village—for use by the North-West Mounted Police (NWMP) as a horse pasture. In January 1884, the CPR acquired Section 15 as part of its twenty-five million-acre grant of land, transferred from the federal government as an incentive to build the transcontinental railway. In 1884, the CPR subdivided and sold townsite lots in Section 15 through its real estate subsidiary, the Canada North-West Land Company. Section 15 became the heart of Calgary, and the future East Village developed as mixed-use area of residential streets, commercial services, and light industrial areas. By 1940, however, the city's Medical Officer of Health condemned the area as part of Calgary's "skid row." The area declined further by 1965, when it was targeted for urban renewal and renamed Churchill Park, after the former British prime minister who died that year. Despite "slum clearance" and construction of high-rise housing complexes, the zone east of City Hall remained a development wasteland for the rest of the twentieth century. After a controversial beginning in 2002–03, the redevelopment of East Village began in earnest.

Sixth Street S.E. forms the boundary between Section 15 and Section 14, and between East Village and Fort Calgary Historic Park. The North-West Mounted Police post was Calgary's birthplace and stood in the present park site at the confluence of the Bow and Elbow rivers from 1875 until 1914. After decades as railway yards and then an industrial zone, it was reclaimed in time for the fort's centennial in 1975.

Across the Elbow River lies Inglewood, which can claim the title of Calgary's oldest neighborhood. The CPR revealed in 1882 that it would follow a southern prairie route past Fort Calgary and not a northern route through Edmonton. Squatters and settlers followed the early lead of the Hudson's Bay Company in building their homes and businesses east of the Elbow, in the certainty that the CPR would place its station there and not in the Section 15 government reserve to the west. The transfer of Section 15 allowed the railway company to place the station on its own property and realize a considerable profit through land sales. Before long, the tents east of the Elbow were folded, and the wooden buildings were jacked up and hauled across the frozen river to lots in Section 15. But Inglewood was included within Calgary's original 1884 town limits, and it developed as an early suburb.

From 1884–1907, Inglewood extended from the Elbow River to 15th Street S.E., the eastern edge of Section 14 and of Calgary itself. However, the CPR cut an arc through the district, severing the southwestern corner that developed separately and was later renamed Ramsay.

Two different groups of business interests developed the original Inglewood and Ramsay districts. West of 11th Street S.E., today's Inglewood and Ramsay were initially developed by Quebec-born businessman Wesley Fletcher Orr (1831–1898) and his partners, who acquired their property from a Métis squatter, Louis Roselle. Orr was assistant editor of the *Calgary Herald* from 1888–89 and later served as Calgary's mayor from 1894–96 and in 1897. Orr named the streets in this area, including Orr Street (part of the original Macleod Trail, and now 8th Street S.E.[1]). New street signs installed in 2002 give original street names as well as their current designations.

The group that developed modern Inglewood east of 11th Street was headed by NWMP Commissioner A. G. Irvine and Major John Stewart, and also included former NWMP Commissioner James F. Macleod. (In 1876, at Macleod's suggestion, Irvine had recommended the name "Calgary" for the Bow River NWMP fort.) Atlantic Avenue (later redesignated 9th Avenue) developed as Inglewood's "main street," and its concentration of remaining historic buildings form part of a Special Heritage Character Area declared by the city in 1991. The area was the recipient of federal and provincial restoration projects in the 1990s.

Both Inglewood and Ramsay were expanded in 1907, when Calgary annexed a vast area surrounding its original corporate boundaries. The Inglewood tour stays within the original 1884 boundaries, but the Ramsay tour includes the 1907 expansion south of 17th Avenue S.E. Originally known as East Calgary or Brewery Flats, Inglewood's present name was adopted in 1911. It derives from Inglewood Addition, part of the 1907 annexation and originally the homestead of Colonel James H. Walker (1846–1936). Walker developed the area and named it for his stately home, Inglewood (2325–23rd Street S.E., now within the Inglewood Bird Sanctuary). Ramsay was named much later, in 1956, when residents of Burnsland, Brewery Flats, Grandview, and Mills Estate consolidated as a new community named for William Thomson Ramsay, an early land agent and property owner.

Unlike the downtown street grid that is oriented to the compass directions, streets and avenues in Inglewood and the north half of Ramsay are set on an angle. Directions in this tour are simplified, and expressed as "east" rather than "southeast," and so on.

Start: The tour begins at the St. Louis Hotel, the east-end institution best known as Ralph Klein's favorite retreat when he was mayor of Calgary in the 1980s.

St. Louis Hotel

Address: 430–8th Avenue S.E.
Style: Edwardian Classical
Architect: J. B. Richards
Year: 1913

This diminutive, working-class hotel belies the magnitude of its original owner, Colonel James H. Walker. Walker bought these lots in 1884, the year he chaired the civic committee to seek Calgary's incorporation as a town. He built the hotel in 1914 in the context of railway development. Two new transcontinentals reached Calgary in 1914: the Canadian Northern Railway and the Grand Trunk Pacific (GTP). (Both were later amalgamated into the government-owned Canadian National Railways.) The GTP purchased nearby Fort Calgary, which was demolished in 1914 and replaced by railway yards. Proximity to a proposed passenger station promised good business for the St. Louis. But a permanent station was never built, and, after the GTP folded into Canadian National, all passenger traffic went to the former Canadian Northern station on 18th Avenue S.W.

A 1950s signband contrasts with the St. Louis' Edwardian Classical design. AUTHOR PHOTO

The St. Louis remained a favorite local watering hole, particularly for those at nearby City Hall—including mayors Rod Sykes (1969–77), Ross Alger (1977–80), and, most famously, Ralph Klein (1980–89), who continued his patronage after becoming premier of Alberta in 1993. Another powerful presence at the hotel was Superman—in the guise of actor Christopher Reeve—when a scene from the movie *Superman III* was filmed at the hotel in 1983.

The façade's original design is overlaid with a 1950s signband, which, along with the 1950s-style basement tavern, dates from the ownership of John Starchuk (1944–72). The hotel served as campaign headquarters for Starchuk's unsuccessful campaign as a Liberal in the 1967 provincial election; two years later, Starchuk managed Sykes' successful quest for the mayoralty. The Blitt family bought the Louis in 1972 and introduced its house specialty, chicken and chips.

Route: Proceed east on 8th Avenue to 4th Street S.E. Cross 8th Avenue, and proceed south to 9th Avenue S.E.

King Edward Hotel

Address: 438–9th Avenue S.E.
Style: Edwardian Classical
Architect: Unknown
Year: 1906 (addition 1907)

Apart from the lavish Palliser Hotel, built by the CPR in 1914, the King Edward is the only existing building that illustrates 9th Avenue's early manifestation as Calgary's hotel row. Louis D. Charlebois (1854–1930) built the three-story brick hostelry in 1906, and the following year he completed a five-story addition, which was larger than the original structure. In 1922, Charlebois and his wife Celima retired to California, where they died in 1930 and 1938, respectively. The King Edward remained property of his estate until Celima's death.

Calgary's "Home of the Blues" was housed in the city's oldest continuously operating hotel. The King Edward closed in 2004 when toxic mold was discovered inside.
KAREN OLSON

The King Eddy's second manager, Scottish-born William Mill (circa 1873–1936), had an excellent background for dealing with his clientele. He had been a warder in a lunatic asylum, then served as a police officer in Edinburgh, Winnipeg, and Calgary before retiring from the Calgary force as an inspector in 1911. Police Chief Thomas Mackie wished Mill every success in the hotel business, but within two years his license was removed for unsanitary conditions, "loose and unsatisfactory" management, and serving drunks. "He was an efficient police officer and popular as a hotel keeper," one reporter noted, "but failed to live up to the license department regulations."[2] Mill went on to manage the National Hotel in Inglewood from 1916 until his death in 1936, a tenure that included Prohibition (1916–24). He is buried in Union Cemetery, with only two burial plots separating him from Calgary's most celebrated tippler—Bob Edwards, publisher of the *Calgary Eye Opener.*

Regina-born Homer S. Meers (1913–2003) owned the King Edward from 1946 to 1962. He used to tell truckers who drank in the bar to leave their keys on the counter if they ever got "loaded," the management would pay their taxi fare home. "You know, I never paid a dollar," he recalled. "Their wives came down and paid the taxi fare, and thanked me very much." If a good customer became a father, Meers gave him a silver dollar to start the child's bank account. "Meet the 'babies' now & then," Meers wrote years later, noting that those grown-up children still had the coins he had given their fathers.[4] He discovered all the old liquor caches, including the bottles and labels that had probably been left behind by Tom Stone. Meers renovated the hotel and paid to have the original fittings— brass beds and porcelain chamber pots, washbasins, and pitchers— hauled to the dump. He decorated the bar with "pretty good" oil paintings by a professional artist who had an outstanding account. Meers considered his bar a "poor man's club" where beer sold for twelve cents a glass.

When Meers took over, the hotel had, like many establishments of the day, a color bar—despite its location close to Calgary's "Harlemtown," as the area around 7th Avenue and 4th Street S.E. was known in the 1940s. Furious, Meers told his staff to serve a beer—on the house—to the first black person who came through the door. Meers boasted proudly of winning the patronage, and the friendship, of members of Calgary's black community.

By the early 1960s, Meers tired of trying to compete with newer establishments and left the hotel business to ranch west of Innisfail. He died in Coquitlam, B.C., at the age of 90. After two decades and a succession of owners, the King Edward was reinvented in 1983 as the city's self-proclaimed "Home of the Blues." The hotel that began as a working-class establishment and had morphed into a cowboy-rock bar was now invaded by blues aficionados who savored its gritty character. The discovery of toxic mold compelled the hotel's closure in the summer of 2004, and the need for a 4th Street S.E. subway under the CPR tracks to connect East Village with Victoria Park left open the possibility of demolition.

Route: Continue east along 9th Avenue. As you pass the 500 block S.E., note that Pearl Miller, Calgary's best-known prostitute, once lived in the now-demolished bungalow at 536–9th Avenue S.E. Cross 6th Street S.E., and enter Fort Calgary Historic Park.

Fort Calgary
Address: 750–9th Avenue S.E.

The site of Calgary's birthplace was reclaimed in the 1970s, and the Fort Calgary Interpretive Centre opened in 1978. Re-creation of the barracks began in 1996.
SHANNON LEE RAE

Although there is evidence within the city limits of First Nations camps and buffalo kill sites from thousands of years ago, Fort Calgary is usually considered as both the place and the time of Calgary's birth. Canada acquired the North-West Territories (NWT) in 1869–70, and the NWMP made their great trek across the west in 1874. The following year, the NWMP's F Troop, under the command of twenty-five-year-old Inspector Ephrem Brisebois, reached the confluence of the Bow and Elbow rivers. Construction of the log fort was contracted out to the Montana-based mercantile

I. G. Baker & Company, and the result was a vertical-log construct that leaked in the rain and allowed snow to drift through the gaps. Following his superiors' examples in the naming of Fort Walsh and Fort Macleod, Brisebois named his command Fort Brisebois. But he was widely unpopular, both to superiors and underlings, and won no friends by appropriating the fort's only stove for himself and his Métis girlfriend. Brisebois was relieved of his command, and, at the suggestion of outgoing NWMP Assistant Commissioner James F. Macleod, the "Bow Fort" was named Fort Calgary. Macleod had visited Calgary Bay on the Isle of Mull in Scotland (where his sister's in-laws owned a mansion called Calgary House), and claimed it as his inspiration for the name. For years, it was generally misunderstood to mean "swift running water," but in 1976, Calgarian Andrew Young determined it was Gaelic for "bay farm" or "enclosed pasture at the harbor." Settlers adopted the name Calgary (without the word "fort"), and it became the name of the post office and railway station in 1883, and of the town when it was incorporated in 1884.

The barracks were solidly rebuilt in 1882, and, until 1914, Fort Calgary remained a highly visible symbol framing the eastern limits of Stephen Avenue (renamed 8th Avenue in 1904), and an important judicial, administrative, and social institution. Fort Calgary was demolished in 1914 and replaced by the yards of the Grand Trunk Pacific Railway, later incorporated into Canadian National Railways.

In 1917, the NWMP Veterans' Association placed a monument at the end of 8th Avenue, but it was knocked over and damaged in 1947; it was moved south to the 9th Avenue corner the following year. Calgarians celebrated the golden jubilee of Fort Calgary in 1925. By then, however, nothing remained of the fort, and an Historic Sites and Monuments Board cairn was unveiled that year in Central Park (now Memorial Park) proclaiming Fort Calgary as a national historic site.

Plans for a Bow River expressway in the 1960s led Alderman John Ayer to wonder where Fort Calgary had been and what remained of it. Commissioned by the Glenbow Museum, University of Calgary archaeology student Ron Getty sought—and found—

remnants of the original fort in the summer of 1968. After a subsequent archaeological dig in 1970, the industrial site was cleared, and Fort Calgary Historic Park was landscaped and dedicated during the fort's centennial year. The Memorial Park cairn was relocated to the fort site in 1978, and, that same year, the Fort Calgary Interpretive Centre was opened. Reconstruction of the 1880s-era barracks began in 1996.

Route: Cross the bridge, and proceed east along 9th Avenue S.E.

Deane House

Address: 802–9th Avenue S.E.
Style: American Foursquare
Architects: Wilson and Lang
Date: 1906

The Deane House's square plan and open front verandah are essential elements of the American Foursquare style. Shannon Lee Rae

The twice-moved Deane House is the only existing structure from the Fort Calgary garrison, which was established in 1875, reconstructed in the 1880s, and demolished in 1914. The two-story, wood frame house was built in 1906 for $6200 as the residence of Superintendent Richard Burton Deane (1848–1930), the commanding officer of Fort Calgary from 1906–14. Born in India and raised in England, Deane joined the Royal Marines and retired with the rank of captain before emigrating to Canada in 1882. After serving as an aide to the governor general, Deane took a commission with the NWMP (renamed the Royal Northwest Mounted Police in 1904). After the North-West Rebellion in 1885, Deane acted as jailor for Louis Riel and other prisoners of the second failed Métis uprising.

Deane's first wife died in 1906, before the family took up residence in the house; his second wife died in 1914, the year he retired to England. (His third wife survived him, but was unable to collect a pension and ended her days in poverty.) The Grand Trunk Pacific Railway razed Fort Calgary in 1914 and transformed the site into railway yards; the house was moved nearer the Elbow River and became the stationmaster's residence. In 1929, the house was sold and moved across the Elbow to its present location, and *Popular Mechanics* magazine reported on the feat in its July 1930 issue. New owner C. L. Jacques converted it into a rooming house, which, by the 1940s, had become known as Gaspé Lodge. In its four decades, Gaspé Lodge was reportedly the site of several murders and suicides, and some consider the building haunted.

The city bought the structure in 1973 and transformed it into the Dandelion Gallery, an artists' and writers' cooperative. That year marked the centennial of the Royal Canadian Mounted Police (as the Mounties have been known since 1920), and, to mark the anniversary, the RCMP Veterans' Association restored the much-altered veranda. In the early 1980s, the Fort Calgary Preservation Society renovated the building into a restaurant and teahouse. Appropriately, given the building's rough past as a boarding house, it is a frequent venue for murder mystery dinner parties. The Deane House became a Registered Historic Resource in 1978.

Route: Enter the Deane House lawn and follow the concrete
   walk to the right (east). The Hunt House stands at the
   rear of the property.

Hunt House

Address: 890–9th Avenue S.E.
Style: Folk house
Architect: None
Date: circa 1875–82

This log "folk house" is probably the oldest existing building in Calgary. Its wood shingling was added later. SHANNON LEE RAE

This log Métis cabin, built with square nails and chinked with clay,
is probably the oldest existing building in Calgary. It was built
between 1875 and 1882, possibly by Louis Roselle, a Métis buffalo
hunter and Hudson's Bay Company employee. It was one of only
two Métis cabins remaining in Inglewood in 1908, by which time it
had become a private residence. The other, adjacent cabin was
moved to the Calgary Brewing and Malting Company grounds in
1931–32, where it remains as an historical artifact. William J. Hunt, a
Royal Canadian Air Force engineer, bought the house in 1947 and
lived here with his wife Eileen until his death in 1974. He bequeathed
the house to the city. It became a Provincial Historic Resource in
1977. It is currently used as storage for the Deane House Restaurant.

Route: Return to 9th Avenue, and proceed east to 8th Street
S.E. (originally Orr Street, for Wesley Fletcher Orr).
Cross 8th Street.

Dick Block (McGill Block)
Address: 902-904–9th Avenue S.E.
Style: Edwardian Classical
Architect: Unknown
Date: 1910 (reconstructed 1986)

The McGill Block is the first major landmark visible to eastbound commuters crossing the 9th Avenue bridge. Its round-headed windows are a Romanesque influence.
SHANNON LEE RAE

In 1888, eight-year-old Albert Adrian Dick (1880–1970) and his family moved from Manitoba to Calgary, where Bert's uncle Frank was the fire chief. Bert entered the real estate business in 1904, and in 1910 he built this eponymous three-story brick building. The following year, he started building the Alexandra Hotel (demolished in 1980 and replaced by the performing arts centre) and a palatial home in Mount Royal for himself and his seventeen-year-old bride, the former Vera Gillespie (1894–1973). The Dicks honeymooned in

Europe and England, and returned as first-class passengers on the ill-fated *Titanic*. Both survived and spent the rest of their lives in Calgary, answering reporters' questions every April as the city's only *Titanic* survivors.

The building became city property during the Great Depression and was renamed for the McGill Apartments that operated on the upper floors. It is the first substantial building seen by eastbound commuters crossing the 9th Avenue bridge from downtown, and longtime tenant Frenchy's Sporting Goods was a local landmark from 1958–93. The McGill Block was gutted by fire in November 1986, and many of the original bricks were used in its reconstruction.

Route: Continue east along 9th Avenue S.E.

Alexandra School (Alexandra Centre)
Address: 922–9th Avenue S.E.
Style: Free Classical
Architect: William M. Dodd
Date: 1902 (additions 1907, 1956)

A mural on the west side of the Alexandra Centre's 1956 addition evokes a street scene of the past. SHANNON LEE RAE

177

Built to replace the original East Ward School, Calgary's second sandstone school (there were eventually eighteen) opened in January 1903 as the New East Ward School. The four-room school was doubled in size in 1907 and named for Queen Alexandra, the consort of King Edward VII. William ("Bible Bill") Aberhart, the preacher, educator, and politician who led the Social Credit party to its first provincial victory in 1935, served as principal of Alexandra School in 1910. A concrete gymnasium, built in 1956, mars the school's appearance as seen from 9th Avenue. Alexandra School closed in 1962, and became a multi-purpose community facility in the mid-1970s.

Route: Continue east along 9th Avenue, and cross 9th Street S.E. (originally Lorne Street, named for Orr's son). Turn left, and proceed north along 9th Street to 8th Avenue S.E. (formerly Stewart Street, for Major John Stewart). Cross 8th Avenue.

Suitor House (Calgary General Surgical Associates)

Address: 1004–8th Avenue S.E.
Style: Queen Anne Revival
Architect: Unknown
Date: 1907

Every side of this three-story brick, sandstone and wood home is designed distinctly from the others, advertising the diverse skills of the carpenter who built it and lived within. Quebec-born David Suitor (1858–1938) and his wife Annie moved to Calgary in 1902, and David established himself as a building contractor, alderman (from 1907–09), and president of the Calgary Poultry and Pet Stock Association. He built this house in 1907 and lived in it with his family until 1922. It was renovated into a commercial structure in 1979.

Each side of the Suitor House is designed distinctly from the others, advertising the skills of the carpenter who built it and lived within. SHANNON LEE RAE

Route: Turn right, and proceed east along 8th Avenue to the intersection with 11th Street S.E. (originally King Street).

Van Wart House

Address: 1036–8th Avenue S.E.
Style: Victorian folk house
Architect: Unknown
Date: 1886

New Brunswicker John Van Wart (1838–1920) joined the gold rushes in California and British Columbia before settling in Calgary as a merchant in 1883. He built this wood-frame house around 1886, and lived here with his family until 1906—except for one last call to adventure in the Alaska gold fields when he was sixty-two years old. Between 1906 and 1922, this was the home of rancher Thomas Burns—whose more famous brother Patrick founded a ranching and meatpacking empire—and Thomas' son John, a future president of his uncle's corporate empire. It later became a boarding house and was converted back into a private residence in 1991.

The vertical, peaked windows of the Van Wart House are a Gothic Revival influence. Shannon Lee Rae

Route: Continue east along 8th Avenue to the corner of 12th Street S.E. (originally McLeod Street, a misspelling of Col. James F. Macleod's name).

A. E. Cross House (Rouge Restaurant)

Address: 1240–8th Avenue S.E.
Style: Queen Anne Revival
Architect: J. L. Wilson
Date: 1891

Montreal-born Alfred Ernest (A. E.) Cross (1861–1932) is best remembered as the founder of the Calgary Brewing and Malting Company, a major Inglewood employer and manufacturer of a favorite product, and as one of the Big Four ranchers who backed the original Calgary Stampede in 1912.

Cross studied business, agriculture, and veterinary science before moving to Alberta in 1884. He initially worked as a veterinarian, ranch hand, and bookkeeper at Senator Matthew Henry Cochrane's eponymous ranch west of Calgary, but soon acquired his own land near Nanton and founded the A7 Ranch, which grew to become one of the largest in the province. After an 1888 ranching accident, Cross personally withdrew from active ranching (while maintaining ownership in the A7) and went east to study the brewing industry. Alberta was still part of the NWT, which had nominally been a prohibition zone since 1875. But the prohibitory law had fatal loopholes, and bootlegging flourished throughout the west, including Calgary. When the NWT acquired self-government in 1892, one of its first new laws was for a licensed liquor system. Cross' brewery opened that very year. Cross was elected to the NWT Assembly in 1898 as a Conservative. By the time prohibition returned to Alberta in 1916, Cross had already begun investing in the province's budding oil industry.

A rooftop hand railing with elaborately figured newel posts on the Cross House evokes a "widow's walk." The enclosed front entrance and upper balcony were later additions. SHANNON LEE RAE

In 1899, just before his marriage to Helen Rothney (Nell) Macleod (daughter of the late James F. Macleod, former NWMP Commissioner), Cross purchased this farmhouse that had been built eight years earlier for railway engineer Matthew Neilson in 1891. The Crosses named their acreage the Brewery; here they kept farm animals and an orchard and garden, and it was here also that they entertained and raised their five surviving children.

In 1912, A. E. bought a Mount Royal lot and proposed building a family mansion. But he brought Nell to inspect it on a windy day, and a gust blew off her hat. Nell judged the hill too windy and told her husband she preferred to remain in what was still called "Brewery Flats." This house remained the Cross home until Nell's death here in 1959. The family donated it to the city in 1973, and it became a Provincial Historic Resource in 1977. Following its use by the city's horticultural division and the Calgary Horticultural Society, it became the A. E. Cross Garden Café in 1991. It was renamed Rouge Restaurant in 2003, and the wooden home's beveled siding, painted grey in the nineteenth century, was repainted red.

Route: Cross 12th Street S.E. and continue east along 8th Avenue. Note the Rhubarb Patch Inglewood Senior Citizens Apartments, named for Magnus Brown's rhubarb patch that was once located on this block. Residents were free to pick rhubarb as late as the 1960s.

Cross 13th Street S.E. (originally Irving Street) and keep to the left, where the road becomes New Street. Continue along New Street, and cross New Street once the sidewalk appears on the opposite site (be cautious, as there is no crosswalk). The next stop is just past the sign for the diminutive New Bow Lane.

Stewart House

Address: 26 New Street S.E.
Style: Queen Anne Revival
Architect: C. W. Moberly
Date: circa 1884

In partnership with NWMP Commissioner A. G. Irvine, Major John Stewart (1854–1893) subdivided and sold a large portion of what is now Inglewood, and his wood-frame home was meant as a showpiece for the fine residential area he hoped to promote. Stewart served on the civic committee that secured Calgary's incorporation in 1884, and, the following year, he helped form the Rocky Mountain Rangers during the North-West Rebellion. He also owned a ranch at Pincher Creek, developed coalmines in partnership with his two brothers, and operated a mail stage service between Calgary and Fort Macleod. Stewart married Isabel Skead in 1887, and they had four surviving children before his premature death from kidney failure six years later.

The house next became property of meatpacking king Patrick Burns, who used it as the staff residence for P. Burns & Co.'s foreman. The house had long since decayed before architect Jack Long (1925–2001), a former alderman, bought it in 1969. The home's rehabilitation as Long's office and residence became an example of Inglewood's possibilities years before the district's revitalization began. It became a Provincial Historic Resource in 1980. Long sold the house in 1992 and it remains a private residence.

Just as Major John Stewart intended his home to be a showcase for Inglewood's development, its 1970s rehabilitation by architect Jack Long demonstrated the area's renewed potential. SHANNON LEE RAE

Route: Retrace your path to confluence of New Street, 8th Avenue and 13th Street, and cross 8th Street.

St. Andrew's Presbyterian Church (St. Vincent Liem Catholic Church)

Address: 1405–8th Avenue S.E.
Style: Gothic Revival
Architect: Unknown
Date: 1911

St. Vincent Liem Catholic Church, 2004. SHANNON LEE RAE

This beautiful brick church was originally named St. Andrew's Presbyterian. It replaced that congregation's original 1906 edifice at 1339–9th Avenue S.E. This was one of many Presbyterian churches that declined to join with Congregationalists and Methodists in the new United Church of Canada in 1925, although some congregants left St. Andrew's for nearby Trinity United. The congregation moved to larger quarters in 1961 and sold this building to the Roman Catholic diocese. The edifice then served as St. Andrew's

Roman Catholic Church, a predominantly Italian congregation. In the mid-1980s it became St. Vincent Liem, serving Catholics of Vietnamese origin.

Route: Cross 13th Street, turn left, and proceed southwest along 13th Street to 9th Avenue.

Blyth Hall (Inglewood Food Mart & Video)

Address: 1340–9th Avenue S.E.
Style: Edwardian Commercial influence
Architect: Unknown
Date: 1923

An identification block on the 9th Avenue façade still shows the building's name, Blyth Hall. The corner store's large red Coca-Cola buttons have been removed. SHANNON LEE RAE

A common façade now unifies the two single-story brick buildings that comprise Blyth Hall, which once appeared distinct from each other. Charles Riddock (1878–1935) built the corner structure in 1923 to house his business, the Calgary Cartage Company. As a professional building mover, Riddock relocated portions of Bankhead to Banff in the mid-1920s and moved the Deane House across the Elbow River in 1929. Riddock named the building for his mother-in-law, Jessie Blyth. The East Calgary Community Club used the building as a dance hall from about 1925–28. It was converted into a confectionery store in 1934. The storefronts to the west were built in the mid-1930s.

Route: Turn around the corner and proceed northwest along 9th Avenue S.E.

Carson Block

Address: 1336–9th Avenue S.E.
Style: Edwardian Commercial
Architect: D. S. McIlroy
Date: 1912

Twice in 1912, the unfinished Carson Block made headlines in local newspapers. Reinforced concrete construction was still new to Calgary when brothers James and Edward Carson built this two-story residential/commercial block at the height of the city's pre-World War I boom. The building's concrete floors collapsed while it was still under construction, and an official investigation pitted Alderman Adoniram Judson Samis against Building Inspector Richard Harrison. The two men had already feuded over construction of Samis' eponymous block near City Hall (on the present site of the Calgary Municipal Building). Samis' committee charged Harrison with incompetence; in a heated City Hall meeting, the enraged building inspector swung five blows at the alderman, landing three on Samis' head. "Mr. Harrison is suspended from his office," blurted Mayor John W. Mitchell once Harrison stormed out and called in a stenographer to write Harrison a memo. Samis rose from his crouched position, smiled, and said "Never touched me." Then Harrison returned, threw his resignation letter on the table, and taunted Samis. "Sometime I'll get you, and I'll knock your head off."[5]

Two symmetrically placed pediments frame the Carson Block on either end, with a swag—a classical detail—between them. SHANNON LEE RAE

Like many buildings at the time, the Carson Block became city property in 1920, probably through non-payment of taxes. It returned to private ownership in 1939, and from 1946–53 it housed the Calgary Public Library's Inglewood branch. The façade was restored in 1996.

Route: Continue northwest along 9th Avenue S.E.

Haskins Block (The Collectors' Gallery of Art)
Address: 1332–9th Avenue S.E.
Style: Edwardian Commercial
Architect: Unknown
Date: 1908 (enlarged 1911)
Built in 1908 and expanded in 1911, this two-and-a-half-story brick building originally housed a retail store on the main floor and Robert Haskins' Metropolitan Rooms upstairs. It was also used as a

pool hall, a dance hall, as a lodge for the Independent Order of Good Templars, early Social Credit party meetings, and at one time for Catholic mass by St. Ann's parishioners. The building became city property shortly after the Great Depression began and sat vacant and vandalized for some time. The city contemplated demolishing the building in 1934 but instead rented it to James A. Fox, who—in contravention of the old saw about who should not be in charge of the henhouse—transformed it into the Fox Quality Hatchery. The building was sold around 1940, and, in an apparent gesture of wartime spirit, the new owner renamed the building the Victory Block. The mansard roof was apparently added in the 1940s. The ground floor façade has been altered.

The mansard roof addition is out of character for the Haskins Block but creates a striking combination with its Edwardian Commercial façade. SHANNON LEE RAE

Route: Continue northwest along 9th Avenue S.E.

Blow Block

Address: 1312–9th Avenue S.E.
Style: Edwardian Commercial
Architect: Unknown
Date: 1911

Yogi Bear has indicated the Zoo turnoff to motorists since about 1960. "The Boys," Fred Thompson and Harry Flumerfeldt, once operated their clothing store just west of the Blow Block, on the later site of Spolumbo's Fine Foods & Deli. SHANNON LEE RAE

Building contractor David C. Blow (circa 1868–1931) hailed from Mountain, Ontario, and followed his better-known cousin—Dr. Thomas Henry Blow, a physician, Conservative politician, and champion of higher education—to Calgary. David Blow built this eponymous three-story commercial building in 1911, and, in 1913, its offices were converted into apartments. Blow also managed the contemporary two-story Dougall Block (1314–9th Avenue S.E.) next door for absentee investor R. J. Dougall, and the two buildings had a common entrance to their upper floors. Blow was killed in a duck-hunting accident in 1931.

Since about 1960, a mural of Yogi Bear on the building's west side has indicated a left turn to motorists bound for the Calgary Zoo. Façade restoration in 2000 renewed Yogi and also revealed a ghost sign for "The Boys," clothiers Fred Thompson and Harry Flumerfeldt. Riff Raff Hair Studio and World Antiques currently occupy the storefronts.

Route: Proceed northwest along 9th Avenue, cross 12th Street S.E., and continue northwest along 9th Avenue.

Canadian Bank of Commerce (CIBC)

Address: 1230–9th Avenue S.E.
Style: Classical
Architect: V. D. Horsburgh
Date: 1911

This two-story brick bank building has housed the Canadian Bank of Commerce, the Imperial Bank of Canada, and the offspring of their 1961 merger, CIBC. It is the longest-serving bank building in the city. SHANNON LEE RAE

The longest continuously operating bank in the city was designed by the Bank of Commerce's staff architect, and it included a five-room suite for the branch manager. By 1937, the Commerce bank moved to a new location, and the Imperial Bank of Canada opened its branch here. The two institutions amalgamated in 1961, becoming the familiar Canadian Imperial Bank of Commerce (CIBC). The exterior was restored in 1999.

Route: Continue northwest along 9th Avenue S.E., and cross 11th Street S.E.

Fire Station No. 3 (Hose & Hound Neighbourhood Pub)

Address: 1030–9th Avenue S.E.
Style: Edwardian Classical with Romanesque influences
Architect: Unknown
Date: 1906

Fire Hall No. 3's elaborate cornice and central pediment form a strong Classical reference. The arched bays are a Romanesque influence. SHANNON LEE RAE

Horse-drawn fire wagons were still in use when the Calgary Fire Department built this satellite station in 1906. Whenever its men were called to service, 9th Avenue traffic ceased while the horses crossed from their paddock across the street. The station's last two horses—the only ones still used by the department at the time—retired in 1933.

Legend has it that a favorite monkey mascot was killed by a dog while the men of No. 3 were away fighting a fire and lies buried in the station's yard. Whether or not this is true, history does record a monkey tale. Fire Chief James "Cappy" Smart kept a menagerie of animals at the old Fire Hall No. 1 downtown. But the monkey he acquired, dubbed "Barney the Monk," proved mean, so Smart sent the animal away—to Fire Hall No. 3. Firemen tethered Barney outside for spectators' amusement, but, on a Sunday in May 1911, the animal attacked a boy who was offering peanuts, and Smart ordered the monkey destroyed. This came only two days after Smart's two boxing bears had been put down after one had killed a child at Fire Hall No. 1.

The firemen froze a rink west of the hall each winter, and children from nearby Alexandra School put on their skates in warmth inside. The firefighters also gave the children haircuts. After the station closed in 1952, it served as a kindergarten and the community hall. Since 1982, it has housed a series of restaurants and pubs, including the Firehall Restaurant and the Hose and Hydrant Pub.

Route: Cross 11th Street, then cross 9th Avenue, and then cross 11th Street again. Proceed south on 11th Street to 10th Avenue (originally Rosselle Street west of 11th Street, and Ford Avenue east of 11th Street).

National Hotel (National Condos)

Address: 1042–10th Avenue S.E.
Style: Edwardian Commercial, with Classical influences
Architect: Unknown
Date: 1907

Part of the National Hotel was converted into apartments during World War II. Conversion of the hotel into the National Condos began in 2004. SHANNON LEE RAE

This working-class hotel opened in July 1907 under the ownership of Arthur S. Marsh, who with his brothers operated the adjacent East End Livery Barn. An adjoining stable offered convenience to hotel guests before the motor age. Unfortunately, it also offered unwanted odors.

From 1910 to 1966, the National was part of a phenomenon known as the "tied house." Brewery companies could guarantee their markets through ownership of hotels that sold the brewery's products. The National became one of dozens of hotels owned by A. E. Cross' Calgary Brewery and its holding companies. By the late 1950s, the provincial government turned against this kind of vertical monopoly and required brewers and distillers to sell all their hotel properties by 1967.

The National opened a lucrative beer parlor when eight years of prohibition ended in 1924, but other aspects of the hotel's business suffered. Reduced business meant the closure of the third-floor rooms in the 1920s and of the dining room in the 1930s. Railway workers and steady hotel roomers used the kitchen and pantry to prepare meals for themselves. The city suffered a housing shortage during World War II, and the north wing of the hotel was renovated into the National Apartments in 1943.

The "Nash" was renovated in 1998 and transformed into a blues bar, but went into receivership and closed the following year. Conversion of the hotel into the National Condos began in 2004.

Route: Turn right (west) on 10th Avenue, and proceed west.

East End Livery Barn/MacLean's Auction Mart (Vacant)

Address: 1036–10th Avenue S.E.
Style: Livery barn
Architect: None
Date: 1908

Built as the East End Livery Barn, this rare remaining stable house Maclean's Auction Mart from 1930–46 and 1962–98. SHANNON LEE RAE

A livery stable next to an hotel was a ubiquitous configuration before the automobile age. Guests arriving by horse-drawn vehicles could stable their horses nearby, and those who came by rail could easily rent a horse and wagon. "Progress" has left this as the only known example of this phenomenon in the city and quite likely in the province. Built in 1908 as the East End Livery Barn, its early operators included Arthur S. Marsh and his brothers (who also ran the National Hotel, 1908–10), and Asa Hillman and his brothers (some of whom also lived in the barn, 1910–30). Alexander "Sandy" MacLean (circa 1872–1932) bought it around 1930 and moved into the loft, from which he accidentally fell to his death two years later. Sandy's son Donald, an auctioneer, operated MacLean's Auction Mart here until 1946, and his brother George, followed by George's son Gary, operated it under the same name from 1962–98.

Route: Return east along 10th Avenue S.E. to 11th Street. Cross 11th Street S.E., turn left (north), and proceed north along 11th Street to 9th Avenue S.E. Turn right on 9th Avenue.

Burn Block

Address: 1217–9th Avenue S.E.
Style: Edwardian Commercial
Architect: Unknown
Date: 1912

The Burn Block's combined use of light and dark colored bricks (and even red mortar between them) creates an excellent polychromatic effect. SHANNON LEE RAE

Contractor Lawrence R. Burn (circa 1864–1929) built this brick, three-story office and commercial building in 1912, and made it his home until about 1919. Born in Ottawa, Burn settled in Calgary in 1901, fought in World War I with the 137th Battalion, and later became building superintendent at the Exhibition Grounds (today's Stampede Park), where he was responsible for building the 1919 grandstand that remained in place until 1973. He eventually moved with his family to San Francisco.

Early occupants included the Palmetto Candy Works, the Vienna Bakery, a Masonic Hall, and one of the earliest locations of Jenkins' Groceteria. The Burn Block's upstairs offices were converted into apartments in the 1930s, and the building was damaged by fire in 1973 and 1987. The façade was restored in 1996.

Route: Proceed southeast on 9th Avenue S.E.

Seablom Block

Address: 1223–9th Avenue S.E.
Style: Edwardian Commercial
Architect: Unknown
Date: 1910

Swedish-born businessman Oscar W. Seabloom (born Oscar Sjöblom, 1875–1916), a partner with Maxwell Fraser in the Seabloom-Fraser Contracting Company, built the two-story Seablom Block (reflecting a variant spelling of Seabloom's anglicized name) in 1909–10. Seabloom was the builder and Fraser the money man. The two went on to build the larger Fraser-Seabloom Block in 1912. Notable early occupants of the Seablom Block included a Masonic lodge (from 1915–18) and the office of John M. Erickson, who with his wife Nola founded the Canadian Chautauqua circuit and managed it until 1935. Named for Lake Chautauqua, New York, where the phenomenon began in 1874, Chautauqua was an itinerant event that operated, circus-style, from a tent. Lecturers, preachers, and performers offered education, inspiration, and entertainment. From 1921–27, the Seablom Block housed Chautauqua's local prop and stage shop. Merchant David Smolensky later bought the building and operated David's Dry Goods and Grocery here until his death. The Dragon Pearl, a Chinese restaurant, has been located here since the early 1980s. The façade was restored in 1997.

Seablom Block, 2003. Stylistic details on this typical Edwardian Commercial building include window keystones and sandstone sills, and a tin-pressed cornice. The storefronts have been modified and the second-floor windows replaced.
SHANNON LEE RAE

Route: Continue southeast on 9th Avenue S.E.

Fraser Block
Address: 1225–9th Avenue S.E.
Style: Edwardian Commercial
Architect: Unknown
Date: 1911

Relief lettering in the Fraser Block's cornice, giving the building's name and construction date, is angled downward for better viewing from the street. SHANNON
LEE RAE

Businessman Maxwell Fraser (1879–1915) built this four-story brick building in 1911, and it enjoyed a short-lived record as the tallest building on Inglewood's 9th Avenue strip—until Fraser and partner Oscar Seabloom built the nearby Fraser and Seabloom Block the following year. Fraser hailed from London, Ontario, and operated sugar and lumber businesses in Mexico before settling in Calgary in 1908. Like his partner in the Seabloom-Fraser Contracting Company, Fraser died young. He joined Lord Strathcona's Horse regiment at the outbreak of World War I and died on the battlefields of France in 1915. Only months after its 1993 restoration, the top floor and roof of the Fraser Block were damaged in an explosion and had to be repaired.

Route: Continue southeast on 9th Avenue S.E.

Aull Block

Address: 1227–9th Avenue S.E.
Style: Edwardian Commercial
Architect: Unknown
Date: 1908

In the timeless tradition of doctors investing in real estate, Ontario-born physician Erastus Aull (died 1944) speculated in real estate during Calgary's pre-World War I boom. He invested his earnings in this two-story brick building.

One of the Aull Block's early occupants was Henry Marshall Jenkins, who transformed his Inglewood grocery store, Jenkins and Cornfoot, into a Southern Alberta groceteria chain. In 1931, Aull sold this building to the Sheftel brothers—Ben, Harry, Harvey, and Leo—members of a Jewish family that came from the Soviet Union in 1922. Renamed the Sheftel Block, it housed the family's East Calgary Empress Grocery until 1955. The building returned to its original name in 1993 when its brick façade was stripped of its stucco covering, dismantled, and then restored to its original appearance. The storefront is now occupied by Modern Country Interiors.

Finials decorate the Aull Block's cornice at both ends. SHANNON LEE RAE

Route: Continue southeast on 9th Avenue S.E.

Garry Theatre (From the Ground Up Design Limited)

Address: 1229–9th Avenue S.E.
Style: Moderne
Architect: N. Masters
Date: 1936

This Moderne community theatre was built on the sandstone foundation of an earlier commercial building that dated back to 1905. The most notable tenant in that early building was Jenkins and Cornfoot, a grocery store that owner Henry Marshall Jenkins later transformed into a province-wide grocery chain with nearly fifty outlets.

Ben and Harry Sheftel were among the businessmen who formed the Garry Syndicate Ltd. that built the Garry Theatre in 1936. Like the contemporary Plaza in Hillhurst and the Tivoli in Mission, this was a small-scale community theatre, as opposed to the lavish downtown movie palaces of the 1920s. It opened November 6, 1936, with "Forbidden Heaven," followed by the George Burns-Gracie Allen vehicle "The Big Broadcast of 1936." The theatre changed ownership in the 1940s and was later renamed the Rialto. By the late 1970s it had become the Hyland International Cinema, its Art Deco sign and canopy long gone, and its program shifted to adult and foreign-language films. Playwright Sharon Pollock spearheaded its revival as a live theatre in 1992, and, from 1998–2003, it was the home of Loose Moose, a local improvisational theatre company established in 1977. The building was converted into retail space in 2005.

The Garry Theatre began as a cinema in 1936 and was converted to live theatre in 1992. Its original appearance has been considerably altered. SHANNON LEE RAE

Route: Continue southeast along 9th Avenue, and cross 12th Street S.E. Proceed southeast along 9th Avenue.

East Calgary Telephone Exchange (Inglewood Silver Threads)
Address: 1311–9th Avenue S.E.
Style: Utilitarian (Classical design with Romanesque referencing)
Architect: Allan Jeffers, Provincial Architect
Date: 1909

The former East Calgary Telephone Exchange has a rare local example of pressed-metal roofing, resembling brick construction. SHANNON LEE RAE

Calgary's first automatic telephone substation is identical to the former West End Substation built later at 1010–14th Avenue S.W. To ensure a consistent temperature for the sensitive equipment within, the building was constructed as two separate shells—an outer, windowless brick structure and an inner, terra cotta one. The space between the two walls provided an unexpected function: as an illicit homeless shelter, accessible by removing a grille.

After it original use ceased, windows were added and the building became a kindergarten from 1966–71. It became property of the Inglewood Community Association in 1973, and now houses the Inglewood Silver Threads seniors' group. The building became a Provincial Historic Resource in 1981.

Route: Continue southeast along 9th Avenue S.E.

Fraser & Seabloom Block

Address: 1329–9th Avenue S.E.

Style: Combined influence of Edwardian Classical and Richardson Romanesque

Architect: Unknown

Date: 1912

Sandstone detailing, arched upper windows and a split cornice distinguish the Fraser & Seabloom Block. Shannon Lee Rae

With its sandstone details and arched upper windows, this four-story building is one of the most distinctive along 9th Avenue S.E. Embossed lettering at the top of the façade immortalizes the partnership of Maxwell Fraser and Oscar W. Seabloom, who built it in 1912. The building was declared a Registered Historic Resource in 1996, and its façade was restored that year.

Route: Continue southeast along 9th Avenue, and cross 13th Street S.E.

Gresham Block
Address: 1403–9th Avenue S.E.
Style: Edwardian Commercial
Architect: Unknown
Date: 1912

Removal of the cornice has altered the Gresham Block's original appearance.
Shannon Lee Rae

During World War II, Calgary teenager Dave Thomson worked as a CPR messenger while attending high school. Like his fellow messengers, Thomson wore a blue uniform and cap as he rode his bike around town delivering telegrams. The worst part of the job was delivering wartime casualty notices, and Dave—who eventually became a public school teacher in Calgary—recalls one he delivered to the Gresham Block. "I delivered a lot of casualty telegrams," Dave said years later, "but that's the one I remember."[6] He took the message to a woman whose soldier son was missing; he never learned whether the young man had survived. "Do you have any relatives in town?" Dave asked the woman. She did—a daughter living a block away, in Seven Oaks Court apartments. Dave immediately went to see her. "Your mother shouldn't be alone," he told her, and walked the young woman to her mother's Gresham Block apartment. By the time Dave got back to the CPR office, the family had called to commend him for his kindness.

An absentee English investor, John Stewart Dismorr of London, England, built this commercial/residential block, whose commercial tenants included grocery stores (Piggly Wiggly from 1929–38, followed by Safeway from 1939–40, and Jenkins Groceteria No. 3 from 1941–48), Exclusive Dairies (1933–66), and the Inglewood Café (1967–86).

Route: Proceed southwest along 13th Street to 10th Avenue S.E. Cross both roads to the southwest corner.

Seven Oaks Court

Address: 1339–10th Avenue S.E.
Style: Classically influenced
Architect: Unknown
Date: 1913

Hundreds of laborers began working at the CPR's new Ogden Shops in 1912. Builder Edward Akhurst built this brick apartment block the following year, and its twenty-nine suites filled a much-felt need for worker housing. Its tenants were largely CPR workers, warehousemen, and factory foremen. False keystones above the windows provide ornamentation, and the prominent gables on both principal façades contribute to the building's landmark quality.

The principal façades of Seven Oaks Court are highly symmetrical, and the prominent gables give it a landmark quality. Shannon Lee Rae

Route: Cross 13th Street S.E.

Trinity Methodist Church (Lantern Community Church)

Address: 1401–10th Avenue S.E.
Style: Gothic Revival
Architect: J. B. Henderson
Date: 1912

This United Church congregation originated in 1906 as the Third Methodist Church, but became commonly known as the "Green Church"—descriptive of the green-painted frame edifice built that year, just east of the present structure. Third Methodist became Trinity Methodist in 1907, and the present brick building was constructed in 1912. The original church was sold and moved a short distance east, where it became a sheet metal shop. Fire damaged the church and destroyed the organ in 1921. Industrialist W. H. Cushing, a former mayor and provincial minister of public works, helped finance the church's reconstruction. When Trinity Methodist joined the new United Church of Canada in 1925, it was renamed Cushing Memorial United Church in memory of Cushing's late wife. But Cushing remarried in 1929, and the church was renamed again, adopting the present name. The congregation folded in 2003 and the building was sold. It now functions as the Lantern Community Church.

Trinity United Church closed in 2003 and the building was sold. SHANNON LEE RAE

Route: Proceed southeast along 10th Avenue to 14th Street S.E. Cross both 10th and 14th, proceed southeast along 10th Avenue to its intersection with 17th Avenue, and cross 17th Avenue.

Calgary Brewing and Malting Company

Address: 1537–9th Avenue S.E.
Style: Utilitarian
Architect: Child and Wilson (original 1892 plant)
Date: 1892 (with later additions)

Rancher Alfred Ernest Cross headed the group of businessmen who established the Calgary Brewing and Malting Company in 1892, the year prohibition ended in the NWT and licensed liquor sales began. (When prohibition returned to Alberta from 1916–24, the brewery sold soft drinks for domestic consumption but continued brewing beer for export.) The Calgary Brewery marketed its beers using a distinctive buffalo head label. Like other breweries in the province, it built up a chain of hotels where its product could be marketed. By the 1950s, the provincial government came to regard this practice as a monopoly and passed legislation requiring breweries to sell their hotels by 1967.

Calgary Brewing and Malting Company, circa 1905–06. GLENBOW ARCHIVES NA-2307-38

Besides its capacity as one of Inglewood's largest employers, the brewery was also an important component in the district's social and sporting life. It provided Depression relief work through development of the Brewery gardens, fish hatchery, and trout ponds. The Calgary Brewery Cabin, a Métis or settler cabin originally located near the Hunt House, was relocated to the Brewery gardens in the 1930s as a relic of Calgary's origins. Further community endeavors included the Horseman's Hall of Fame museum and the salt-water aquarium that opened to the public in the 1960s. The museum closed in 1975, and the aquarium was shipped to Montreal.

The Calgary Brewing and Malting Company was sold to Canadian Breweries Ltd. in 1961, and, in 1989, it was taken over by Molson's Breweries. The plant was closed permanently in 1994.

Route: Inglewood tour ends. Proceed to Ramsay tour, which begins at the former 815 Snack Bar, just east of the Macdonald Bridge at the confluence of Macdonald and Bellevue avenues and Maggie Street.

815 Snack Bar (vacant)

Address: 815 Macdonald Avenue S.E.
Style: Moderne
Architect: Unknown
Date: circa 1939

The neon ice cream cone above the 815 Snack Bar has been a sweet tooth siren for generations. The building's flat roof adds to its Moderne appearance. Shannon Lee Rae

When the Ogden streetcar line opened at the end of 1912, it crossed the Macdonald Bridge and passed this triangular-shaped lot before turning south on 8th Street S.E. A cottage built around 1902 forms the core of this vintage snack bar, where teamster Edward J. Matthews lived with his family and stabled his horses. George F.

Mitchell converted it for commercial use around 1939 when he opened Pop's Confectionery. Olaf Gunderson operated it as Ole's Grocery & Confectionery between 1946–57, and built front and rear additions and removed the original cottage's pitched roof. It became a dairy bar around 1957, and under a variety of names (lastly as the 815 Snack Bar) it served the sweet tooth of Ramsay residents for decades. The building is currently vacant.

Route: Turn right on Maggie Street S.E., and proceed south. There is only one crosswalk, on the right hand side.

Maggie Street's "painted lady," 2004. Shannon Lee Rae

Maggie Street

This quaint, narrow one-way street (southbound) was named for Maggie Beatty, a daughter of nineteenth-century mayor Wesley Fletcher Orr, who as head of the group of businessmen that developed Ramsay was in a position to name its streets. Maggie Street is lined with diminutive houses and tiny garages; the most delightful is the "painted lady" at 1140 Maggie Street, built around 1915 as the home of stonemason John V. Monaghan. As it proceeds south, Maggie Street becomes more steeply inclined uphill. The much-steeper, curiously named Bison Path veers off to the right.

Route: Continue south on Maggie Street to 17th Avenue S.E., and turn left (east). Descend the steps, and continue east on 17th Avenue to 8th Street S.E. Cross both roads.

Black & White Meat & Groceries
Address: 1702–8th Street S.E.
Style: Moderne
Architect: Unknown
Date: 1948

Built in 1948, this corner grocery exemplifies the Moderne style that had been popular over a decade earlier. Racing stripes, or "speed whiskers," appear above the projecting awning. SHANNON LEE RAE

Merchant Henry Benner built this one-story stucco building to house the corner grocery he had operated a few blocks to the north since 1935. The style, complete with thin racing stripes or "speed whiskers" above the rounded awning, belonged more to the 1930s than the late 1940s, but war and depression had put off much-needed construction during those decades. Post-war prosperity allowed the city to make up for lost time.

In a reversal of typical family-owned groceries, the residence here was below the store rather than above. Benner and his wife sold the store in 1963.

Route: Proceed east along 17th Avenue to 11th Street S.E. Note that 17th Avenue was Calgary's southern city limit from 1884–1907. The sidewalk on the south side, next to the metal-clad building with the Calgary Co-op Fur Farmers' Association signage, descends down to the 11th Street level. Turn right on 11th Street, and proceed south.

Calgary Co-operative Fur Farmers' Association

Address: 1701–11th Street S.E.
Style: Industrial
Architect: Unknown
Date: circa 1912

Two buildings comprise the complex on this site: a two-story, tin-covered warehouse and a smaller single-story brick structure. Their order of construction is unknown, but the site was developed around 1912 as the Canadian Western Natural Gas Company's Warehouse No. 2. Five years later, during World War I, it became an experimental facility to produce helium in commercial quantities for the British government. The gas was intended for use in lighter-than-air-aircraft, which had proved their military utility during the war. The plant was placed under guard, and its function kept secret until after the conflict ended. It still had not reached production capacity when armistice was declared on November 11, 1918.

Signage on the Calgary Co-operative Fur Farmers' Association's building was painted out after its occupancy ended in the 1970s. There was enough of it left for John Holt to repaint the sign when he converted the abandoned building into a residence and artists' studios in the 1990s. Shannon Lee Rae

The gas company continued to use the buildings until about the mid-1920s, and, in the 1930s, the Calgary Casket Company operated here, followed by Central Flour Mills. In 1940, the main building became the feed mixing warehouse of the Calgary Co-operative Fur Farmers' Association. When fire broke out in November 1948, fifty cans of tomato juice (an ingredient in the feed-mixing formula) exploded, splattering the floors with what looked like blood. The association repaired the gutted building and continued to use it until the 1970s. It then fell vacant for a quarter of a century, until businessman John Holt bought the warehouse in 1993 and converted it into a residence, rental office, and artists' studios. Holt acquired the adjacent brick building in 1997 and turned it into an artists' studio.

Route: Proceed south along 11th Street to 19th Avenue S.E., turn right, and proceed west along 19th Avenue about two-thirds of the block.

McKay Lodge

Address: 1016–19th Avenue S.E.
Style: American Foursquare
Architect: Likely a pattern-book design
Date: 1911 (rear addition 1926)

Unemployed men knew they would find hospitality at McKay Lodge during the Great Depression. SHANNON LEE RAE

During the Hungry Thirties, an unemployed man who found charity or a meal at a family home would mark the fence or gatepost with chalk, signaling to fellow unfortunates that here they would find welcome. McKay Lodge was one of those homes.

Ontario-born Robert J. McKay (circa 1877–1950) came to Calgary in 1901 and got a job with the CPR. By 1905, he worked his way up to locomotive engineer and became one of the first to drive the trains through the spiral tunnels at Field, B.C. Both of Calgary's daily newspapers ran a story on McKay's final run in 1942. Well-wishers greeted him at every stop between Field and Calgary. In Calgary, a crowd of sixty was on hand when McKay pulled in on Engine No. 5925. "They shouted and cheered as the short, jolly man clambered down from his cab, to kiss his wife," the *Albertan* observed. "For some reason or other, the ladies always find retiring engineers very attractive. In traditional manner, they rallied around to kiss Mr. McKay."7

McKay and his wife Margaret built this two-and-a-half-story home in 1911, and in the late 1920s they built an addition and converted it into McKay Lodge apartments, while continuing to live in it until 1947. McKay handled grievances for union members, and railway men frequently came to McKay Lodge to consult with him. When an army of unemployed men rode the rails into Calgary as part of the On-to-Ottawa Trek in 1935, McKay took his young granddaughter to their demonstration, explained what it was all about, and told her she should remember it.

The McKays sold the lodge to David and Effie McRae. As a widow in the 1950s, Mrs. McRae operated the house as the McRae Nursing Home.

Route: Continue west along 19th Avenue, and cross 9th Street S.W.

Alberta Corner Store

Address: 922–19th Avenue S.E.
Style: Simplified Edwardian Commercial
Architect: Unknown
Year: 1912

This period corner store, covered in yellow stucco and decorated with seven large red Coca-Cola buttons, was built around 1912 and owned by Aaron Schnitka from 1912–29. Schnitka's son Abraham later became the King's Printer in Alberta and a personal friend of Premier William Aberhart. Schnitka's grandson, Bob Smithens, founded Smithens' Auction.

Large enamel Coca-Cola buttons give the Alberta Corner Store a period chic.
SHANNON LEE RAE

Route: Cross both roads.

Beers House
Address: 1001–19th Avenue S.E.
Style: False-front commercial building
Architect: Unknown
Date: 1908

This 1908 cottage, with its original rear stable and later storefront addition, is unremarkable in Ramsay; many buildings of this type and vintage remain. What is outstanding is the owner's attention to its history and her effort to revive it.

Soon after artist Rhonda Thurn bought this house from its antique dealer occupant in 1998, she learned from neighbors that it was once a meat market. Intrigued, she researched its history and learned the original owner was carpenter Joseph Beers, who probably built the house himself. Ernest Wood converted it into the English Meat Market, and it later went under a series of names as a meat shop and grocery store. Thurn sometimes hosts unofficial exhibits at her home showcasing fellow local artists, and she seized on an idea that would emphasize the house's landmark character. She painted "Beers House, est. 1908" on the front elevation that already had the appearance of a storefront. The novelty gives the house substance as a gathering place, but often draws strangers who think it's a pub and wonder what type of beer she has.

The exterior décor of the Beers House reflects its original owner, its date of construction, and its history as a commercial building. SHANNON LEE RAE

Route: Return east along 19th Avenue to 11th Street S.E., and cross.

Western Steel Products Ltd. (Ramsay Design Centre)

Address: 1902–11th Street S.E.
Style: Utilitarian (Free Classical influence)
Architect: George Fordyce (1926 addition)
Date: 1918 (additions circa 1921, 1926)

Western Steel Products Ltd. (later renamed Westeel) was founded in Winnipeg in 1905. For a dozen years, its Alberta branch manager was the delightfully named Polycarp Spurgeon Woodhall (1872–1945). Woodhall had worked in the sheet metal and hardware business in his native Ontario and settled in Calgary with his wife Elizabeth in 1902. He built the original phase of this structure in 1918 to house his Sheet Metal Manufacturing Co. Ltd., which under his management had become Western Steel's local branch by 1921. The office and workshop addition fronting 11th Street S.E. was built in 1926. During World War II, Western Steel repaired aircraft and damaged oil and gas tanks for the Dominion government, and manufactured parts for Boeing B-28 Catalina flying boats. Like Rosie the Riveter, the iconic industrial worker of wartime posters, many of Western Steel's wartime employees were women. Westeel remained in business here until the 1970s, and the building was renovated into the multi-purpose Ramsay Design Centre in the 1990s.

The Ramsay Design Centre is an early example in this district of the adaptive reuse of industrial buildings by artists and designers. SHANNON LEE RAE

Route: Proceed south along 11th Street to 20th Avenue S.E., turn left, and proceed east along 20th Avenue. As you reach the railway tracks, look both ways for trains— and look to the left for the former Standard Soap Company factory.

Standard Soap Company (Local Motive)

Address: 1902–11th Street S.E.
Style: Utilitarian
Architect: Unknown
Date: 1905 (addition 1907)

Like other former industrial buildings in Ramsay, this former soap factory has been converted for design and office use. It was a typical Edwardian-era factory, with load-bearing brick walls and a loading platform that fronted on a railway spur line.
SHANNON LEE RAE

In 1905, meat-packing baron Patrick Burns became president of the newly established Standard Soap Company, which offered a natural industrial use for animal by-products from Burns' abattoirs. Mayor John Emerson, who was also vice-president of the company, authorized the city's agreement to sell the land once the company had built a $10,000 factory, operated it for a year-and-a-half, and employed at least ten people. These terms were met by 1907, and that year an addition to the original brick factory was constructed. The Calgary-based company had branches in five other cities across the western provinces, but, in 1908, it was taken over by the Royal

Crown Soap Company of Winnipeg. Lever Bros. Ltd. absorbed Royal Crown in the early 1940s, and the factory was sold in 1946. A variety of businesses and industries later used the building, but it eventually became vacant. A project to convert the former factory into a design centre was announced in 2002.

Route: Retrace your steps back to 11th Street S.E., noting the fading painted signs on the rear of the C. C. Snowdon building to your left. At 11th Street, turn left, and cross 20th Avenue. Proceed south a short distance along 11th Street.

C. C. Snowdon Oils (Stanton Studios/Farrell Guitar Repair)

Address: 2010–11th Street S.E.
Style: Edwardian Commercial
Architect: Unknown
Date: 1911 (additions to 1914)

A prominent arch and pressed-metal cornice are among the Edwardian features of this combined office/warehouse complex. Traces of a 1988 fire are still visible.
SHANNON LEE RAE

In 1901, twenty-year-old Campbell Camillus (C. C.) Snowdon (1881–1935) left his native Montreal to represent the Canadian Oil Company in western Canada. He came to Calgary in 1908 as the company's western manager. He soon went into business for himself as a wholesale importer, manufacturer, and refiner of oils—at first as a pioneer in the west and later on a nation-wide scale. This complex of brick buildings was constructed incrementally between 1911–14, and it produced oils, chemicals, and cleaning compounds with such trademark names as Numidian, Sliptivity, and Velox. Snowdon lived in Mount Royal with his wife Isabella and their children, and there he opened his beautiful garden at 925 Durham Avenue S.W. to the public.

C. C. Snowdon Oils survived its founder but was eventually taken over by another firm. This complex was vacant from 1983–87 and was badly damaged by fire in 1988. In the 1990s, part of the building served as the Calgary Biker Church.

Route: Cross 11th Street S.E., turn left, and proceed south along 11th Street to 21st Avenue S.E. Cross 21st Avenue.

Shamrock Hotel
Address: 2101–11th Street S.E.
Style: Edwardian Commercial (originally)
Architect: Unknown
Year: 1924

This 1924 view of the Shamrock Hotel shows its wood-frame construction and the adjacent harness shop under common ownership. GLENBOW ARCHIVES

In 1910, Dublin-born harness maker Bill Cummins (1890–1933) arrived in Calgary and worked at his trade for P. Burns and Company. He later opened the East Calgary Harness Shop on this site. When Prohibition ended in 1924, he built and operated the Shamrock Hotel. (Shamrock was one of the product labels of the nearby P. Burns & Co. meatpacking plant, and the hotel served as a watering hole for many of its employees.)

An avid sportsman, Cummins sponsored hockey, lacrosse, and football teams, and named each of them the Shamrocks. "There was hardly a kid in East Calgary during Bill Cummins' day that wasn't wearing a Shamrock sweater," observed one Calgary old-timer in 1964.[8] After Cummins passed away, his widow Bridgid operated the Shamrock until her own death in 1941, and the hotel remained in family hands for many years after. The building was stuccoed and modernized in 1948, and successive renovations have rendered it unrecognizable. But the green beer still served in the tavern every St. Patrick's Day cannot be mistaken.

Route: Cross back to the north side of 21st Avenue S.E., turn left, and proceed west along 21st Avenue. Cross 9th Street S.E.

Tinchebray House (Raido House)

Address: 922–21st Avenue S.E.
Style: French Provincial
Architect: Unknown
Year: 1913

Originally known as Tinchebray House, this was the rectory for the Priests of St. Mary of Tinchebray, who administered the adjacent St. Ann's Catholic Church until they returned to France in 1916. In 1919, it was renamed St. Ann's Convent, occupied by the Sisters of St. Josepho of Peterborough (1919–21) followed by the Ursuline Sisters (1921–23). It then served again as the parish rectory until 1951, when the Sisters Adorers of the Precious Blood bought the building and used it as the Monastery of the Precious Blood for the next thirty years. From 1975–2002 it served as Sunrise Residence, a residential addiction treatment centre for First Nations. It became Raido House, a transitional home for homeless teenagers, in 2003. It is a rare example of its style in Calgary.

This building's Second Empire style reflects the French origins of its original occupants, a French Catholic order of priests. Pitched details over the dormer windows, and brick detailing over the windows below, are an Italianate influence. SHANNON LEE RAE

Route: Continue west along 21st Avenue S.E., and cross 8th
Street S.E. Turn left, and proceed south along 8th
Street.

Ramsay Elementary School

Address: 2233 Spiller Road S.E.
Style: Free Classical
Architect: Hugh McClelland (probably assisted by William A.
Branton)
Year: 1912

*Ramsay Elementary School is the only remaining sandstone school not marred with
an unsympathetic addition.* SHANNON LEE RAE

This school was called Ramsay long before the district that sur-
rounds it adopted the name. William Thomson Ramsay came to
Calgary in the 1880s as an agent for the Canada Northwest Land
Company, and he became a significant property-holder in what
later became the Ramsay district. He sold this parcel in what was
then known as Grandview to the public school board in 1912, and
presumably this school (as well as nearby Ramsay Street) was
named for him.

In 1956, Grandview residents joined with their neighbors in Burnsland, Brewery Flats and Mills Estate to incorporate the Grandview Community Association. Since the name was already in use in Edmonton, the east Calgary group chose a new name: Ramsay.

Completed in 1913, Ramsay Elementary was one of about eighteen sandstone schools built in a twenty-year period prior to World War I, and one of three built from an identical design. (The others were King George and Sunalta). It is the only remaining sandstone schools not marred in appearance by a later, unsympathetic addition. Distinguished alumni have included professional athlete Eddie Wares (who played hockey for the Detroit Red Wings and Chicago Black Hawks), Fire Chief Charles A. Harrison (who held the office from 1964–72), and his brother, Chief Inspector Bob Harrison of the city police force.

Route: Continue south on 8th Street to 24th Avenue S.E., cross, and turn left (east). Proceed east on 24th Avenue S.E.

Riverside Iron Works / Dominion Bridge (Ramsay Crossing)

Address: 803–24th Avenue S.E.
Style: Utilitarian (Simplified Edwardian Classical)
Architect: Rex Millar
Date: 1927 (with later additions)

In 1913, industrialists Frederick L. Irving and George A. Hannah established Riverside Iron Works, a machine and repair shop named for the northeast Calgary district where it was located. By the time it moved to this sprawling, purpose-built complex in 1927, it had become a major steel manufacturer with over 225 laborers. Riverside Iron Works exemplified Alberta's industrial growth of the 1920s. However, in 1929, Irving sold his controlling interest to the Dominion Bridge Company of Montreal. The new owners expanded the site to nearly twenty-one acres and added a massive steel shop. During World War II, the shipbuilding industry placed heavy demands on Dominion Bridge. After the war, the company provided steel for massive building projects such as Elveden Centre and the Calgary Tower. The company closed its Calgary operation in 1987, and the site has become a mixed-use complex for industry, designers, artists, and filmmaking props and sets.

Buildings in the former Riverside Iron Works/Dominion Bridge complex were designed for heavy industrial use. They now accommodate artists, designers, and filmmakers, as well as continued industrial use. SHANNON LEE RAE

Tour ends.

Notes

1 Calgary's well-known southern thoroughfare, Macleod Trail, originally passed through Ramsay and not downtown as it does now. The trail originated as Calgary's lifeline to Fort Macleod, and thence to Fort Benton, Montana. Ox-drawn "bull trains" hauled supplies from Fort Benton to Calgary before the CPR arrived in 1883. South of Cemetery Hill, Macleod Trail approximates its original north-south route. As it continued north, the trail skirted Cemetery Hill to the east, then jogged east of what is now Stampede Park into present-day Ramsay, and continued to a ford at the Bow River. The construction of Victoria

Road over Cemetery Hill in 1912 shifted traffic to 2nd Street S.E. through downtown. In 1967, the city renamed Victoria Road and 2nd Street as Macleod Trail, and designated the old stretch as Spiller Road (as it passes by Cemetery Hill, for well-known local scout leader Edward Spiller) and as 8th Street S.E. (through Ramsay, the stretch that Orr had named Orr Street).

2 "King Edward Hotel to be Closed Up," *Morning Albertan* 22 Dec. 1913: 1.

3 Homer Meers, personal interview, 1995.

4 Glenbow Archives, Homer Meers fonds M7475.

5 "Building Inspector Harrison Punches Alderman A. J. Samis Three Times and Resigns Job," *Calgary Daily Herald* 29 Mar. 1912: 1.

6 Dave Thomson, personal interview, Jan. 2004.

7 "40 Years With Railroad Brings Last Engine in," *Albertan* 31 Mar. 1942: 6.

8 "Traces Calgary's Growth," *Albertan* 29 June 1964:23.

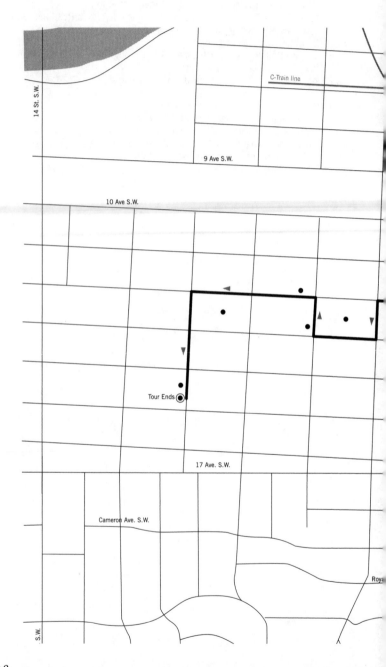

14 St. S.W.

C-Train line

9 Ave S.W.

10 Ave S.W.

Tour Ends

17 Ave. S.W.

Cameron Ave. S.W.

Roya

S.W.

The Beltline

For generations, Calgarians have referred to the residential and commercial area south of downtown as the Beltline. It overlaps with the districts of Connaught and Victoria Park (officially amalgamated in 2003 as the Beltline Communities of Victoria and Connaught), and takes its name from the Blue Line streetcar, established in 1909 and known unofficially as the belt line. (Victoria Park was named for Queen Victoria at the time of her death in 1901 and originally referred to the agricultural grounds now known as Stampede Park. Connaught took its name from Connaught School, itself named for the Duke of Connaught, Queen Victoria's son and governor-general of Canada from 1911–16.)

The belt line streetcar encircled the district in the following loop, starting at Centre Street and 8th Avenue S.W.: west on 8th Avenue to 1st Street S.W.; south on 1st Street to 12th Avenue S.W.; west on 12th Avenue to 14th Street S.W.; south on 14th Street to 17th Avenue S.W.; east on 17th Avenue to 2nd Street S.E. (now Macleod Trail); north on 2nd Street S.E. to 8th Avenue S.E.; then west on 8th Avenue to the starting point at Centre Street.

The Calgary Municipal Railway, as the streetcar system was called, changed its named to the Calgary Transit System in 1945. The last streetcar ended its run in 1950, but the Beltline identification has endured.

Although the area was first developed in the late nineteenth century, most of the Beltline's historic buildings date from the boom period between 1906–13. Twelfth and 13th avenues developed early as a high-class residential area, but many of its fine homes have since been demolished. Other streets became middle-class areas with wooden homes and walk-up apartment buildings, and commercial buildings cropped up along streetcar routes. Early twenty-first century planning for what has become the Connaught-West Victoria district projects high densification and increased development pressure.

Start: Begin the tour at the Manhattan Lofts (1117–1st Street S.W.), at the northwest corner of 1st Street and 12th Avenue S.W. First Street was originally called

Scarth Street; 12th Avenue was originally Van Horne Avenue, named for William Cornelius Van Horne, general manager of the Canadian Pacific Railway (CPR) and later its president.

Pryce-Jones Department Store (Manhattan Lofts)

Address: 1117–1st Street S.W.
Style: Edwardian Classical
Architect: William Stanley Bates
Date: 1911 (addition 1913)

This building's prestigious origin as a department store accounts for its elaborate windows and prominent signband cornice. SHANNON LEE RAE

On February 14, 1911, Calgary's Pryce Jones department store—the only Canadian branch of a family-owned English firm—opened to the strains of live orchestral music, service in the store's Royal Welsh Tea Room, and the attendance of 100 employees. The inaugural day was for demonstration only, and no sales were made. The store was expanded in 1913, but the store closed permanently three years later, when the family scion resident in Calgary, Lt.-Col. A. W. Pryce Jones, departed the city as commander of the 113th Highlanders. After the war, Calgarians visited what was still known as the Pryce Jones Building in January 1919 to attend the city's War Trophies Exhibition. It later became known as the Traders Building and housed such tenants as Garbutt's Business College and the Caldwell Knitting Company. The Dominion government bought the building in 1942 to serve as headquarters for Military District No. 13. After World War II it continued to house federal offices, including Veterans' Affairs, Income Tax, and Unemployment Insurance. In 1974 it became the Refinery nightclub, where live acts included B. B. King, Jerry Doucette, and the Association. In the early 1990s, it was remade into New York-style loft condominiums and appropriately named the Manhattan.

Route: Cross both streets to the southeast corner of 1st Street and 12th Avenue S.W.

Canadian Bank of Commerce (Formans Men's and Women's Fashions)

Address: 1202–1st Street S.W.
Style: Georgian Revival
Architect: Unknown
Date: 1912

In 1909, the Canadian Bank of Commerce opened its south Calgary branch in the small building that still stands across the street at 1205–1st Street S.W. In 1912 the bank constructed this three-story brick building, complete with apartments for the manager and other staff members, and similar to other branches elsewhere in the country. A 1961 merger with the Imperial Bank of Canada yielded the bank's unwieldy new name, Canadian Imperial Bank of Commerce (eventually simplified to CIBC). The branch closed by the early 1980s, and after intermittent uses it became Formans Men's and Women's Fashions in 2004.

Windows on each floor of this former bank branch have a distinct size and style, separating functional areas visually: the bank on the main floor, offices on the second, and staff residences on the third. SHANNON LEE RAE

Route: Cross 1st Street S.W., and proceed west on 12th Avenue S.W.

Young Women's Christian Association (The Old Y)

Address: 223–12th Avenue S.W.
Style: Institutional Georgian Revival
Architect: D. S. McIlroy
Date: 1911 (addition 1954)

In 1907, a group of women alarmed by the lack of single women's accommodation in the city founded the Young Women's Christian Association of Calgary. Katharine Underwood, the wife of former mayor Thomas Underwood, became its first president. The group raised money to rent a house for temporary use and to buy five lots on 12th Avenue for a permanent building. The cornerstone was laid on June 21, 1910, and the YWCA was officially opened in February 1911. The dormitory was quickly filled, and Thomas Underwood provided additional space in the nearby Underwood Block (1311–1st Street S.W.). YWCA members met women as they arrived at the railway stations, and directed them to stay at the "Y." Besides accommodations, the "Y" offered employment counseling, life skills training, a gymnasium, and bible classes. The mortgage was burned in 1941, and the building was renovated in 1944 and expanded to include a new swimming pool and gymnasium in 1954. It was replaced by a new downtown YWCA in 1971, and the "Old Y," as it became known, was taken over by the city. It was designated a Provincial Historic Resource in 1982 and today provides office space for community groups and non-profit societies. The 1954 addition functions as the Beltline Pool and Fitness Centre.

Restrained classical details and combined use of brick and sandstone define the appearance of The Old Y. A large two-story balcony and arched front porch have been removed. SHANNON LEE RAE

Route: Return east along 12th Avenue S.W. to 1st Street S.W.

Aull Block (Drum and Monkey)

Address: 1201–1st Street S.W.
Style: Simplified Edwardian Commercial
Architect: Unknown
Date: 1925

The "bookends" of this block—the Aull and Radio blocks—both have angled corner entrances typical of commercial buildings between the pre-World War I boom and the 1920s. SHANNON LEE RAE

Dr. Erastus Aull, who owned the adjacent business block to the west, built this single-story brick building in 1925 in place of an original wooden one. The new structure originally housed Kraft the Furrier and a branch of Nippon Bazaar (a downtown business later renamed Silk-O-Lina). The Welcome Café, a Chinese restaurant and confectionery, occupied the corner storefront from about 1940–72; the storefront to the south housed Luey Dofoo's Mid-West Delicatessen from about 1935–48.

When Calgary's nightclub strip lay along 1st Street S.W. in the late 1970s and early 1980s, this was the home of Slack Alice's (later renamed Slack Jack's). It was known as a pickup joint and reportedly provided table-to-table telephone service. The "strip" shifted to 11th Avenue in the 1980s, but nightlife later returned to 1st Street, and the Drum and Monkey opened here in 1999.

Route: Proceed south along 1st Street to 13th Avenue S.W.

Radio Block
Address: 1215-1223–1st Street S.W.
Style: Edwardian Classical
Architect: Unknown
Date: 1923

Like the Aull Block to the north, the Radio Block was built during a slow economic period. The busy 1st Street S.W. shopping district warranted their construction.
SHANNON LEE RAE

Like the word "electric" before it, and "micro" and "quantum" years later, "radio" evoked high technology in the 1920s. Both CFCN (dubbed "The Voice of the Prairies") and the *Calgary Herald*'s CFAC started broadcasting in 1922. Calgarians were thrilled with the new medium and bought radios or built crystal sets from specifications published in the *Herald*. The two-story Radio Block is an excellent example of a 1920s residential/commercial building, and its name evokes the spirit of the times. In place of an upper cornice, the Radio Block sports two horizontal bands, an early occurrence of the "speed lines" later made popular by the Moderne style. The Radio Meat Market occupied one of the storefronts from 1924–40. More recent occupants have included Cherry, the Castle Pub, and King's Arms.

Route: Cross 13th Avenue (originally Kennedy Avenue, for CPR director John S. Kennedy), and proceed south on 1st Street S.W.

Underwood Block

Address: 1311–1st Street S.W.
Style: Edwardian Classical
Architect: Unknown
Date: 1911

Sandstone pilasters and pediments provided visual contrast with the red brick façade of the Underwood Block, seen at centre left in this 1928 photograph. GLENBOW ARCHIVES NA-554-31

The extension of streetcar service along 1st Street S.W. helped establish a business strip that stretched from 10th Avenue south to 17th Avenue. Six years after he built the first Underwood Block (now the Western Block), contractor and former mayor Thomas Underwood (1863–1948) erected this much larger building, one of the first major commercial/residential buildings outside the city core. The five-story building housed apartments, offices, and shops. Early tenants included the Alberta Bible Society, the Baptist Convention of Alberta, the Calgary Musicians' Association, and the YWCA Annex.

The Underwood Block was the scene of a miracle in January 1912, when a baby fell four stories from the building but was unhurt.

A 1989 fire destroyed most of the Underwood Block, but two popular establishments—the Crazy Horse saloon and Mescalero's restaurant—continued to occupy the surviving portion.

Route: Return north along 1st Street to 13th Avenue S.W., turn left (west), and continue west on 13th Avenue.

Haultain School (Calgary Parks Foundation)

Address: 225–13th Avenue S.W.
Style: Neo-Classical
Architect: J. L. Wilson (of Child and Wilson)
Date: 1894

The original South Ward School was built of irregularly sized rusticated sandstone blocks, more than a decade before stonecutting technology arrived in Calgary. The more elaborate sandstone entrance replaced the original wooden one in 1922.
SHANNON LEE RAE

Calgary's first sandstone school is also the oldest surviving school building in the city. The keystone over the portal indicates it was built in 1892, but that erroneous date was already thirty years past when the keystone was carved. Construction began in 1893 and the school was finished in August 1894. It was the first school in the city to have running water and electricity.

In 1910, a much larger sandstone edifice was built to the west and named for Sir Frederick William Gordon Haultain, the Conservative premier of the North-West Territories (NWT) before Alberta and Saskatchewan were carved away from it in 1905. The original building became the office of school board superintendent Dr. Melville Scott, but in 1922 it was renovated to become an annex for Haultain School. Declining enrolment led to the school's closure in 1962, and in 1964 the larger building was destroyed by fire. The remaining Haultain Annex was declared a Registered Historic Resource in 1979. The city purchased the property in 1980 and restored the annex as the new headquarters for Uncles at Large. It now houses the Calgary Parks Foundation.

Route: Proceed west along 13th Avenue to 2nd Street S.W. Cross both roads to the northwest corner, and proceed north to Memorial Park Library.

Memorial Park and Memorial Park Library

Address: 1221–2nd Street S.W.
Style: Classical (Beaux-Arts influence)
Architect: McLean and Wright of Boston, Massachusetts
Date: 1911

The library's park setting was first set aside in 1889 at the suggestion of William Pearce, Inspector of Dominion Land Agencies and Superintendent of Mines. It was initially developed in the 1890s as a tree nursery, but, by 1912, was still described—by Chief Librarian Alexander Calhoun—as "an unsightly wilderness of sand and scrub."[1]

A small bandstand, replaced in 1912 by a larger bandshell, stood at the park's west end until the cenotaph, originally dedicated to the soldiers who perished in World War I and later rededicated to those who died in World War II and Korea, was erected in 1928. The park's real development began during the tenure of Parks Superintendent William Reader, who held that position from 1913–42.

Ionic columns flank the main entrance to the original Calgary Public Library, and details in the carved pediment above include the name of the institution and an open book in relief. SHANNON LEE RAE

Built at the park's east end between 1908 and 1911, the Calgary Public Library was the first such public institution in the province as well as the first in Alberta using a grant from the Carnegie Foundation in the United States. Members of the Calgary Women's Literary Society had gathered signatures to petition for a Carnegie grant, and the Central Park location was decided through a 1908 plebiscite. The library was officially opened on January 2, 1912, and Alexander Calhoun remained its chief librarian until 1945. It became the meeting place for a variety of cultural groups and the original home of the Calgary Natural History Society museum. From 1912–15, it housed classes of the short-lived Calgary College, which aspired to become the University of Calgary.

Both the library and Central Park were renamed Memorial Park in 1928, when the cenotaph was constructed and unveiled. It is one of several military monuments in the park. The "Horseman of the Plains," Calgary's South African War memorial, was unveiled in 1914. The World War I memorial in front of the library replaced an earlier statue of Amazon women in 1924. Tragically, Vancouver contractor Phil Thorsen—who in 1926 had helped place the Boer War memorial on its present granite pedestal—was killed when a large stone fell on him during the cenotaph's construction in October 1928. The cenotaph faces the former Colonel Belcher Veterans' Hospital across 4th Street S.W., and it is an important venue for Remembrance Day ceremonies each November 11.

The Memorial Park Library remained the central branch until 1963, when the new William R. Castell branch opened downtown. From 1964–73 the library maintained only a basement branch here, while the rest of the building was used as the Glenbow Museum's library and archives. It was designated a Provincial Historic Resource in 1976 and reopened as a full library branch in 1977.

Route: From the cenotaph, proceed north along 4th Street S.W. (originally called Ross Street), and cross 12th Avenue. Proceed east along 12th Avenue.

Masonic Temple

Address: 330–12th Avenue S.W.
Style: Art Deco influence
Architect: D. S. McIlroy
Date: 1928

From 1907–22, Calgary's Masonic headquarters were located in Alexander Corner, an 1889 sandstone building at the northwest corner of 8th Avenue and 1st Street S.W. The building was sold in 1922 to make way for an addition to the Hudson's Bay Company store (which was not built until 1929–30), requiring the Masons to find a new home. Members formed the Calgary Masonic Temple Ltd. in

1927 and purchased this property opposite what was still known as Central Park. Mayor Fred E. Osborne turned the first sod, and the cornerstone was laid in June 1928. During the ceremony, the viewing platform, on which seventy masons were standing, collapsed. No one was hurt. Financial constraints resulted in use of cast stone in the façade instead of terra cotta. The building was dedicated on December 28, 1928, and still continues its original function.

The Masonic Temple's brick and cast stone façade emphasizes the vertical dimension, and its flattened, streamlined quality is a hallmark of Art Deco style. The Masonic emblem, which includes a square, compass, and letter G for God, stands in relief at the top of the central bay. SHANNON LEE RAE

Route: Return west along 12th Avenue to 4th Street S.W. Cross both roads and proceed south along 4th Street to 13th Avenue. Cross 13th Avenue to the southwest corner of the intersection.

First Baptist Church

Address: 1311–4th Street S.W.
Style: Gothic Revival
Architect: D. S. McIlroy
Date: 1912 (later additions)

Sandstone and red brick contrast nicely on the First Baptist Church's Gothic Revival façade. Shannon Lee Rae

Calgary's First Baptist Church originated in 1888, when seven of the town's sixteen Baptists met for organizational purposes. After meeting in temporary quarters, the congregation built its first church in 1890 at the northeast corner of what is now 6th Avenue and 2nd Street S.W. (now the site of Bow Valley Square) Within a decade, First Baptist had outgrown its edifice and built a larger church at the northeast corner of what is now 7th Avenue and 1st Street S.W. (now the site of the Len Werry Building), designed by architect D. S. McIlroy and completed in 1901. It was destroyed by fire in 1905 and rebuilt on the same site. The church's leadership established mission churches across the city, including Hillhurst and Westbourne in Victoria Park.

First Baptist grew in tandem with the city's pre-World War I boom, and in 1910 the congregation purchased its present site from lawyer, provincial Conservative leader, and future prime minister R. B. Bennett. When he was paid $25,000 in cash for the six lots, Bennett was reportedly so impressed that he donated $1000 towards the building fund. Former mayor Thomas Underwood, who lived across 13th Avenue behind the Burns mansion, was a prominent member and also contributed to the building fund. Dr. John Clifford, president of the Baptist World Alliance, laid the cornerstone on July 12, 1911, and the Gothic Revival church building was dedicated on May 12, 1912.

The church complex was considerably expanded in the 1950s and 1960s. A youth wing was added in 1951. In 1958 the congregation bought the Seventh Day Adventist Church to the south and replaced it with the Christian Education Building, completed in 1962. The original manse next door to First Baptist was converted into offices in 1957.

Route: Cross 4th Street S.W., turn right, and proceed south along 4th Street.

Hester Apartments

Address: 1306–4th Street S.W.

Style: Eclectic (influenced by Georgian Revival and Tudor Revival)

Architect: Unknown

Date: 1910

The three-story Hester Apartments was one of several high-class apartment buildings in the vicinity of Memorial Park. The commercial block to the south replaced Joseph Gray Hester's upscale home, which was demolished in the 1950s. AUTHOR PHOTO

Joseph Gray Hester, a manufacturer's agent who had previously lived in London and New York, settled in Calgary around 1904 and constructed a fine residence for himself on the south corner of this block. In 1910, Hester built this eponymous high-class apartment block, located half a block south of Central Park and immediately north of his home. It was apparently patterned after Georgian Court, an identical-looking building at 621–5th Avenue S.W., demolished in 1978 and now the site of the Fifth and Fifth office tower. The Hester's most notable tenant was Dr. Rosamond Leacock, Calgary's first pathologist and the sister of humorist Stephen Leacock. She lived in the building from 1912–17.

Hester won an aldermanic by-election in 1912 but left the city within a year. His house was demolished in the 1950s, and a corner dollar store now occupies the site. The apartment building's distinctive wooden balcony, removed at an unknown date, was reconstructed in the 1990s. Hester Apartments became a Registered Historic Resource in 1998.

Route: Continue south to 14th Avenue S.W. (originally Grenfell Avenue). Cross both 4th Street and 14th Avenue, and proceed south along 4th Street.

R. H. Williams Block (Haycock Family Chiropractic)

Address: 1411–4th Street S.W.
Style: Edwardian Commercial
Architect: Unknown
Date: 1928

Robert Harold Williams (1880–1956), an "expert ladies tailor" who once fitted the Queen, left his native Cornwall, England, and settled in Calgary around 1910. He went into partnership with Fred Heath in the Heath Block (which still stands at 615–15th Avenue S.W.) then set up his own ladies' ready-to-wear store, the R. H. Williams Co. Ltd., in 1921. Williams built this two-story brick building in 1928, and here his fashion shop outlived its founder by four decades.

Four upstairs suites boasted "Frigidaire electric refrigeration." The most notable tenant was Eva Reid (1907–1989), the social reporter for the *Albertan* (precursor to the *Calgary Sun*), who lived here in the 1940s and 1950s. Reid had been a youthful devotee of the Social Credit movement and of William Aberhart, Alberta's first Socred premier. (She once boarded with the Aberharts; when she moved out, her room was taken by a new boarder—Ernest Manning.) Reid originally wrote for the *Social Credit Chronicle*, a political organ, and moved to the *Albertan* when it bought the *Chronicle*. A pioneer female journalist, Reid covering the police and society beats concurrently and later wrote a popular column that featured local topics and personalities.

Former R. H. Williams Block, 2003. Well-known Albertan *columnist Eva Reid lived in a second-floor apartment in the 1940s and 1950s.* SHANNON LEE RAE

Route: Cross 15th Avenue S.W. to the southwest corner of 4th Street and 15th Avenue.

Davidson House (Rose & Crown Pub)

Address: 1503–4th Street S.W.
Style: Tudor
Architect: Unknown
Date: Circa 1906

Long before it became the Rose & Crown Pub around 1986, generations of Calgarians knew this large converted dwelling as a funeral parlor. Perhaps its original occupants, David Davidson (1839–1921) and his wife Dora (1842–1930) set the tone. Both died in the house and both had their funerals here. This was an era when funeral services often took place in the deceased's residence.

David had operated a lumber business in Penetanguishene, in his native Ontario, and won two terms in that province's legislature as the Liberal member for Simcoe Centre (1898–1905). In 1905, David and his family moved to Calgary, where he became a rancher and stockbreeder, and built this fine family home. After Dora's passing in 1930, one of her in-laws, lumber merchant Harvey S. Perkins, lived here about five years. Two funeral homes, Park Memorial and McInnis & Holloway, occupied the house between 1935 and 1986.

Half-timbering details on the Rose & Crown Pub are typical of Tudor Revival style. Original occupants David and Dora Davidson set the tone for this house when they had their funerals here. It later served as a funeral home before becoming a pub in 1986. KAREN OLSON

Route: Proceed west along 15th Avenue S.W. for three blocks. Continue west on 15th Avenue to 7th Street S.W. Cross 7th Street to the southwest corner of the intersection.

Nellie McClung House

Address: 803–15th Avenue S.W. (formerly 1501–7th Street S.W.)
Style: Tudor Revival
Architect: Unknown
Year: 1907

Tall chimneys, half-Tudor detailing and multiple gables characterize the Tudor Revival style of the Nellie McClung House. SHANNON LEE RAE

Built by lawyer Harry Woodburne Blaylock, this house is best remembered for the decade-long occupancy by author, social reformer, and politician Nellie McClung (1873–1951), her husband Robert, and their family from 1923–33. Born in Ontario but raised in Manitoba, McClung was active in the temperance and women's suffrage movements before she moved to Alberta in 1915. During her residency in the Tudor Revival house, she sat as a Liberal MLA in the provincial legislature (1921–26) and was one of the Famous Five whose efforts led to the Persons Case in 1929, which advanced the status of women in Canada. She did much of her writing in her second-floor bedroom, and here she entertained politicians, social reformers, and literati. The house was originally oriented to 7th Street and was set on a large parcel with extensive gardens. The McClungs moved to Victoria, B.C., in 1933, and a later owner altered the house in the 1950s, moving its entrance to 15th Avenue. The house became a Provincial Historic Resource in 1978. It was damaged by fire in 1990 and repaired.

> **Route:** Cross 15th Avenue, and continue north along 7th
> Street to 14th Avenue S.W. Cross 14th Avenue.

Wesley Methodist Church (Jubilee Christian Centre)

Address: 1315–7th Street S.W.
Style: Predominantly Romanesque influence, with Classical
and Renaissance details
Architects: Fordyce and Stevenson
Date: 1912 (addition 1956)

*The rounded windows and entrances of the former Wesley United Church typify its
Romanesque influence.* Shannon Lee Rae

Calgary's First Methodist Church was constructed in 1905, and the
following year its Second Methodist and Third Methodist churches—soon renamed Wesley and Trinity respectively—were established. Wesley Methodist Church built its first home that year, at
819–13th Avenue S.W. (since demolished). It quickly proved too
small, and a building fund started in 1911 received contributions
from congregants Senator James A. Lougheed, Public Works
Minister William H. Cushing, and future prime minister R. B.

Bennett, among others. (Another notable member of Wesley was Nellie McClung.) The church's design might have been influenced by a church in Bismarck, North Dakota, the home state of church board member A. Judson Sayre. Cushing, who had served as Calgary's mayor in 1905–06, laid the cornerstone on July 14, 1911, and the church was dedicated on December 17 that year. Reverend A. C. Farrell, who became the congregation's minister in 1913, resigned during World War I to serve as chaplain for the 175th Battalion. During World War II, Reverend J. Rolph Morden, Wesley's minister through most of the 1940s, was also chaplain of HMCS Tecumseh, Calgary's naval training centre.

As early as 1909, the congregation had contemplated amalgamating with nearby Grace Presbyterian Church, and the two congregations sometimes held joint services when the minister of one went on vacation. In 1925, Wesley Methodist became Wesley United with the union of the Congregational, Methodist, and Presbyterian churches into the United Church of Canada. (Grace declined to join, kept its Presbyterian identity, and continues to operated in its beautiful Gothic sandstone edifice at 1009–15th Avenue S.W., built in 1913.)

Wesley's congregation was able to burn its mortgage in 1944, and a west-side addition was constructed in 1956. But the inner-city church declined in membership as families moved to the suburbs, and it was finally closed in 2003. The building presently houses the Jubilee Christian Centre.

Route: Proceed north along 7th Street to 13th Avenue S.W. Cross 7th Street and continue east on 14th Avenue to the Moxam and Congress Apartments.

Moxam and Congress Apartments
Address: 721 and 725–13th Avenue S.W.
Style: Classical
Architect: Unknown
Date: 1912

Moxam and Congress apartments, 2003. The lower balconies of both buildings have been retained, but massive pillars and the wide upper balconies they supported have been removed. SHANNON LEE RAE

Immediately west of the Lougheed mansion stand the Moxam and Congress apartments, two apartment blocks built from an identical design. Built at the height of Calgary's pre-World War I boom, the buildings helped transform 13th Avenue from a street dominated by mansions of the wealthy to a built-up urban area. But Senator Lougheed was behind it himself: he sold five lots to Winnipeg developer John Moxam (1882–1941), who had recently moved to Calgary, and helped finance the construction project. Each building had fourteen spacious apartments intended for well-to-do tenants. Moxam sold the eponymous eastern block to an English investor but briefly lived in it himself before moving to Victoria. Another noted tenant was Charles Comba, general foreman of Calgary's street railway system.

Moxam built the western block, originally named Houlton House, for real estate agent Sydney Houlton. The suites in Houlton House were subdivided in 1938 and the building was renamed Congress Apartments.

Route: Continue east along 13th Avenue S.W.

Beaulieu (Lougheed mansion)

Address: 707–13th Avenue S.W.
Style: Queen Anne Revival
Architect: James R. Bowes, Ottawa (1907 alterations and
additions designed by William M. Dodd)
Date: 1891

From its construction in 1891 until the death in office of its owner, Senator James Alexander Lougheed (1854–1925), this sandstone mansion was home to Calgary's original "power" couple. Lougheed worked as a carpenter in his native Brampton, Ontario, before studying law at Osgoode Hall and making his way to Calgary in 1883. He became the CPR's legal counsel, and invested in downtown real estate that earned him a fortune. In 1884, he married Belle Hardisty (1860–1936), daughter of the chief factor of the Hudson's Bay Company in its Mackenzie district and niece of Senator

Richard Hardisty, who represented the NWT in the upper house. The senator died in an 1889 accident and Lougheed was appointed to replace him. He became the Senate Conservative leader in 1906, and he entered the cabinet after the Tories won the 1911 election. During World War I he became head of the Military Hospitals Commission. Sir James, as he became in 1917, remains the only Albertan ever to have been knighted.

Beaulieu, the Lougheed mansion, was restored in time for Alberta's centennary in 2005. Courtesy of Lougheed House Conservation Society

Thirteenth Avenue lay blocks south of Calgary's developed area in 1891, and family members could probably watch visitors for some time as they crossed the prairie and approached the house. Here the Lougheeds established themselves as the cream of Calgary's society and entertained such distinguished guests as the Duke and Duchess of Connaught (he was the governor general) and their daughter, Lady Patricia, in 1912; and the Prince of Wales (the future King Edward VIII and later Duke of Windsor) in 1919. The Lougheeds built several additions to accommodate their growing family, and they developed a sunken garden to the east of the house. The Lougheeds called their house "Beaulieu" for one of Belle's ancestral family names, but many Calgarians knew it as "the big house."

After Sir James' death, his massive estate became mired in debt. The mansion became city property in 1934 for non-payment of taxes, but municipal authorities allowed Lady Belle to live there for the rest of her life. The spectacle of a public auction of household effects after his grandmother's death made a deep impression on ten-year-old Peter Lougheed, the future premier of Alberta. The house became a youth training centre, and during World War II it housed the Canadian Women's Auxiliary Army Camp. From 1948–79 it was Red Cross House. Generations of Calgarians remember the home's elaborate ceiling, at which they stared while lying down and giving blood.

The provincial government purchased the house in 1979, but it sat vacant until the 1990s, when a provincial advisory board and the Lougheed House Conservation Society began efforts to restore it as a tea house and multi-purpose facility. Apartments had been built on the former garden site in the 1960s, but they were demolished in 1980 for a larger development that was never built. The city bought the former garden site in 1993, and it was restored in 1997. Beaulieu was designated a Provincial Historic Resource in 1977, and in 1995 it was recognized by the Historic Sites and Monuments Board of Canada.

Route: Cross 13th Avenue at the west side of 6th Street S.W.

Ranchmen's Club
Address: 1211–6th Street S.W.
Style: Classical Mannerist
Architect: R. E. McDonnell
Year: 1914

Calgary's exclusive gentlemen's club, with rules patterned after those of Montreal's St. James Club, was established in 1892. The golden age of ranching in southern Alberta was then at its height, and prohibition had finally been repealed in the NWT. After a few years in rented quarters on Stephen Avenue, members built a wooden clubhouse on McIntyre Avenue (now 7th Avenue) in 1896 on the future site of the Bay Parkade (later renamed the Bow Parkade). During the pre–World War I boom, the club sold its downtown headquarters and, in 1914, built a lavish new clubhouse across 13th Avenue from the Lougheed mansion. Designed in Renaissance Revival style, the clubhouse boasted stained glass, oak paneling and, western motifs carved in exterior terra cotta panels. Membership spanned the cream of male Calgary society, but excluded women as full members until 1993.

Elaborate detailing, with figures depicting local fauna and western motifs, adorn the brick and terra cotta façade of the three-story Ranchmen's Club. The interior was gutted and rebuilt in 1980, when the building was incorporated into the adjacent new condominium tower. SHANNON LEE RAE

During a second round of prohibition, from 1916–24, the club could not provide alcohol but set aside a room for members to store their own bottles. A bed was placed in the room, in "compliance" with provincial rules that allowed consumption only in a room with a bed. Everyone knew that this was "Mr. Smith's bedroom."[2]

In 1980, the Ranchmen's Club was incorporated into an adjacent new condominium tower, and the club's interior was gutted and reconstructed.

Route: Proceed north along 6th Street to 12th Avenue S.W.
Cross both roads, and proceed east on 12th Avenue.

The Lorraine

Address: 620–12th Avenue S.W.
Style: Art Nouveau
Architect: James C. Teague
Date: 1913

Ornate terra cotta details, including the large stylized name block, distinguish the Lorraine's façade. Its three-level balcony was not unusual for its time, but on most apartment blocks this feature was built of wood instead of brick. SHANNON LEE RAE

Dr. Omer H. Patrick (1869–1947), the physician-turned-business-man who founded the Calgary Zoological Society in 1928, built this three-story brick apartment block and named it for his son Lorraine. Patrick intended to build a second structure and name it for his daughter Lenore, but the real estate boom collapsed in 1913 and the Lenore was never built. Notable occupants in the thirty-three suite building included Patrick himself, until he moved to

Mount Royal with his wife Lulu; architect Alex Pirie; and Robert C. Marshall, who lived here during his term as mayor (1919–21). Lorraine Patrick owned the building after his father's death, but its attraction as a high-class address had already declined. The Lorraine was gutted by fire in 1998, but the outer walls survived and it was reconstructed inside as an office block.

Route: Return west along 12th Avenue to 8th Street S.W. Cross both, and proceed south on 8th Street to 13th Avenue. Turn right, and continue west along 13th Avenue S.W. to the middle of the block.

Central Collegiate Institute (Rundle College)

Address: 930–13th Avenue S.W.
Style: Scottish Baronial
Architect: R. G. Gordon; Lang and Dowler (1911 addition); William Branton (1940 gymnasium)
Year: 1908 (additions 1911, 1940)

When it opened in 1908 as Central Collegiate Institute, this Scottish Baronial-style building replaced the city's previous high school— City Hall School, a small frame cottage behind City Hall and commonly referred to as "Sleepy Hollow." CCI, as the new high school became known (some quipped that it stood for "Calgary's Collection of Idiots"), evolved as an academic high school; its graduates were expected to pursue a higher education. It was later renamed Central High School. Premier William Aberhart officially opened the school's Egyptian Revival-style gymnasium addition in 1940.

Central closed in 1965, and its traditions are maintained by the suburban school that replaced it—Central Memorial. Alumni included Defence Minister Douglas Harkness, Alberta Premier Peter Lougheed, architect Harold Hanen, and Liberal MLA Sheldon Chumir. The building later became an adult education facility and was renamed Dr. Carl Safran Centre, after the educational psychologist who became the school board's chief superintendent in the 1970s. By the 1990s, the building was rented to Rundle College, a private academy. In 2003, the Calgary Board of Education announced it would convert the facility into its new headquarters.

The Calgary Board of Education announced in 2003 it would develop its new headquarters on the campus of Calgary's oldest existing high school, Central Collegiate Institute. SHANNON LEE RAE

Route: Continue west along 13th Avenue to 9th Street S.W. Cross 9th Street to the northwest corner.

High School Terrace

Address: 1217–9th Street S.W.
Style: English Terrace House
Contractor: Thomas Montgomerie
Date: 1910

The proximity of this two-story, brick terrace-style apartment to the former Central Collegiate Institute—at one time Calgary's only public high school—accounts for its name. It was built by Charles Thomas Gilbert (1867–1952), a baker from Warwickshire, England, who settled in Toronto in 1881 and moved to Calgary in 1898. Gilbert owned bakeries in Calgary, Banff, Claresholm, and Okotoks. The Alberta Bakery in Heritage Park Historical Village is intended to represent Gilbert's Calgary business. Gilbert's real estate activities included building this apartment block and developing Gilbert Estates, a subdivision near Forest Lawn.

Proximity to Central dictated this apartment's name: High School Terrace. The building later became known as Ashley Square, but the original name endures and remains engraved in the east-facing identification block. SHANNON LEE RAE

The building's most notable tenant was Richard Wallace, the city assessor and tax collector, who lived here from 1920 until his death in 1927. William Ferguson Ross, who owned the building from 1942–59, was once president of the Calgary Philatelic Society.

Route: Proceed north along 9th Street to 12th Avenue S.W. Cross 12th Avenue, turn left, and proceed west to the Harvey Block.

Harvey Block
Address: 1008–12th Avenue S.W.
Style: Edwardian Commercial
Architect: Unknown
Year: 1913

Merchant John W. Chittick (1866–1945), who had earlier built the nearby Chittick Block (J. W. C. Block), constructed this typical two-story brick building in 1913 and named it for his son Harvey. The city's booming economy crashed that year, but the Turner Valley oil boom the following spring brought a dramatic, albeit brief, recovery. Calgarians bought oil shares as if they were going out of style, and a robbery in the Harvey Block caught the *Albertan*'s attention. "Ponoka Pete" was the newspaper's characterization of the "bonehead burglar," referring to the mental hospital in that central Alberta town. The thief broke into William McCoy's apartment and stole cut glass, linen, and silverware, "but overlooked a nice fat bunch of oil stock certificates which might have put him on easy street for the rest of his life."[3] Fat chance. Within months the boom faded and many of those stock certificates became worthless, except as wallpaper.

After builder John W. Chittick's death, his son Harvey inherited the Harvey Block. The eastern storefront has been modified, and the central arch is a later addition.
SHANNON LEE RAE

Harvey Chittick and his sister inherited the Harvey Block after their father's death, and they sold it in the 1950s. Harvey taught school at Leduc, Alberta, and retired as that town's high school principal in 1963.

Route: Proceed west along 12th Avenue to 10th Street S.W.
Cross both roads, and proceed west on 12th Avenue to
the centre of the block.

Connaught School

Address: 1121–12th Avenue S.W.
Style: Free Classical
Architects: Lang and Dowler
Date: 1911 (additions 1920, 1953)

Connaught School, 2003. Alumnus Sheldon Chumir (1940–1992) later became a Rhodes scholar, civil rights lawyer, and provincial Liberal politician. SHANNON LEE RAE

When this sandstone school was built, it was customary to name public schools for the neighborhoods in which they were set. But this district had no name, and the pending appointment of Canada's new governor general—Prince Arthur, Queen Victoria's son and the 1st Duke of Connaught and Strathearn—provided inspiration. The school became Connaught, and the neighborhood eventually followed suit. In 1912, the Duke presented the school with portraits of himself and his wife, Luise. As governor general from 1911–16, a period that overlapped World War I, Connaught served as nominal commander-in-chief of the Canadian militia; his wife, a Prussian princess, was the Kaiser's cousin. After the war ended, teacher W. Markle Pecover—a veteran who fought at Vimy Ridge—lectured Connaught students on the subject every April, on the anniversary of that 1917 battle.

Route: Continue west along 12th Avenue to 11th Street S.W. Cross 11th Street, and turn left (south). Proceed south on 11th Street, cross 14th Avenue, and continue south to the J. W. C. Block.

J.W.C. Block
Address: 1407–11th Street S.W.
Style: Edwardian Commercial
Architect: Unknown
Date: 1912

Rare, intact pressed metal ceilings enliven the stores in the J.W.C. Block.
KIRSTEN OLSON

John Wesley Chittick (1866–1945), a merchant from Walkerton, Ontario, arrived in Calgary by 1907 and established a general store in the extant single-story building immediately north of the present J. W. C. Block. Chittick became a commission merchant for farm products and also invested in real estate: he built the two-story, brick J.W.C. Block in 1912 and the nearby Harvey Block, named for his son, the following year. Chittick later retired to the west coast, and by the 1930s this building became known as the Mahood Block, for its next owner, Dublin-born pharmacist Joseph E. Mahood (circa 1892–1959). A formal man, Mahood stood erect and always wore a three-piece suit. He lived in the building and operated his pharmacy here from 1924 to 1950. "Your 5¢ Order Will Be Delivered as Cheerfully as Your $5.00 Order," he advertised. Current occupants are Prints Charming and Kaleidoscope Color & Glass Gallery.

Route: Continue south on 11th Street S.W.

Brigden Block

Address: 1413–11th Street S.W.
Style: Edwardian Commercial
Architect: Unknown
Date: 1912

London-born Walter James Brigden (circa 1873–1961) settled in Calgary in 1906 and initially operated a grocery store at the north end of this block (1401–11th Street S.W.) By 1910 he bought four lots at the block's southeast corner and developed them incrementally. He first built the corner grocery (1421–11th Street S.W., now the Kalamata Grocery) in 1909, then the two-story wooden block just north of the store (1415-19–11th Street S.W., now Steeling Home and Peaseblossom) in 1910. In 1912 he built the two-story Brigden Block, and, around the corner, the Norwood Apartments (a three-story brick walk-up that still stands at 1208–15th Avenue S.W.) For years, Bridgen operated a shoe repair shop in his namesake building.

In 1996, restaurateur Brad Myhre opened the retro-1940s Galaxie Diner in the Brigden Block, and its décor was remodelled in 2000 as a set for the Chevy Chase movie *Snow Day*. Myhre took over the adjacent space in 2003 to house the Palace of Eats, another retro luncheonette that serves Montreal smoked meat. It perpetuates the name of the original Palace of Eats, which opened in the 1920s in the Alberta Block (which still stands at 805–1st Street S.W.) and was renamed Jimmies, for new owner Jimmie Condon, in 1934.

Walter James Brigden built all four structures at the southeast corner of this block. From left to right: the Norwood Apartments (built in 1912); a grocery store and residence (built in 1909, and occupied by the Kalamata Grocery since 1968); a two-story wooden commercial/residential block (1910); and the Bridgen Block (1912).
SHANNON LEE RAE

Tour ends.

Notes
1 Jennifer Bobrovitz, "Industrialist financed library," *Calgary Herald* 3 Aug. 1997: E5.
2 Hugh A. Dempsey, *Calgary: Spirit of the West* (Calgary: Glenbow and Fifth House Publishers, 1994) 70.
3 "A Bonehead Burglar Leaves Oil Stock," *Morning Albertan* 21 May 1914: 1.

Tour Begins

4th St. S.W.

8th Ave. S.W.

5 St. S.W.

Warehouse District and Victoria Park

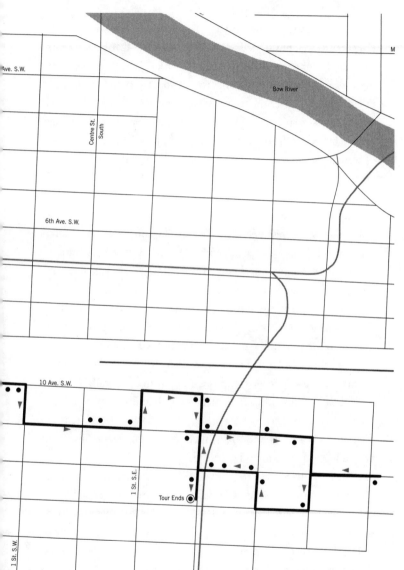

With its location on both the east-west transcontinental Canadian Pacific Railway (CPR) line (completed in 1885) and its north-south subsidiary between Edmonton and Fort Macleod (built in 1891–92), Calgary was well positioned to become a regional distribution centre for manufactured goods. The Calgary Board of Trade (later renamed the Calgary Chamber of Commerce) negotiated a preferred freight rate in 1902, and over the next dozen years the city's warehouse district flourished. Spur lines directed freight cars from the right-of-way, located between 9th and 10th avenues, to the back lanes between rows of warehouses that primarily lined 9th, 10th, and 11th avenues (and portions of 8th Avenue) between 13th Street S.W. and 4th Street S.E. Dozens of warehouses served hundreds of companies, and warehousing and jobbing became a major component of the city's economy. The buildings represented a massive capital investment by eastern Canadian and American firms, and at least one British corporation.

Most of the warehouses date from before World War I, reflecting the overheated economy before the war and the economic reversal of 1913. The city prospered again after World War II, but the decreasing importance of railways for distributing goods led to decline in the warehouse district. Many of the buildings fell vacant or were demolished in the 1970s, and others began new life as offices or furniture stores. Few warehouses built north of the railway tracks survive; most remaining examples line 10th and 11th avenues, and the CPR right-of-way forms northern boundary of the warehouse district. By the 1980s and 1990s, many remaining warehouses had been adaptively reused and gentrified.

West of 4th Street S.W., the warehouse district lies within the historic neighborhood of Connaught, a mixed-use area heavily developed between 1906–13, and which has since undergone high-density redevelopment. East of 4th, it overlaps Victoria Park, one of Calgary's earliest residential suburbs. Both Connaught and Victoria Park lie within Calgary's original town boundaries of 1884. The two districts amalgamated in 2004 as the Beltline Communities of Victoria and Connaught, taking the commonly used name that originated with the old Beltline streetcar route.

Warehouse District and Victoria Park

Originally part of a broader area called East Ward, which extended to present-day Inglewood, Victoria Park quickly formed a distinct identity between 4th Street S.W. and 6th Street S.E., and from the CPR tracks south to 17th Avenue. East of Macleod Trail (formerly 2nd Street S.E.), it lies immediately north of the exhibition grounds, which were first developed in 1889, annexed to the city a dozen years later, and named Victoria Park soon after Queen Victoria's death in 1901. The district took its name from the fair grounds, while the grounds themselves later abandoned the moniker and were officially renamed Stampede Park in 1975. The Calgary General Hospital was built in what is now the Victoria Park district in 1895 and remained the city's chief public hospital until the completion of a new General in Bridgeland in 1910. Victoria Park also lay adjacent to the city's commercial core, making it an attractive residential area for merchants and managers, since it was only a short distance from their downtown businesses. Working-class families found the same advantage, and the early departure of the managerial class for swankier neighborhoods contributed to Victoria Park's eventual blue-collar character. Calgary's first streetcar route was built through Victoria Park in 1909, connecting downtown with the exhibition grounds via 2nd Street S.E. and transforming that route into a commercial area.

In the decades following the 1913 collapse of Calgary's boom, little new construction took place in the district, apart from some renewed industrial development in the 1920s. Many houses became duplexes, apartments, or boarding houses, and immigrants and migrant workers contributed to the district's changing demographics. The physical decline of Victoria Park's aging housing stock was already apparent by the 1940s, and by the 1960s inner-city decay, crime, and social problems had become entrenched. Since the 1960s, the district has experienced development pressure from the Calgary Stampede, which has expanded north from 17th Avenue and will ultimately include all of eastern Victoria Park south of 12th Avenue S.E. Like Connaught, Victoria Park faces high-density redevelopment.

Qualico Developments, which restored the Louise Block in 2000, placed this identification sign at the northeast corner of 12th Avenue and Macleod Trail.
SHANNON LEE RAE

Start: Begin the Warehouse district tour in front of the former Ford Motor Company Building (902–11th Avenue S.W.).

Ford Motor Company of Canada Ltd. (Cohos Evamy & Partners)

Address: 902–11th Avenue S.W.
Style: Industrial (simplified Classical influence)
Architect: Wells-Grey Ltd. Engineers
Year: 1922

Except for a Depression-era shutdown in the early 1930s, this two-story brick warehouse served the Ford Motor Company of Canada from 1922 until the late 1950s. Its strong industrial design was sufficient to bear the weight of cars in its second-floor showroom. It was here, late in 1927, that Calgarians got their first glimpse of the Model A, the new roadster that succeeded Ford's original standard-bearer, the Model T. For years, a whistle mounted on top of the building loudly sounded at the start and end of each shift and lunch hour at the Ford plant. The Glenbow Museum used the building as a storage warehouse from about 1961–76. Since then, it has housed Cohos Evamy & Partners, a prominent architectural firm.

Cohos Evamy & Partners, a prominent architectural firm, adapted the former Ford warehouse as its headquarters in the 1970s. Identification blocks, recessed in the brick parapet, once contained signs for the Ford Motor Company. SHANNON LEE RAE

Route: Cross 8th Street S.W. to the northeast corner of 8th Street and 11th Avenue S.W.

General Motors Company warehouse (Brewsters Brew Pub)

Address: 834–11th Avenue S.W.
Style: Industrial (simplified Classical influence)
Architect: Unknown
Year: 1931

Built to the same scale as rival Ford Motor Company's building across the street, this two-story brick warehouse served the General Motors Company from its construction in 1931 until the mid-1950s, when GM moved out of the city core to Blackfoot Trail. A series of occupants followed until Brewsters Brewing Company, a microbrewery and restaurant chain established in Regina in 1989, transformed this warehouse into its first Calgary branch. The building is now known as the Corner Block.

Built eight years after the Ford building, the General Motors warehouse was built by the same contractor (Bentall Construction) and to a comparable scale and appearance. Despite its functional design, the warehouse has some classical elements, such as an abstract cornice line and engaged pilasters (flattened pillars that suggest the building's interior structure). KAREN OLSON

Route: Proceed east along 11th Avenue S.W. to the end of Brewsters' parking lot.

Alberta Government Telephones Warehouse (The King & I Thai Cuisine)

Address: 822–11th Avenue S.W.
Style: Industrial (simplified Classical influence)
Architect: Unknown
Date: 1921

Alberta Government Telephones (AGT), the publicly owned phone company established in 1907 and privatized in the 1990s as TELUS, built this brick warehouse as its stores and plants building in 1921. Across the province, early AGT employees enjoyed an enthusiastic social life together, which included dinners, dances, and sports. In 1922, local staff even formed the Calgary Telephone Society, which barred shop talk and organized strictly social events. According to Tony Cashman, AGT's onetime corporate historian, this building housed two bowling lanes and "may have been the only telephone warehouse in the world with a hardwood floor on the second storey for dances."[1]

Like the nearby Ford warehouse, the AGT stores building became a storage facility for the Glenbow Museum from about 1961–88. The King & I Thai Cuisine restaurant has been the main tenant since 1988.

Cast-in-place concrete, visible on the west side of this 1921 building, demonstrates a transitional technology, a departure from load-bearing brick walls that typify warehouses built a decade earlier. SHANNON LEE RAE

Route: Continue east on 11th Avenue, and cross 7th Street S.W.

Sherwin Williams Paint Company warehouse (Royop Block)

Address: 738–11th Avenue S.W.
Style: Industrial (simplified Classical influence)
Architect: Unknown
Date: 1913

The original building on this site was a 1905 residence, notable as the home of Ernest L. Richardson, longtime manager of the Calgary Exhibition and later of the Calgary Exhibition and Stampede. It was demolished to make way for this three-story red brick warehouse, built for the Sherwin Williams Paint Company that remained its chief occupant until 1965. It later housed the McArthur Furniture Store (1972–82), and Heaven's Fitness (1992–2004). The Royop Corporation acquired the building in 2004 and announced plans to add two high-tech storeys.

The former Sherwin Williams warehouse is unusually elaborate from the street, but, in typical fashion, cheaper bricks were used on the rear face. SHANNON LEE RAE

The public façades are unusually elaborate for the warehouse district and include limestone trim, a well-detailed arched entrance, and a hint of crenellation, reminiscent of a castle, in the parapet high above. In contrast, the rear façade is typical in its use of lesser quality bricks and the presence of a loading dock, built at the height of railway boxcars that came along the spur line between 10th and 11th Avenues. In the 1990s, in a clever example of adaptive reuse, the coffee shop at the ground floor used the dock as an outdoor patio. The loading dock was removed in 2005.

Route: Cross to the south side of 11th Avenue, turn left (east), and proceed east to 5th Street S.W.

Roberts Block (The Keg)

Address: 601-607–11th Avenue S.W.
Style: Edwardian Classical
Architect: Rex Arlo Millar
Date: 1911 (addition 1912)

Two symmetrical buildings comprise the Roberts Block, which has housed the Keg restaurant since 1974. A ghost sign on the east face dates from the Calgary Furniture Company's occupancy in 1912. SHANNON LEE RAE

Louis Melville Roberts (1879–1958), an Iowa-born lawyer and businessman, built this eponymous three-story brick warehouse in 1911 and doubled its size the following year. Its original occupants included A. McKillop and Company Ltd. (a wholesale boot and shoe business), Alberta Empress Company Ltd. (a wholesale food business later taken over by Safeway), and the Calgary Furniture Company Ltd. During Alberta's eight dry years of Prohibition (1916–24), the only legitimate source of alcohol was the Alberta Government Liquor Vendor, which moved into this building in 1919. It was likely the most popular place in Calgary for tipplers who wished to avoid the city's bootleggers.

Roberts was a member of the prestigious Lougheed and Bennett law firm, and represented High River as a Liberal in Alberta's second legislature (1909–13). He left the city in the 1920s. During the Great Depression, Roberts faced a high vacancy rate in this building, diminished revenue, and foreclosure proceedings, but evidently managed to hang onto the building.

Fire tore through the Roberts Block in 1937, 1954, and 1958, and it was repaired each time. The Vancouver-based Keg'N Cleaver restaurant chain (later renamed The Keg) opened its first Calgary outlet here in 1974.

Route: Cross 11th Avenue S.W., and proceed north along 5th Street to 10th Avenue S.W.

Simington Company warehouse (Kipling Square)

Address: 601–10th Avenue S.W.
Style: Industrial (simplified Classical influence)
Architect: Unknown
Date: 1914

Stone doorways, string courses, window heads and cornice bands contrast with red brick in Kipling Square's façade. The recessed, glassed-in penthouse dates from the 1980 renovation. SHANNON LEE RAE

The Simington Company, a wholesale grocery business, built this two-story warehouse in 1914 and soon added a three-story annex. The raised courtyard to the west was once a street-level loading area, designed for horse-drawn vehicles; west-facing bay windows now cover the former loading bays. Between 1930 and 1979, the building housed Western Grocers Ltd., a wholesale house that supplied the Red & White Stores, a chain of stores that were once ubiquitous in small town Alberta.

In 1979, architects Paul Tarjan and Associates transformed the Simington warehouse into Kipling Square, a retail complex and the first of many adaptive reuse projects in the warehouse district. It once housed the Polo Club restaurant, which featured a bar purchased from a San Francisco hotel and a brass dumbwaiter that carried drinks between the restaurant's two levels.

Route: Cross 5th Street S.W.

Hudson's Bay Company warehouse (The Hudson)

Address: 535–10th Avenue S.W.
Style: Industrial (simplified Classical influence)
Architect: Unknown
Date: 1912

Just as the Hudson's Bay Company was building its massive department store at 7th Avenue and 1st Street S.W., the Bay also constructed this five-story brick warehouse along the railway spur line. The building served its original function until 1924, when the provincial government rented it to house the new Alberta Liquor Control Board, established at the end of Prohibition that year. Safeway Stores Inc. (later renamed Canada Safeway) bought the warehouse in 1935 and kept its offices here for nearly sixty years. In 1993, it was converted into Calgary's first New York-style loft condominium projects, and named after the department store that first built it.

In 1993, the old Hudson's Bay Company warehouse was converted into Calgary's first New York-style lofts and renamed The Hudson. Rather than damage the brick façade by sandblasting, the developer repainted it to resemble brick finish. SHANNON LEE RAE

Route: Proceed east along 10th Avenue, and cross 4th Street S.W. (originally Ross Street).

J. I. Case Company warehouse (Tantra Nightclub and Lounge)

Address: 355–10th Avenue S.W.

Style: Industrial

Architect: Unknown

Date: 1907 (additions 1932 and 1952)

This brick and stone warehouse, built in 1907 and later enlarged, housed the J. I. Case Company, an American agricultural implement firm, from 1907–72. In 1985 Case amalgamated with International Harvester, becoming Case International.

For as long as Case occupied the building, the company's trademark American eagle symbol dominated the corner of 10th Avenue and 4th Street S.W. The eagle was modeled after Old Abe, a live bird that served as mascot of Company C, Eighth Wisconsin Regiment, during the U.S. Civil War. Jerome Case was in Eau Claire, Wisconsin, at the time the company was formed there, and he adapted its mascot—named for President Abraham Lincoln—as his corporate logo. (Two decades later, industrialist Peter Prince moved his sawmill from Eau Claire, Wisconsin, to Calgary, where he named it the Eau Claire and Bow River Lumber Company. Calgary's modern Eau Claire district takes its name from the mill.)

"Tantra" refers to Buddhist or Hindu mysticism, and the Tantra Nightclub has placed a relief female figure, styled in Indian motif, in the Case eagle's old place.
SHANNON LEE RAE

The façade is made of blond colored bricks, fired at low temperature. They later proved softer and less durable than ordinary brick. The building later housed Collegiate Sports (circa 1978–82), Claudio's restaurant, The Drink nightclub, and, since 2003, Tantra Nightclub and Lounge.

Route: Proceed east along 10th Avenue S.W. (originally called Pacific Avenue east of 4th Street S.W.).

G. F. & J. Galt Company/Canadian Consolidated Rubber & Pacific Cartage and Storage (Wigelo Building)

Address: 323-325–10th Avenue S.W.
Style: Industrial (simplified Edwardian Classical influence)
Architect: Unknown
Date: 1910 (east building); 1913 (west building)

Bricks in the original 1910 façade are darker than those of the larger 1913 addition. Giant murals on the building's east and west faces replaced ghost advertising signs in the 1980s. Vern Schwab, the owners' lawyer and an art aficionado, chose a Paul Klee image for the west wall, and a depiction of Taos Mountain in New Mexico, site of an artists' colony, for the east. SHANNON LEE RAE

Like other large warehouses in the district, this imposing five-story brick building comprises two structures built in quick succession: an eastern one built in 1910 to house the Winnipeg-based G. F. & J. Galt Company, a wholesale grocer and tea importer, followed by wholesale grocers Campbell, Wilson & Horne Ltd.; and a larger western one built in 1913, and occupied by the Canadian Consolidated Rubber Company and the Pacific Cartage and Storage Company, which contracted its services to the CPR. The combined complex housed many firms at a time, some for decades (such as Merchants Hardware Specialties from 1919–73).

The building's form neatly demonstrates its original warehouse function. The rear loading dock is the most intact example in the district. Its projecting canopy sheltered workers as they unloaded freight on a loading dock built at boxcar level. After goods were processed on the ground floor, the freight elevator—identifiable by the top of the elevator bay, the highest point of the building—carried goods to storage areas on the upper floors. Facing 10th Avenue, the attractive ground level entrance established the building's public face, and reflects the display function of the wholesalers who used this warehouse. The imposing rusticated sandstone base creates a massive effect at street level.

By the 1960s, the eastern portion was named the Cristobal Building, while the western one became the Bal-Cristo Building. The current owners bought the property in 1970 and called it the Wigelo Building, an amalgam of the owners' surnames. Many Calgarians knew the building as the home of its anchor tenant through the 1970s and 1980s, Nu-Trend Furniture. It still houses office and commercial tenants, as well as artists' studios. A two-story eastern annex built in the 1950s has housed the Cannery Row seafood restaurant since 1982.

Route: Proceed east along 10th Avenue to 2nd Street S.W. (originally Hamilton Street). Turn right, and proceed south along 2nd Street to 11th Avenue S.W.

Metals Ltd. (The Vintage)

Address: 322–11th Avenue S.W.
Style: Industrial (simplified Classical influence)
Architects: Fordyce and Stevenson
Date: 1929

Originally four stories tall, this corner warehouse was purpose-built for Metals Ltd., a plumbing and heating supply firm that remained as late as the 1950s, by which time it had become the Empire Brass Manufacturing Company. The building later became a furniture factory, and from 1969–93 it housed Cristy's Arcade, a landmark furniture store owned by prominent Calgary businessman and philanthropist Hyman Belzberg. On an early December morning in 1982, Belzberg was kidnapped from the parking lot. He was released twenty-four hours later, after his family paid a $1.8-million ransom. Traced phone calls soon led police to the kidnappers.

The four-story Metals Ltd. warehouse later became Cristy's Arcade Furniture and has since been transformed into an eight-story retail and office complex. The original upper cornice still remains. Construction of a large western addition in 2003 is visible at left. SHANNON LEE RAE

In 1998, Gibbs Gage Architects designed the building's transformation into The Vintage, an eight-story office complex. A sympathetic eight-story addition was constructed to the west in 2003.

Route: Cross 2nd Street S.W.

J. H. Ashdown Hardware Company warehouse (Lewis Lofts)

Address: 240–11th Avenue S.W.

Style: Simplified Classical, with Romanesque features in its round-headed windows

Architect: J. H. G. Russell of Winnipeg; Hodgson and Bates, associate architects

Year: 1909 (additions 1910, 1913)

Rounded arches typify the Romanesque style that influenced this building's design. The seam between the original corner warehouse and its 1913 addition is still visible. SHANNON LEE RAE

The Winnipeg-based J. H. Ashdown Hardware Company entered the Calgary market in 1889 and built this brick warehouse twenty years later. Patterned after the firm's Winnipeg warehouse, the building originally stood only four stories tall and was half its present width. Increased business during Calgary's massive pre-World War I boom moved Ashdown's to build two additional floors in 1910 and to double the size of the building in 1913. Ashdown's closed its Calgary operation in 1972, and, as Lewis Stationery's warehouse for the next twenty years, this building became one of the last remaining large warehouses that still served its original purpose. It was converted into the Lewis Lofts in time for the 1995 Designers' Showcase, an annual charity fundraiser in which local designers demonstrate their talents in one room of a designated building.

Route: Proceed north on 2nd Street to 10th Avenue S.W.
Turn right (east), and proceed east on 10th Avenue.

Walter M. Lowney Company of Canada/Scott Fruit Company (MacCosham Place)

Address: 211-215–10th Avenue S.W.
Style: Industrial (simplified Classical influence)
Architect: Unknown
Date: 1912

The brick and sandstone façade of MacCosham Place is simple and stylized, with a corbelled brick upper cornice. SHANNON LEE RAE

This office and retail centre takes its present name from its 1937–75 occupancy by the MacCosham Storage & Distributing Company, an

Edmonton-based cartage firm established by R. V. "Vic" MacCosham in 1913. MacCosham's entered the Calgary market in 1937 through acquisition of Johnston's Storage and Cartage Company, which had been located in this warehouse since 1915. In 1945, MacCosham's built a second warehouse near the confluence of the Bow and Elbow rivers, and operated out of both buildings for the next thirty years. Archaeological work in the early 1970s revealed that the second warehouse had been built over the remains of Fort Calgary. In 1975, the fort's centennial, MacCosham's sold both warehouses and moved to a suburban industrial park. The 1945 warehouse was demolished to create Fort Calgary Historic Park, while the older 10th Avenue structure was restored as MacCosham Place in 1980.

Though remembered as MacCosham's, this warehouse always housed multiple businesses, and between 1912 and the 1950s its tenant list would have seemed a "dream team" to candy lovers: chocolatiers Lowney's, Neilson's, Fry-Cadbury, and Rowntree, as well as Canada Dry Ginger Ale and the Empress Manufacturing Company, whose food products included jams. For purists, there was the B. C. Sugar Refining Company, and, for those who favored savory, the Vancouver Pickle Company. Perhaps another longtime tenant, Hygiene Products Ltd., did a good business here selling toothbrushes and toothpaste. Another early and longtime tenant was the Scott Fruit Company (1912–29).

Route: Continue east on 10th Avenue S.W.

Calgary Gas Co. Ltd. workshop (Back Lot bar)

Address: 207–10th Avenue S.W.
Style: Utilitarian
Architect: Unknown
Date: 1907

This diminutive, two-story frame building seems out of place among the more substantial brick and sandstone warehouses that transformed the district within a few years after it was built. It stands on what was once a large block of lots owned by contractor and businessman Thomas Underwood, Calgary's mayor in 1902–04. The building's unadorned original appearance probably reflected its use as the workshop of the Calgary Gas Company Ltd., whose president was meat-packing king Patrick Burns. In 1911, Eugene Coste's newly formed Canadian Western Natural Gas Company bought out its eight-year-old counterpart, and Coste's firm took over the Calgary Gas Company offices in the Underwood Block (now known as the Western Block) next door.[2] Atco Gas, the city's chief home heating supplier, took over Canadian Western Natural Gas in the 1990s.

A series of small businesses occupied this small building before it became the Back Lot, a gay bar, around 2000.

Calgary Sales, a hotel and restaurant supply firm, occupied the former Calgary Gas Company workshop in the 1960s. CALGARY HERITAGE AUTHORITY

Route: Continue east on 10th Avenue to 1st Street S.W. (originally Scarth Street).

Underwood Block (Western Block)

Address: 1001–1st Street S.W.
Style: Edwardian Commercial
Architect: Francis J. Lawson
Date: 1905

The Western Block was important in establishing 1st Street S.W. as a commercial district. Interlocking letters (UB) in a leaded glass window over the main entrance are the only remnant of the building's original identification as the Underwood Block. SHANNON LEE RAE

Viewed from 10th Avenue or from 1st Street S.W., this two-story brick block looks like a typical building from its time, with ground-level storefronts and apartments upstairs. At the rear, however, the building contains a relic of the horse-drawn transportation era, unique in the city. An open entryway from the back alley, with a bridge-like set of apartments overhead, leads into a courtyard loading area built on a scale for horse-drawn vehicles. The courtyard is now used as a parking lot.

In its early years, the building was set alongside Calgary's second Chinatown. At a time when many Calgarians were hostile to their Chinese neighbors, Thomas Underwood (1863–1948), an

English-born carpenter and building contractor, Calgary's four-teenth mayor (from 1902–04), and a deacon of the Baptist Church, befriended members of the Chinese community—albeit with a missionary purpose. The original Chinatown had been located at the corner of Centre Street and 9th Avenue, near the CPR station. Underwood's generosity of spirit helped shift it to the area around 10th Avenue and 1st Street S.W., where he owned a large block of property. He built a two-story Chinese Mission on one of his 10th Avenue lots (on the present site of MacCosham Place) in 1901 and served as its president for twenty years. Proposed railway develop-ment along 1st Street S.W. threatened this second Chinatown and prompted its move to the present Chinatown site in 1910. (The rail-way project, which would have seen the Canadian Northern Railway enter downtown along 1st Street S.W., was never constructed.)

In 1905, Underwood built this original Underwood Building on what had previously been a slough, and it was key in establishing 1st Street S.W. as a commercial strip. It housed offices the Calgary Gas Company and its successor, Canadian Western Natural Gas, as well as the Diamond Coal Company, in which Underwood had invested. When he built a new, larger Underwood Block a few blocks further south in 1911, Underwood renamed this building the Western Block. It was repaired after a serious fire in March 1919, and continues as a small-scale retail, office and residential building. Perhaps its best-known tenant was Olivier's, a candy factory and confectionery locat-ed here from 1924 until the 1970s. Quebec-born businessman Gaspard Frederic Olivier (1886–1965) lived in the building with his family from 1924 until his death. Son Maurice "Bud" Olivier sold the business in 1971, and it remains in business in the Inglewood district.

Route: Proceed south along 1st Street S.W., and duck into the lane to observe the Western Block's courtyard. An art gallery in the building, the Sugar Gallery, is accessi-ble from the back alley. Return to 1st Street, and con-tinue south to the corner with 11th Avenue S.W. Cross 1st Street, and proceed east along 11th Avenue. At the northwest corner with Centre Street (originally McTavish Street), you will pass the Mustard Seed Street Ministry's newer building. Cross Centre Street (where the S.W. designation becomes S.E.) to the old warehouse on the northeast corner, which also houses the Mustard Seed.

Relief lettering in the signband originally identified this warehouse as the Northern Electric & Mfg. Co. Limited. Its classical influence is readily apparent through such features as expressed columns and strong cornice (since removed) that evoke ancient Greek and Roman design. At ground level, the attractive carved stone façade reflects the importance of office and display functions. Glenbow Archives ND-8-296

Northern Electric Co. warehouse (Mustard Seed Street Ministry)

Address: 102–11th Avenue S.E.
Style: Classically-influenced
Architect: William M. Dodd (eastern building); Lawson and
Fordyce (western building)
Year: 1913

The rise and decline of Nortel Networks lay in the distant future when the Northern Electric Company—precursor to Northern Telecom, later renamed Nortel—built this warehouse. City directories characterize Northern Electric's business as "radio, sound systems, electrical supplies, wires and cables"—just a hint of the high-technology siren that briefly transformed Nortel into an international dynamo before its spectacular fall when the tech bubble burst in the late 1990s.

The Dominion government bought the building in 1942, and it housed the Royal Canadian Ordnance Corps until the end of World War II. For nearly half a century after the war, it housed federal government offices and laboratories, including the departments of Agriculture, Forestry and Veterans' Affairs. The Mustard Seed Street Ministry, a Christian humanitarian organization with roots in the First Baptist Church, bought the building in 1992. The Mustard Seed provides meals, clothing, and shelter to the homeless, as well as education, skills training, and worship services.

Route: Continue east along 11th Avenue S.E.

Ganong Bros. Ltd. and Calgary Saddlery Company (Centre 110)

Address: 110–11th Avenue S.E.
Style: Industrial
Architect: Lawson & Fordyce (western building)
Date: 1909 (eastern building); 1912 (western building)

"Candy is dandy," observed poet Ogden Nash, "but liquor is quicker." The western building on this site (106–11th Avenue S.E.)

had it all. It originally functioned as a liquor warehouse, but quickly became the Calgary home of Ganong Bros. Ltd., the New Brunswick-based candy manufacturer founded in 1873. Ganong was famed as the inventor of the "chicken bone," a cinnamon-flavored hard candy with a chocolate "marrow" centre. The eastern building (110–8th Avenue S.E.) was built to house the Calgary Saddlery Company, a successor to one of Calgary's earliest saddlery businesses. The two structures were combined in the 1970s as the headquarters of General Distributors Ltd., the Canadian distributor of Sony products owned by businessman Harry Cohen (1912–1990) and his brothers. Cohen's wife Martha is the namesake for the Martha Cohen Theatre in Calgary's performing arts centre. The building remains an office block. An applied stone façade unites the two buildings as Centre 110, but obscures their original appearance.

The Calgary Saddlery Company warehouse, seen here around 1910, forms the eastern portion of Centre 110. GLENBOW ARCHIVES PA-2356-1

Route: Proceed east along 11th Avenue S.E.

Customs Examining Warehouse (Cantos Music Museum)

Address: 134–11th Avenue S.E.

Styles: Chicago and Classical influences

Architect: Department of Public Works (supervised locally by Leo Dowler, Dominion architect in Calgary)

Date: 1916

Strong features of the former Customs Examining Warehouse include its heavy, rusticated sandstone base; close-set pilasters, or columns, topped by ornamented capitals and linked at the top by stone arches; and a strong pressed-metal cornice, with tooth-like dentils suggestive of wooden beams. SHANNON LEE RAE

In its day, the Customs Examining Warehouse was a key element of the warehouse district. Here duty-bearing merchandise, which mostly arrived by rail, was inspected and cleared on its arrival in Calgary. The short spans between the shallow vertical columns—typical Classical features called engaged pilasters—express the building's structure, and reveal its incredibly high load-bearing capacity: 200 pounds per square foot, more than double the modern standard. The rusticated sandstone base gives the warehouse a massive feel, appropriate to an important institutional building. When it was designated a Provincial Historic Resource in 1979,

Minister of Culture Mary LeMessurier characterized the Customs Examining Warehouse as "the largest and most impressively designed building of its type in Alberta."[3] It remained a federal government office building until 1982, when the city bought it for use by the police department. The building was sold to private owners in 1997. In 2002, it became home to the Cantos Music Museum, which holds a world-class collection of musical instruments.

Route: Cross 1st Street S.E. (originally Osler Street), turn left (north), and proceed north on 1st Street to 10th Avenue S.E. Turn right (east), and proceed east along 10th Avenue to Macleod Trail (originally Drinkwater Street, later known as 2nd Street S.E., and, since 1967, Macleod Trail).

Tudhope, Anderson Co. warehouse (Demcor Building)

Address: 239–10th Avenue S.E.
Style: Industrial (simplified Classical influence)
Architect: William M. Dodd
Date: 1906

Calgary's oldest remaining warehouse was also among the first to undergo "adaptive reuse" when it was converted into modern offices and a restaurant in the early 1980s. The Tudhope, Anderson Co., an agency that represented eight different agricultural implement manufacturers, occupied the building from 1906–21. Later occupants included the Hedley Shaw Milling Co., Oliver Agricultural Implements, James Storage & Cartage, and, finally, Bekins Moving & Storage, before the building's restoration in 1980. A 1993 pink and turquoise color scheme was sandblasted off a decade later. The two round-headed rear loading bays have been closed in with concrete block and glass, forming Palladian-style windows that match the arched front entrance and east-facing rounded window. The front façade has been severely modified.

The large display windows in the former Tudhope, Anderson Co. warehouse have since been considerably altered. Calgary's oldest remaining warehouse was one of the first to undergo adaptive reuse in the 1980s. Shannon Lee Rae

Route: Cross Macleod Trail S.E. The next building, the Bell Block, is the first on the tour not built as a warehouse.

Bell Block

Address: 1002 Macleod Trail S.E.
Style: Edwardian Commercial
Architect: Unknown
Date: 1909

In July 1909, the first leg of the new Calgary Electric Railway (soon renamed the Calgary Municipal Railway) linked the downtown core to the exhibition grounds by way of 2nd Street S.E., as this stretch of Macleod Trail was known for decades. (Originally, the historic Macleod Trail completely bypassed downtown. It skirted east of Cemetery Hill as it entered Calgary from the south and made its way north through the Ramsay district to the Bow River and beyond. In 1967, the City Council officially changed 2nd Street S.E. into Macleod Trail and renamed the original route: one section became Spiller Road and another section became 8th Street S.E.)

The Bell Block's symmetrical façade features a central bay bounded by columns, with an arched entrance, central pediment, and tall flagpole. SHANNON LEE RAE

Ralph A. G. Bell (1861–1953), a retired North-West Mounted Police officer and veteran of the 1885 North West Rebellion, built this namesake commercial/residential block in 1909, just as the streetcar was transforming the former Drinkwater Street into a commercial strip. In its three floors, the Bell Block contained thirty apartments and eight storefronts; one of the first commercial occupants was the International Correspondence School. Alderman Richard A. Brocklebank, the contractor who built Memorial Park Library, the Odd Fellows Temple, the YWCA, and Stanley Jones School, lived upstairs in 1912–13. The Bell Block remains a combined retail/apartment block.

Route: Proceed south along Macleod Trail.

Louise Block
Address: 1018 Macleod Trail S.E.
Style: Edwardian Commercial
Architect: Unknown
Date: 1910

The Louise Block formed a transition between the warehouse district and Victoria Park's commercial zone along 2nd Street S.E. (now Macleod Trail). It had west-facing storefronts on 2nd Street and south-facing loading bays on 11th Avenue. SHANNON LEE RAE

Like the contemporary Bell Block, the Louise Block was built soon after the streetcar transformed 2nd Street S.E. into a major commercial thoroughfare. Frank Fairey (1864–1926), a contractor and developer who built extensively in Victoria Park (including the nearby Fairey Terrace), named this residential/commercial block for his wife (died 1945). Its west-facing storefronts reflect 2nd Street's commercial nature. The south side originally had loading bays, reflecting 11th Avenue's character as part of the warehouse district.

One of the most notable occupants of the second-floor suites was Thomas Arthur Presswood ("Tappy") Frost (1865–1927), one of the most colorful aldermen in Calgary's history. During his four-year tenure on City Council, the English-born Baptist minister kept a gun in his City Hall office, threw an opponent out a window, and faced sanction for taking a pickaxe to a 17th Avenue sidewalk to expose a contractor's shoddy work. When oil was discovered at nearby Turner Valley in 1914, Alderman Frost went on a one-man, two-city tour (Winnipeg and Toronto) to promote Calgary and its new source of wealth. In Toronto, Frost stood on the street ladling crude from a wooden bucket. He resigned from the council in 1916 to fight in World War I.

The Louise Block survived a 1966 fire, and its exterior was restored in 2000. It has been declared a Registered Historic Resource.

Route: Continue south along Macleod Trail to 11th Avenue S.E. Turn left (east), and proceed east on 11th Avenue.

Massey-Harris warehouse (Ribtor Hardware)

Address: 318–11th Avenue S.E.

Style: Utilitarian (influenced by Edwardian Classicism, with simplified details)

Architect: Massey-Harris head office, Toronto (supervised locally by J. A. Cawston)

Date: 1912

The Massey-Harris Company (later renamed Massey-Ferguson Ltd.) used this building from 1912–79, the longest any warehouse in the district served its original occupant. SHANNON LEE RAE

Of Calgary's many warehouses built for agriculture implement dealers, this four-story brick and sandstone building housed its original occupant the longest. Massey-Harris, a well-known Canadian manufacturer of agricultural implements, entered the Calgary market at the dawn of the twentieth century and built this substantial warehouse for light assembly, distribution and sales, and as its southern Alberta headquarters. The Massey name is well known in Canada through two great-grandsons of company founder Daniel Massey: Vincent Massey, Canada's first native-born governor-general (from 1952–59); and Raymond Massey, the famed Hollywood actor and star of television's "Dr. Kildare."

Massey-Ferguson, as the company was renamed in the 1950s, sold the building in 1979. Since then it has housed Ribtor Sales, a popular, locally owned camping and hardware store first established in 1949. The name is an amalgam of "Riback" and "Hector," family names of the company's founders.

Route: Continue east along 11th Avenue to its northeast corner with 3rd Street S.E. (originally Hardisty Street).

Pilkington Paint & Glass (Critical Mass)

Address: 402–11th Avenue S.E.
Style: Edwardian Commercial
Architects: Hodgson, Bates and Beattie
Date: 1913

Stark juxtaposition marks the adaptive reuse of the Pilkington Brothers Ltd. warehouse, built as one of the British glass manufacturer's fourteen warehouses across Canada. After Pilkington's departure in 1967, the building housed DeFehr and Sons, a furniture business, until the 1980s. In 1995, after years of vacancy, a developer began converting the two-story brick warehouse into residential and commercial lofts. The project eventually stalled, and in 2000 the building was transformed as the state-of-the-art home of the website design firm Critical Mass. The interior was stripped to its bare essentials, and graffiti from the building's vacant years left intact. A low-rise floor covers all electrical wiring and computer cables, and modular furniture forms partitions that can be easily changed.

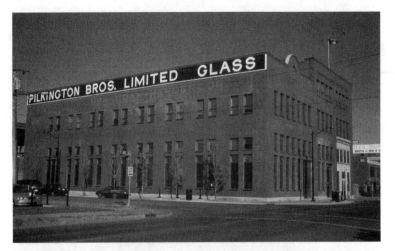

An elaborate Tyndall stone façade forms the office entrance and display windows on the Pilkington's east wing. The west wing's façade is relatively unadorned except for an attractive oculus, or round window, centered at the top. SHANNON LEE RAE

Route: Continue east along 11th Avenue S.E. to Olympic Way (originally Dewdney Street and later designated 4th Street S.E.) Cross 11th Avenue S.E., turn right (west), and proceed west on 11th Avenue to the middle of the block.

Victoria School and Victoria Bungalow School (ArriVa Condos)

Address: 411–11th Avenue S.E.

Style: Free Classical

Architect: William Dodd (original 1903 wing and 1907 addition); Hugh McClelland with William A. Branton (1912 addition)

Date: 1903 (additions 1907, 1912)

The original Victoria School was built in 1903 in the subdivision first known as East Ward but quickly renamed Victoria Park. Like other sandstone schools built between 1892 and 1920, it was designed to evoke the grandeur of the British Empire in the consciousnesses of public school students and their parents. Architect

William Dodd, who also designed Calgary's historic City Hall, worked on both the original four-room wing and its four-room extension in 1907. A 1912 addition, also built of sandstone, still remains, but the earlier wings were demolished in 1961 and replaced by modern classrooms and a gymnasium. All schools closed during the worldwide Spanish Influenza epidemic in 1918–19, and Victoria became one of four city schools used as emergency hospitals. During World War II, the Ration Division of the War Time Prices and Trade Board accepted registrations and issued sugar ration books in the school's auditorium.

Victoria School was built in stages on what had once been the Athletic Association grounds. SHANNON LEE RAE

The adjacent bungalow school built in 1919 represents a later, more frugal era of school building. Bungalow schools were less substantial than their sandstone counterparts, but more permanent and institutional in appearance than the early cottage schools, which had been designed for temporary use and eventual conversion to residential use. Administratively, the sandstone school and bungalow school operated as separate institutions. The 1962 addition connected the two buildings.

Declining enrolment led to the closure of Victoria's junior high in 1989 and its elementary school six years later. The school board leased the campus to a charter school for several years, and sold it to a developer in 2004. Development plans call for retention of the sandstone building and relocation of the bungalow school to the south side of the block.

Route: Return east along 11th Avenue to Olympic Way, and cross. Turn right (south), and proceed south on Olympic Way to 12th Avenue. Cross 12th Avenue, turn left (east), and proceed east along 12th Avenue, crossing 5th Street S.E. Continue east on 12th Avenue to the Rundle Ruins.

Calgary General Hospital (Rundle Ruins)

Style: Romanesque
Architect: Child and Wilson
Date: 1895 (additional buildings constructed 1899, 1903, and 1905)

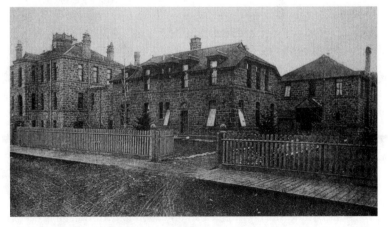

A complex of three buildings eventually formed the Calgary General Hospital. The Rundle Ruins include remnants of all three. GLENBOW ARCHIVES NA-1114-5.

These picturesque ruins are all that remain of the second Calgary General Hospital, which operated on this site until 1910 and was all but demolished in 1973.

Nothing is left of the first General, which operated in a two-storey yellow house on 7th Avenue S.W. from 1890–95. It had eight beds, and operations were performed on a dining room table—in the hospital dining room. A lean-to served as the morgue.

The second General opened May 22, 1895, with a capacity for thirty-five patients. The General quickly expanded into a three-building complex, but could not keep up with Calgary's growing population. By 1907 the hospital was impossibly overcrowded, and a new General was completed in Bridgeland in 1910. The Victoria Park complex, briefly used for military purposes, became Calgary's Isolation Hospital in 1911. During the deadly worldwide epidemic of Spanish Influenza at the end of World War I, fifty flu patients crowded the old buildings, with as many more in tents outside.

By the 1930s the aging buildings were crumbling, and one nurse remembered chasing bats down the corridors with a broom. But it took until 1953 for the General to build a new isolation ward. That year, "Operation Measles" moved patients to the new quarters, and the Isolation Hospital closed forever.

In 1955, the old hospital received new life as Rundle Lodge, a United Church seniors' home named for pioneer missionary Robert Rundle. By 1968, however, Rundle Lodge was labelled a deathtrap, and in 1971 a new facility was built directly behind the old. Plans to demolish the old hospital found stiff opposition, and a bitter public debate followed. Preservationists hoped to convert it into an artists' centre or medical museum. Opponents considered Rundle Lodge an eyesore. There were public hearings, government reports, newspaper editorials, and television specials. Grade 3 and 4 pupils studied the history of Rundle Lodge and participated in an essay contest. Anne Murray declined an invitation to perform at a benefit dinner, but impressionist Rich Little showed up. "Rich Little voiced support for preservation," a *Herald* reporter wrote, "but nobody was quite sure if it was the opinion of John Wayne, Archie Bunker, Pierre Trudeau—or the real Rich Little."[4]

The preservation campaign failed, but the cause was not entirely lost. Portions of the sandstone walls were left deliberately as a ruin, a sentinel of history in the midst of an inner-city park. It lies within the future Stampede expansion area.

Route: Return west along 12th Avenue S.E. to Olympic Way. Cross Olympic Way, turn left (south), and continue south on Olympic Way to 13th Avenue S.E. (originally Kennedy Avenue).

Westbourne Baptist Church (Victory Outreach Centre)
Address: 436–13th Avenue S.E.
Style: Gothic Revival
Architect: Unknown
Date: 1910

This humble outreach church near Stampede Park belies its significance to the province's history. This is where William "Bible Bill" Aberhart launched a public career that ultimately led to the premiership of Alberta. SHANNON LEE RAE

Named for its London counterpart that provided a grant to build it, Calgary's Westbourne Baptist Church served its original congregation from 1910–67. The small brick building later housed a Pentecostal congregation, followed by an organization called Religious-Divine Worship. It has housed the Victory Outreach Centre since 1992. The building lies within the future Stampede expansion area.

From 1915–29, an evangelical layman, Crescent Heights High School principal William Aberhart, ministered at Westbourne Baptist. It was here that he launched his radio ministry, the "Back to the Bible Hour," in the 1920s. By the end of that decade, Aberhart launched the Calgary Prophetic Bible Institute and built its headquarters on 8th Avenue S.W. (on the present site of Sears). Westbourne's congregants were split between those who followed Aberhart and those who questioned his leadership. Aberhart went on to found the Social Credit party and serve as Alberta's premier from 1935–43.

Route: Proceed west along 13th Avenue to 3rd Street S.E. Turn right, and go north along 3rd Street S.E. to the southeast corner of 3rd Street and 12th Avenue S.E.

Dafoe Terrace
Address: 1204–3rd Street S.E.
Style: Georgian Revival
Architect: Unknown
Date: 1910

Brothers John C. Dafoe and Alexander Norman Dafoe (manager of the exhibition grounds, today's Stampede Park) built this terraced apartment block in the context of Calgary's housing shortage during the pre-World War I boom. It later became one of several boarding houses operated by Bella Singer (1880–1984), a Russian Jewish immigrant who used her savings to sponsor the immigration of relatives from Europe. She established a pyramid system that called on each sponsored relative to sponsor another, and for that relative to sponsor yet another. Though Singer's efforts brought an estimated 200–300 Jewish immigrants to Canada, she was unable to save her two sisters or their families from the Holocaust. Singer sold the building in the 1940s, and lived to become Calgary's oldest Jewish citizen. Her son Jack is the namesake of Calgary's Jack Singer Concert Hall.

Arched stone entrances and multiple gables distinguish Dafoe Terrace, built in the context of Calgary's pre-World War I housing shortage. SHANNON LEE RAE

Businessman Mike Giammarco bought the Dafoe in 1978 and renovated it. In the 1990s, responding to changing demographics, he began converting its family suites into commercial and restaurant space and bachelor apartments. Dafoe Terrace was declared a Provincial Historic Resource in 1987. It lies within the future Stampede expansion area.

Route: Cross both 3rd Street S.E. and 12th Avenue S.E.

Fairey Terrace
Address: 1111–3rd Street S.E.
Style: Jacobethan Revival
Architect: William M. Dodd
Date: Circa 1903

Typical for its style, Fairey Terrace is set back slightly from the street. Each of its apartments, later converted for business and retail use, had outside entrances.
SHANNON LEE RAE

Contractor Frank Fairey (1864–1926) was an active developer in Victoria Park's early history, and this two-story, terrace-style brick apartment building, which he built and continued to own for the rest of his life, was one of the first of its kind in the city. Transplanted from England, this row-housing style addressed the city's housing shortage and offered a low-maintenance, high-class address that did not require servants to maintain it. Early tenants included both professionals and skilled laborers. Mike Giammarco bought the building in 1981, and converted it for office use in 1999. It was designated a Provincial Historic Resource in 1987.

Route: Proceed west along 12th Avenue S.E. to the middle of the block.

Moyes duplex (Rock Central)
Address: 322-324–12th Avenue S.E.
Style: Queen Anne Free Classic
Architect: Unknown
Date: 1907

Doric columns, a two-story veranda and a central dormer characterize the duplex that has become known as Rock Central. Each year at Stampede time, local musicians at Rock Central provide an alternative to country music. SHANNON LEE RAE

This two-story brick duplex was originally a high-class residence, one of many such fine homes in early Victoria Park occupied by the managerial class. Traveling salesman Alexander H. Moyes was one of the first occupants of this semi-detached brick dwelling constructed in 1907. Later occupants included CPR engineer Thomas Elliott and his wife Minnie (from 1910–28) and CPR conductor Thomas Clarke (from 1912–13). Harry Isenstein, a Jewish immigrant who lived here from the 1920s to the 1950s, returned to Russia in 1921 and brought dozens of relatives to Canada. Furniture dealers Abe and David Chetner bought the duplex in the 1930s, and Abe lived here with his family for decades. In the 1990s, the house's youthful residents cultivated its image as Rock Central, a venue for small outdoor rock concerts and pancake breakfasts each year at Stampede time.

Route: Proceed west along 12th Avenue S.E.

Sales house

Address: 314–12th Avenue S.E.
Style: Queen Anne
Architect: Unknown
Year: Circa 1905

The former Sales residence, shown here in 1905, was converted into apartments in the 1940s. GLENBOW LIBRARY

This two-story wood frame house was another of Victoria Park's early high-class dwellings, originally the home of clothing merchant Enoch Samuel Sales (1860–1930), founder of the Sales Clothing Company. Sales was a militia captain, treasurer of the Alberta Rifle Association, and, according to his obituary, "one of Calgary's most famous rifle shots."[5] He built this house by 1905, and here he died at the age of 70. It was later converted into apartments, which it remains.

Route: Proceed west along 12th Avenue S.E., to Macleod Trail, and cross Macleod. Turn right (north) and proceed north on Macleod to 11th Avenue S.E. Turn left (west) and proceed west a short distance on 11th Avenue.

Calgary Labor Temple (Flamingo Block)

Address: 229–11th Avenue S.E.
Style: Utilitarian
Architects: Fordyce and Stevenson (1954 and 1959 additions)
Date: 1912 (additions 1954, 1958)

The Flamingo Block's two-toned brick façade distinguishes the original single-story structure from its 1954 second-story addition. Skilled tradesmen donated their labor to build it and apparently demonstrated their skills in the geometric pattern of brickwork. SHANNON LEE RAE

In 1912, a group of trade unionists in Calgary formed the Calgary Labor Temple Company Ltd. to build and operate a union hall. Initially built as a single-story "temporary" brick building, the Calgary Labor Temple suffered financial difficulties in its early years. It served as the long-term home of the Calgary Trades and Labour

Council, which eventually represented more than sixty unions. The platform of the new Co-operative Commonwealth Federation (a federal party, later reorganized as the New Democratic Party) was developed in the Calgary Labor Temple in the summer of 1932.

The Great Depression and World War II delayed execution of an expansion plan designed in 1931 by architects Fordyce and Stevenson. It was finally completed with a second-story addition in 1954 and a rear addition in 1958. In the 1980s, the company was dissolved and the building sold for commercial use. It was renamed the Calgary Merchandise Mart, later renamed the Flamingo Block after a longtime occupant, the Flamingo Palace Restaurant.

Route: Return east along 11th Avenue to Macleod Trail, and turn right (south). Continue south, and cross 12th Avenue S.E.

Curtis Block

Address: 1203-1217 Macleod Trail S.E.
Style: Edwardian Commercial
Architect: Unknown
Date: 1909

The sprawling Curtis Block comprises three typical Edwardian buildings along the commercial Macleod Trail strip. Romanesque windows at the corner are probably a legacy of the storefront's origins as a Merchant's Bank branch. Early twentieth-century banks preferred Romanesque style, and landlords built to suit them as tenants.
SHANNON LEE RAE

Rancher James Haines Curtis (1864–1921) built this complex of three contiguous two-story brick buildings in 1909, forming part of the commercial strip that developed along 2nd Street S.E. with the advent of the streetcar. In 1913 Curtis' wife Alice (1877–1957), a teacher, became president of the Connaught Mothers' Club, reportedly the first parent-teacher association in western Canada. The Merchant's Bank of Canada originally occupied the corner storefront. The most significant residential tenant was William J. Oliver (1887–1954), a well-known photographer whose studio work and news photographs for both the *Albertan* and the *Calgary Herald* now form an impressive visual document at the Glenbow Archives. Oliver was a butcher's apprentice in his native Kent, England, when he won a camera in an advertising promotion after correctly guessing the weight of a lump of coal. He became an accomplished amateur photographer by 1910, when he left England on the *Lusitania*. Oliver came to Calgary intending to work for P. Burns & Co. in the meat business, but quickly launched his professional photographic career. He lived briefly in the Curtis Block around 1911. The building remains a residential/commercial block.

Route: Continue south along Macleod Trail to 13th Avenue S.E.

Deutsch-Canadier Block (Eastern Block)

Address: 1227 Macleod Trail S.E.
Style: Edwardian Commercial
Architect: Unknown
Date: 1912

In 1909, Joseph Schuster and Charles Pohl confidently moved their German-language printing and publishing business, Der Deutsch-Canadier Ltd., from Edmonton to Calgary. They built this typical two-story brick building along the new streetcar line and made it the headquarters for their two newspapers, *Der Deutsch-Canadier* (billed as "Western Canada's Largest German Paper") and *Deutsch-Canadischer Farmer* ("The only German Farm Journal West of Ontario"). Their job printing press, according to their advertisement, could print in "English, German, French, Italian, Polish and other Languages."

A south-facing mural on the Eastern Block portrays Calgary's downtown skyline.
SHANNON LEE RAE

In 1913, *Der Deutsch-Canadier* boldly declared its intention to be "a link between all German-Canadians in Western Canada."[6] In fact, its days were already numbered. Schuster died in an automobile accident in 1912, and that year Pohl moved the company to another Victoria Park address. The company was liquidated early in 1914, and the outbreak of war between the British and German empires that August aroused strong anti-German sentiments. *Der Deutsch-Canadier* published its last in December, and Pohl left town about the same time. The building was renamed the Eastern Block.

Longtime occupants included British Pork Butchers (1922–46) and the Black & White Grocery (1946–66). The best-known residential tenant was Andrew Davison, who lived in the building for a short time around 1914. Davison was a linotype operator for the

Calgary News-Telegram, a daily newspaper that ceased publication in 1918. He won election to city council in 1921, and his record sixteen-year tenure as mayor (from 1930–46) has yet to be matched.

The building remains a commercial/residential block.

Tour ends.

Notes

1 Tony Cashman, *Singing Wires: The Telephone in Alberta* (Edmonton: The Alberta Government Telephones Commission, 1972) 290.
2 Coste's firm was originally called the Canadian Western Natural Gas, Light, Heat and Power Company Ltd.
3 *Calgary: A Decade of Heritage* (Calgary: Heritage Advisory Board and the City of Calgary Planning and Building Department, [1987]): 51.
4 "Rundle fund dinner sweet—financial reward sour," *Calgary Herald*, 14 June 1972: 34
5 "Prominent Clothier Dies on Wednesday," *Calgary Daily Herald* 20 Nov. 1930: 21.
6 Alexander Malycky, "German-Albertans: A Bibliography. Part 1," *Deutschkanadisches Jahrbuch/German-Canadian Yearbook* (Toronto, Ont.), vol. VI (1981): 336. Malycky refers to "Zum neuen Jahrgang," *Deutsch-Canadier*, 4 Dec. 1913: 4.

Uptown 17th Avenue, Lower Mount Royal, and 14th Street S.W.

By and large, this tour follows the southern and western boundaries of Calgary's original corporate limits, established in 1884 and vastly expanded in 1907. In 1884, the town of Calgary comprised Sections 14, 15, and 16 in Township 24, Range 1 west of the Fifth Meridian. Until 1907, the southern boundary corresponded to modern 17th Avenue, and the western boundary to 14th Street S.W. With some departures, this tour follows those two major roads.

In a pattern similar to 16th Avenue north (the Trans-Canada Highway), 17th Avenue south originated as a section road and emerged as a significant commercial strip and transportation thoroughfare. It was Calgary's point of entry for farmers from the Springbank district west of town. Seventeenth Avenue also formed the border between Calgary and Rouleauville, a predominantly Roman Catholic village settled in the 1880s, incorporated in 1899, and annexed in 1907. Street names in Rouleauville had a Catholic character, and its residents knew 17th Avenue as Notre Dame Road. Early developments along modern 17th Avenue included Crown Prosecutor John R. Costigan's residence, constructed around 1893 at what is now the avenue's northwest corner with 1st Street S.W., far south of what was then Calgary's built-up area, and Western Canada College, a boys' preparatory school constructed outside the city limits in 1903. Streetcar service to 17th Avenue commenced on August 13, 1909, and before long 17th Avenue formed part of the Blue line (commonly known as the Belt line), which encircled much of Connaught and Victoria Park between 12th and 17th avenues, and between 14th Street S.W. and 2nd Street S.E. The streetcar prompted 17th Avenue's development as a mixed residential and commercial strip. Like Kensington Road N.W. in Hillhurst, and 9th Avenue S.E. in Inglewood, 17th Avenue ultimately developed into a funky shopping alternative to downtown and suburban malls, with unique and offbeat stores. In 1984, local merchants formed a Business Revitalization Zone, placed ornamental streetlights, park benches, and banners, and promotionally branded the strip as "Uptown 17th." It has a long history of boisterous nightlife, never more in evidence than during the 2004 Stanley Cup playoffs, when the Calgary Flames came within a single game of winning the National Hockey League's championship trophy. Seventeenth Avenue became the "Red Mile," as police shut the street down and thousands of red-clad citizens celebrated their team's victories.

East of 4th Street S.E., 17th Avenue overlaps Victoria Park, an early suburb that took its name from the adjacent exhibition grounds. The fair grounds were called Victoria Park following Queen Victoria's death in 1901, but later became known as the Stampede grounds, and were officially renamed Stampede Park in 1975. The tour begins at Victoria Park's fire station, continues with an introduction to Stampede Park, and then moves west along 17th Avenue. Where appropriate, the tour makes forays onto adjacent street to nearby points of interest. West of 4th Street, 17th Avenue enters Connaught, another historic mixed-use district largely settled during Calgary's pre-World War I boom. (In 2004, the community associations amalgamated as the Beltline Communities of Victoria and Connaught.) At 9th Street S.W., the tour turns south into Lower Mount Royal, which lies at the northern base of an exclusive subdivision developed by the Canadian Pacific Railway in 1907. Apartment blocks have replaced many of the fine homes in Lower Mount Royal since the 1960s, but others still remain.

Finally, the tour emerges onto 14th Street S.W. and explores the fringe area between the earlier Connaught district and the post-1907 suburbs of Bankview (southwest of 14th Street and 17th Avenue S.W.) and Sunalta (west of 14th Street between 17th Avenue and the Bow River). Until the Mewata Bridge was constructed in 1954, 14th Street reached a dead end to the north at the Bow River, which limited its historic development.

The tour concludes at the Pumphouse Theatres in Sunalta, an old waterworks installation dating back to 1913.

Start: Begin at the Macleod Trail pedestrian overpass that leads to Victoria Park / Stampede LRT station and to the Calgary Exhibition and Stampede Grounds. The overpass provides a perspective on the old stockade fence to the grounds and to the grounds themselves.

Calgary Exhibition & Stampede Grounds

Stampede Park looking southeast, 1948. GLENBOW ARCHIVES NA-2864-488TT

Even before the town of Calgary was incorporated in 1884, citizens organized the Calgary District Agricultural Society. They wanted to stage an annual fair that would showcase the agricultural and stock-raising promise of southern Alberta. For the idea to succeed, Calgary needed its own fairgrounds. Major James Walker, a leading Calgary citizen, cast his eye on a government-owned, ninety-four-acre property bounded on two sides by the Elbow River.

A stroke of luck practically delivered the land to Walker. While inspecting farms in the area, Deputy Interior Minister A. M. Burgess fell from his horse and fractured his collarbone. Walker happened to be driving by in his farm wagon and rescued Burgess. As the civil servant convalesced in Walker's home, the Major convinced him the fairground idea was a good one. Burgess pushed the idea back in the nation's capital, and three years later the government sold the land for $235—only $2.50 per acre.

Organizers mortgaged the grounds for $3000 to begin improvements. The Exhibition was off to a good start, but by the mid-1890s poor weather, ruined crops, and an economic depression killed the fair. The mortgage was foreclosed, and the grounds became a cow pasture and occasional sports field. Even in those difficult times, area farmers organized their own, unofficial fairs.

In the late 1890s, Canada's future prime minister, R. B. Bennett, bought the fairgrounds as speculative property. But there was a restriction on the title: the grounds could never be subdivided or sold as town lots.

The economy improved by 1899, when the Inter-Western Pacific Exhibition Company—formed from the ashes of the old Agricultural Society—revived the Exhibition. In 1901, Bennett sold the grounds to the City for $7000. The City annexed the property, named it Victoria Park after the Queen who had just passed away, and signed a long-term lease with the company.

A precursor to Canada Olympic Park's ski jump tower? Ski-jump atop the grandstand, 1921. GLENBOW ARCHIVES NB-16-504

The revitalized Exhibition transformed the grounds. Newer and better buildings replaced the old; added attractions like trick roping, wild horse races, and the now-familiar midway widened the fair's appeal. The city won its bid to host the 1908 Dominion Exhibition, an annual educational, industrial, and agricultural showcase held in a different Canadian city each year. American cowboy and showman

Guy Weadick participated in the show, and four years later he returned to stage the first-ever Calgary Stampede.

With success after success under its belt, the Calgary Industrial Exhibition Company, as the organization was renamed, converted the grounds to year-round use for sporting events and livestock sales and shows. For a few years in the 1920s, the Exhibition even sponsored a Calgary Winter Carnival, complete with a ski-jump tower on top of the grandstand.

Finally, in 1923, the Stampede took its place as a permanent feature of the Exhibition, and the grounds became in fact—if not yet in name—Stampede Park. (The name was officially changed in 1975.)

Main Gate

The stockade gate was completed in 1950, the 75th anniversary year of Fort Calgary, which it was meant to evoke. CALGARY EXHIBITION & STAMPEDE ARCHIVES

Between 1908 and 1950, visitors formed their initial impressions of the grounds at the original entrance gateway at 17th Avenue and 2nd Street S.E. (now Macleod Trail), which predated the Stampede itself. Calgarian George Stanley Rees, the architect of the 1908 Dominion Exhibition, designed an entirely new set of buildings for the grounds, including ceremonial entrance gates. Contractor John McClune built the classically derived structure, which included sandstone columns, a rounded, central sandstone arch, and a wooden cupola topped by a flagpole. More than a hundred thousand people passed through those gates in July 1908—Guy Weadick among them. Weadick organized the original Stampede in 1912, and, again, nearly 100,000 people made their way through that entrance—at a time when Calgary's population was only about half that number. Between 1908 and 1949, nearly eight million people went through the gate's turnstiles.

In 1950, the entrance gates made way both for progress and for history. By that time annual attendance averaged nearly 400,000, and a $35,000, seven-door gate structure replaced the original building in time for the 1950 Stampede. That year marked the 75th anniversary of the founding of Fort Calgary, the North-West Mounted Police fort that became the nucleus of the original Calgary settlement. As part of its anniversary celebrations, the Stampede built its new main entrance to resemble a fort stockade, evoking Fort Calgary in particular and the city's western heritage in general. Inside the palisade walls, a replica Fort Calgary housed log buildings representing historic western structures, including an authentic 1893 Mounted police post and a replica Hudson's Bay Company trading post. That area of the park is now known as Weadickville.

The stockade served as the main entrance until the early 1980s, when Light Rail Transit development and the construction of the Roundup Centre changed Stampede Park's dimensions and obscured the outer walls of the stockade. Today's main entrance is roughly in the same location, accessible by the pedestrian overpass at the Victoria Park/Stampede LRT station.

After 1950, the original gates were gone, but not forgotten. A Calgary businessman acquired the central sandstone arch, which he relocated to a development site on the old Banff highway (next to the present intersection of Crowchild Trail and Nose Hill Drive N.W.) The project was never built, and for years the sandstone arch stood alone on the prairie. It's gone now, but the circumstances of its disappearance remain a mystery.

Stampede Corral

Style: Art Deco and International influences
Architect: John Stevenson
Date: 1950

The Corral was part of the Calgary Exhibition and Stampede's post-World War II modernization. The stylized mural of a cowboy riding a bucking bronco was originally outlined with neon tubes for nighttime effect. CALGARY EXHIBITION & STAMPEDE ARCHIVES

One of the oldest remaining buildings in Stampede Park is visible from the overpass—the Stampede Corral, completed in 1950 as the first step in the Stampede's post-World War II modernization. The $1,350,000 arena—the largest west of Toronto's Maple Leaf Gardens when it was built—accommodated nearly 9,000 spectators and was equally equipped for "hockey, skating, ice shows, horse shows, home shows, boxing, wrestling, name bands, dancing, religious gatherings, banquets, bingo and celebrity concerts."[1] Fortunately, Stampede directors chose the name Corral over such suggestions as the "Rodeodrome" and the "Stampedeoriem."

The Corral was built on the site of the old Industrial Building, once the main exhibition building on the grounds. Built in 1908 for the Dominion Exhibition, the original structure boasted a central dome and enclosed balcony. When it was completely destroyed by fire in May 1931, organizers briefly considered canceling the Exhibition, which was only weeks away. Instead, the Stampede took to heart the motto "On with the show!" In only five weeks, a new pavilion arose on the future site of the Big Four Building; named the Bessborough Building, it created much-needed jobs for unemployed men during the Great Depression.

Victoria Pavilion

Style: Utilitarian (Free Classical references)
Architect: Unknown
Date: 1919

The Victoria Pavilion, longtime home of Stampede Wrestling, is the oldest remaining functional building in Stampede Park. CALGARY EXHIBITION & STAMPEDE ARCHIVES

Although it is not visible from the overpass, note that the oldest remaining building on the grounds is the Victoria Pavillion, which stands just south of the Pengrowth Saddledome. It was built in 1919 as a cattle pavilion, curling rink, and judging ring and has housed everything from livestock shows and auctions to political rallies and the world-famed professional Stampede Wrestling. Both the Victoria Pavillion and the adjacent 1928 Admonistration Building have been covered by a metal façade.

Route: Return across the overpass to the west side of Macleod Trail, descend the overpass, proceed south along Macleod to the south side of 17th Avenue S.W. Turn right (west) and proceed west to 17th Avenue.

Mayor Silas A. Ramsay house (National Forensic and Medico-Legal Services Inc.)

Address: 221–17th Avenue S.E.
Style: Homestead
Architect: Pattern book design
Year: 1912

Nothing about this stuccoed house suggests its origin as the home of Calgary's fourteenth mayor. SHANNON LEE RAE

This two-story stucco house is undistinguished, except for its 1912–14 occupant: Silas Alexander Ramsay (1850–1942), who had served as Calgary's fourteenth mayor in 1904–05. Seventeenth Avenue was Calgary's southern city limit during Ramsay's tenure, and the site of his future home lay in the adjacent village of Rouleauville. But for the signal decision of his tenure—changing named streets and avenues to numbers—17th Avenue might still have been named Notre Dame, as the burghers of Rouleauville called it before the city annexed their village in 1907.

Ramsay left his native Quebec in 1870, when, at the age of twenty, he served in the Wolseley expedition to quash Louis Riel's Red River Rebellion at Fort Garry (now Winnipeg). Ramsay established a machinery business in Calgary in the 1880s and served in the 1885 North West Rebellion as a dispatch rider. Ramsay served on the City Council from 1894–98 and 1901–03 before he became mayor. He retired in 1921 and settled in Vancouver, where he died two decades later. The house became a commercial address in the late 1970s and since 1993 has housed National Forensic and Medico-Legal Services Inc., which provides forensic psychiatric services, both criminal and civil.

Route: Proceed west on 17th Avenue to 1st Street S.E. (originally Osler Street). Turn right (north), and cross 17th Avenue.

Ed's Restaurant

Address: 202–17th Avenue S.E.
Style: Simplified Queen Anne
Architect: Pattern book design
Year: 1909

To a generation of Calgarians, the name Ed's is synonymous with Buffalo-style chicken wings. How appropriate that the presumed builder of this converted residence, contractor (and alderman) M. Ross Wallace, was "a well-known poultry fancier."[2] Early occupants of this 1909 house included widow Agnes Flanagan, barber Percy

McNaughton, carpenter Montague Spicer, and John A. Letroy, a traveling salesman for the Western Lightning Rod Company. Between 1952 and 1967, this was the home and workplace of Swiss-born landscape gardener Ernest Brunner (circa 1896–1972). The house was converted into apartments in the late 1960s and became a commercial property in the 1970s. Mr. Ed's Feedbag (later changed to Ed's Restaurant) opened here in 1984.

Contractor M. Ross Wallace, a poultry fancier, is believed to have constructed the Queen Anne house that now houses a restaurant best known for its chicken wings.
SHANNON LEE RAE

Route: Proceed east on 17th Avenue S.E.

The Embarcadero (former James J. Hall residence)

Address: 208–17th Avenue S.E.
Style: Eclectic
Architect: Pattern book
Date: 1907

Ontario-born builder James J. Hall (1851–1922) settled in Calgary in 1907 and joined the city payroll, serving as construction superintendent on paving projects and, in 1908–09, Calgary's modern new waterworks—the gravity water system.

This brick home once belonged to James J. Hall, who built and operated Calgary's gravity-fed waterworks. It now houses a restaurant named for San Francisco's waterfront. SHANNON LEE RAE

Hall's waterworks began at Twin Bridges, nearly twenty kilometers west of the city, where an intake drew water from the Elbow River. Water flowed by gravity pressure through a wooden flume that dropped more than ninety meters in elevation between the intake and the South Calgary Reservoir, located at what is now the southwest corner of Crowchild Trail and Richmond Road S.W. The project provided a lasting nickname for the well-known alderman who championed its construction: John "Gravity" Watson. Hall became the system's superintendent, a position he still held at the time of his death. The gravity system remained in use until the completion of the Glenmore dam and reservoir in 1933.

The Hall family lived in this two-story brick house from 1907 to about 1916. It was divided into apartments by the late 1960s and, in 1977, became a commercial address. In 1995, it became The Embarcadero Wine and Oyster Bar, named for San Francisco's waterfront.

Route: Return west on 17th Avenue to 1st Street S.E. Cross
1st Street S.E., turn right (north), and proceed north
along 1st Street to 15th Avenue S.E. (originally Rose
Avenue).

McCall house (Printy Rubber Stamp Company)

Address: 1501–1st Street S.E.
Style: Worker's cottage
Architect: Pattern book design
Date: 1912

*With its symmetrical design, pyramidal roof, and shed dormers on each side, James
McCall's house is a typical example of a pre-World War I worker's cottage.* SHANNON
LEE RAE

James Ferguson McCall (1868–1952), who lived in this house
between 1926 and 1952, has at least three claims to fame in this city.
The Scottish-born machinist served as chief engineer and superintendent of the city's street lighting plant in Victoria Park from its
inauguration in 1905 until his death nearly a half-century later. He
helped place the 1914 South African War memorial in Central Park

(now Memorial Park) on its present granite pedestal in 1926. And he was the father of Captain Fred R. G. McCall (circa 1896–1949), the World War I flying ace for whom Calgary's first international airport, McCall Field, was named. The younger McCall enlisted in 1916. Before the war ended, he shot down thirty-seven enemy aircraft and shook hands with the king. Fred McCall demonstrated his skills as a barnstormer after the war. When his engine failed during a demonstration flight over the Calgary Exhibition grounds in 1919, with Exhibition manager Ernest L. Richardson's two sons on board, he famously landed his plane on top of the carrousel. Capt. McCall lived in this house for a brief period in the 1930s.

The house's original occupant was contractor Joshua C. Warwick in 1912. It later became apartments, and was converted into a commercial building in the 1980s. Since 1997 it has housed the Printy Rubber Stamp Company Inc.

Route: Turn left (west) on 15th Avenue S.E., and proceed west.

Colgrove Apartments

Address: 129–15th Avenue S.E.
Style: Classical influence
Architect: Unknown
Date: 1912

Patterned on an apartment block in New York City, the brick, three-and-a-half story Colgrove Apartments—built in 1912 and named for owner and builder Robert J. Colgrove—boasted specially made carpets from England and an electric-powered security system that allowed tenants to open the main doors by pressing a button in their suites. Tradesmen used separate entrances and stairways, guaranteeing that ladies need never encounter them in the public spaces. Harvey Bricker and his wife bought the nineteen-suite building from Colgrove in 1929 and renamed it the Bricker Apartments. It later became known as the Darlington Apartments.

The front of the building has no signage to identify it, but a ghost sign at the rear still reads "Colgrove Apartments / Suites to Let."

Classical details on the Colgrove Apartments include a fan-shaped central pediment and columns that form the structure of its three-level wooden balconies. The crenellated parapet provides a mediaeval element, suggestive of a castle. SHANNON LEE RAE

One of the building's most notable occupants was former millionaire Frederick C. Lowes (1880–1950), the flamboyant real estate developer who lost his fortune after the real estate bubble burst in 1913 and lived here in reduced circumstances during the 1930s. Lowes was admitted to the Ponoka mental hospital in 1938, and his wife continued living here in the 1940s.

Route: Continue west on 15th Avenue S.E. to Centre Street (originally McTavish Street). Cross Centre Street, turn left (south), and continue south to 17th Avenue. Turn right (west), and continue west on 17th Avenue to 1st Street S.W. (originally Scarth Street). Cross 1st Street.

Highway Esso Service Station (Ideal Rentals)

Address: 202–17th Avenue S.W.
Style: Moderne
Architect: H. K. Knowles, Imperial Oil Co., Toronto
Date: 1928

The former Highway Esso Service Station is a rare extant example of a Moderne service station from the 1920s. SHANNON LEE RAE

As a building type, the service station was only twenty years old in Canada at the time Imperial Oil built this structure in 1928. With little to draw upon except for the livery stable, architects were free to apply new concepts to a twentieth-century building type without reference to historical tradition. Oil companies developed a trademark "look" for their stations, making them easily recognizable. The Highway Esso Service Station, one of four new downtown Esso stations built that year (and the only one still standing), is a classic example: a clean white surface, horizontally organized, and unified by a band of narrow horizontal strips affectionately known as "speed whiskers." It is a rare early example of its kind in the city. As a landmark, however, it paled in comparison with Texaco's Big Chief station built across 17th Avenue in 1938, a masterpiece of Art Deco that was gutted by fire and demolished in 1980.

The original building on this site was Crown Prosecutor John R. Costigan's residence, located far from Calgary's built-up area when it was constructed around 1893. Costigan's house was moved to its present location (221–17th Avenue S.W.) in 1928 to make way for the new Esso station. The gas station closed by 1970, when the building became Ideal Tent & Party Rentals.

Route: Proceed west on 17th Avenue S.W.

L. Draper Groceries (Vacant)

Address: 226–17th Avenue S.W.
Style: Edwardian Commercial
Architect: Unknown
Date: 1906

This circa 1906 photograph shows L. Draper Groceries, a typical commercial store-front of its day. One atypical characteristic is its escape from the wrecker's ball.
COURTESY OF MIRIAM PODLUBNY

This diminutive false-fronted wooden store has survived the decades as an intact example of its era and type. Features typical of its Edwardian Commercial style include a recessed entrance and large, clerestory windows (now boarded up), which provided maximum natural lighting into a long, narrow store that had no side or rear windows.

From 1906–36, it housed L. Draper Groceries, owned by Luke Draper (1861–1941) and his wife Eliza (1864–1954). Luke was born in Athens, Ontario, and later sojourned in North Dakota before moving to Calgary with his wife in 1890 and building this store in 1906. In 1927, L. Draper Groceries sold the very first biscuits manufactured by the newly established Independent Biscuit Company in Victoria Park, managed by G. Stanley Draper, the grocer's son.

The Drapers lived in a gabled house just west of the store, now the site of First Memorial Funeral Services' parking lot. Luke died in the house only weeks after the couple's diamond wedding anniversary. The store later became known as the Standard Grocery & Confectionery. By the 1980s it became the Sound Exchange, a records and tapes shop. It has been vacant since about 1990.

Route: Continue west on 17th Avenue to 2nd Street S.W. (originally Hamilton Street).

Jacques Funeral Home (First Memorial Funeral Services)

Address: 240–17th Avenue S.W.
Style: Spanish Eclectic influence
Architect: John Stevenson
Date: 1936

In 1930, fifty years after his father settled in Calgary and opened its first jewelry store, George L. Jacques (1894–1937) purchased Mrs. Alice Powers' boarding house and converted it into Jacques Funeral Home, billed as "The Little Chapel on the Corner." When that proved too small, he demolished the house and built what is believed to be Calgary's first architecturally designed mortuary (as opposed to a pattern book or contractor-designed building). Jacques had lived in Los Angeles in the 1920s, which might account for the California Mission-style influence in this stucco-covered Moderne building. After Jacques' death, his widow Vera (1898–1999) was left to run the business and raise their thirteen-year-old son Murray. For many years, Vera Ireland (as she became after remarrying in 1950) produced a Sunday afternoon musical program, "Chapel Chimes," on CFAC radio. Vera and Murray continued to own and operate the business until 1981, and later owners continued to operate it as Jacques Funeral Home until the 1990s, when it became First Memorial Funeral Services. Members of the Jacques family remain in the industry as owners of Heritage Family Funeral Services.

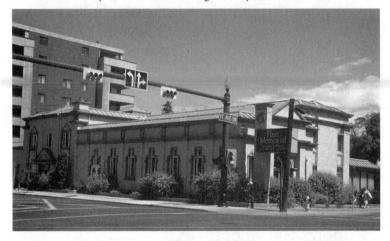

With its central entrance, window placement, and pilasters, Calgary's first architecturally designed funeral home resembles church architecture. SHANNON LEE RAE

Route: Cross 17th Avenue S.W., and turn left (east).
Proceed east on 17th Avenue.

Costigan Residence (Tequila Nightclub)

Address: 221–17th Avenue S.W.
Style: Simplified Queen Anne
Architect: Unknown
Date: Circa 1894

This two-story brick house was built in 1893 at the northwest corner of 1st Street S.W. (then known as Scarth Street) and 17th Avenue (Notre Dame Road) and moved to its present location in 1928. Its original occupants were John Ryan Costigan (1855–1902), Calgary's

first crown prosecutor, and his wife Ada (1858–1954). The Costigans
were Roman Catholics, and the house stood just opposite the city
limit from the Catholic village of Rouleauville. One of Costigan's
early cases was the 1889 "Jack the Ripper" case, in which William
"Jumbo" Fisk was convicted of murdering a teenage Cree prostitute—but only after a second trial. Judge Charles B. Rouleau
refused to accept the first jury's verdict of "not guilty" and ordered
a retrial. After John Costigan's death, which occurred in the house,
Ada made ends meet for herself and her three children as the music
instructor at Western Canada College (on the present site of
Western Canada High School) and St. Hilda's College.

*This 1928 photograph shows the former Costigan house being moved across 17th
Avenue to its present location. Professional house mover York Shaw did a steady
business moving houses in Calgary. The streetcar had to be rerouted and overhead
power lines taken down.* GLENBOW ARCHIVES NA-2186-10

This fine house had other notable occupants. Former rancher
George Hope Johnston (1857–1938), who lived here from 1900 to
1908, later worked in the sheriff's office and for many years was an
editor for the *Albertan*, the forerunner of the *Calgary Sun*. Colonel
Sam Steele (1849–1919) lived here between 1907 and 1910 when he

commanded Military District 13. A veteran soldier and North-West Mounted Police (NWMP) officer, he was the namesake for Fort Steele, B.C. Steele fought in the Fenian Raids in 1866, in both of Louis Riel's rebellions (1870 and 1885), the South African War (1899–1902), and World War I. (As commander of the NWMP's E Troop in 1883, Steele had been the senior officer of Major Thomas Dowling—Ada Costigan's father.)

The house was moved from its original site in the spring of 1928 to make way for a new Esso station (which still stands at 202–17th Avenue S.W.) At its present, new location, the former Costigan residence became a boarding house operated by Nelson and Emma Green. It became a nightclub in the 1980s, known variously as The Area and Mertz. From 1989 to 2000 it housed the Republik, a live music club where noted acts included Big Sugar, Goo Goo Dolls, Green Day, Hole, and Our Lady Peace. It became the Tequila Night Club in 2003.

Route: Return west along 17th Avenue to 2nd Street S.W.
Cross both roads, and continue west along 17th Avenue.

Model Milk Company (Victoria's Restaurant/Arena Coffee Bar)

Address: 308–17th Avenue S.W.
Style: Art Deco influenced
Architect: Unknown
Date: 1934 (additions 1936 and 1958)

Concrete milk bottles, raised in relief on this building's ornamental pediments, speak to its original use as James Colpitts' Model Milk Company (commonly known as Model Dairies). Born in Colpitts Settlement, New Brunswick, Jim Colpitts (1881–1941) ran a New York fish market before moving to Springbank, west of Calgary, in 1921. He became a dairy farmer and fox rancher, later establishing Model Dairies in 1930 to market his products in Calgary. Built in 1934, this facility housed state-of-the-art pasteurization equipment.

Model Dairies was the first in Calgary to use trucks for distribution. The milk bar, which had a separate entrance from the dairy business, lives on in the memory of generations who enjoyed its excellent milkshakes and the largest five-cent ice cream cones in the city. In 1965, rival Palm Dairies bought the company. Victoria's Restaurant, a gay-friendly establishment, has been a main floor occupant since 1983.

Elaborately detailed concrete pediments seem to reach for the sky. Each bears a milk bottle in relief. KAREN OLSON

Route: Continue west on 17th Avenue to 5th Street S.W., and cross 5th Street.

Nettleton Grocery and Boarding House (Magic Room)

Address: 602–17th Avenue S.W.
Style: Dutch Colonial Revival
Architect: Unknown
Year: 1907

With its rare gambrel roof and its gabled dormers overlooking a prominent corner, this two-story building has been a landmark almost since 17th Avenue was the city limit. It became Joseph H. Nettleton's grocery store in 1911, while Mrs. Nettleton ran a boarding house upstairs. The building became the centre of a shocking story in October 1912. One of Mrs. Nettleton's tenants was a young private detective named Mildred Dixon. A real estate salesman named John C. Davis feared that his wife Minnie was cheating on him; he hired Dixon to shadow her. Dixon quickly recognized what was going on: there was no affair; Davis was paranoid and abusive; and he posed a danger to his wife. Dixon quit the case, warned Minnie, and helped Minnie move into Dixon's boarding house room until she could arrange a safe house for her. Davis learned where his wife was staying and rented his own room in a neighboring building. Through an intermediary, Davis promised he would return to his native United States and never bother her again. He asked to meet one more time. When he entered Dixon's apartment, Davis pulled out a revolver and shot the detective, mortally wounding her. He then killed his wife and committed suicide. All three were buried in unmarked graves in Union Cemetery. A month after the tragedy, Davis' business partner learned that the dead man was really Spencer Holder, a bigamist from Alabama where he already had a wife and two children.

The Magic Room beauty spa has occupied the former Nettleton Boarding House since the early 1990s. AUTHOR PHOTO

The Nettletons moved on by 1918, and the building later housed a series of groceries known as Viccars, Sharp's, and the Pedlars Wagon. From 1974–88, it was the Gold Studio of Photography, and it now houses the Magic Room beauty salon.

Route: Proceed west on 17th Avenue to 6th Street S.W.
Cross 17th Avenue, turn right (west), and continue west on 17th Avenue.

Western Canada High School

Address: 641–17th Avenue S.W.
Style: Modern Gothic
Architect: William Branton, Calgary School Board architect
Date: 1929 (addition 1958)

Western Canada College lay outside the city limits when it was built in 1903. When it closed in 1926, university advocates hoped it would be the site of a future campus.
GLENBOW ARCHIVES NA-3516-1

College Lane, which bounds this campus to the west, speaks to this school's origin as Western Canada College. Its eastern boundary is 5A Street, created when the college's masters subdivided part of the property in 1912. College authorities had suggested the street be named University Street—probably revealing their aspirations for the institution—but the city demurred.

Western began in 1903 as a prestigious, British-style private boarding school for boys, built on land donated by the Canadian Pacific Railway. When it closed in 1926, advocates of university development in the city hoped the facility would become the campus of a future University of Calgary. Instead, the public school board bought the property and commissioned its architect, William Branton, to design separate western and eastern buildings to house parallel academic and technical high schools, respectively. They were constructed in 1928–29, and, in 1938, the two schools were amalgamated as Western Canada High School. The main college building was demolished in 1958 and replaced by a school administration building that linked the two original wings.

Route: Continue west on 17th Avenue S.W., cross College Lane, and continue west to 7th Street S.W. Cross 17th Avenue S.W.

Jenkins' Groceteria No. 12 (Buy-Rite Grocery/Nellie's Kitchen)
Address: 738-740–17th Avenue S.W.
Style: Edwardian Commercial
Architect: Unknown
Date: 1926

After studying the business methods of a Seattle chain in 1918, Calgary merchant Henry Marshall Jenkins (1881–1945) transformed his Inglewood grocery store into Canada's first self-service groceteria, in which shoppers picked their own groceries off the shelf instead of having the clerk fill their order. Within a decade, Jenkins' business had expanded to seventeen stores in Calgary and another thirteen across Southern Alberta. He branched out into wholesaling by taking over Calgary-based Louis Petrie Ltd., and brought in founder Louis Petrie as a director of Jenkins' Groceteria Ltd. Jenkins survived Safeway's intrusion into the local market in 1929, but his son Ronald eventually sold to Winnipeg-based Western Grocers in 1959.

This typical corner store originally housed one of the city's ubiquitous Jenkins' Groceteria outlets. SHANNON LEE RAE

Jenkins and Petrie built this small brick building to house Jenkins' Groceteria No. 12, which remained in the corner storefront until 1952. That year, J. Leslie Hill, an alderman and vice-president of the Alberta Social Credit League, moved his Buy-Rite Grocery Store into the space. Founded in 1936, this landmark independent business still occupies the corner at the dawn of the twenty-first century. Nellie's Kitchen, a popular breakfast spot, has occupied one of the other two 17th Avenue storefronts since 1992.

Route: Cross both 17th Avenue and 7th Street S.W. Proceed south on 7th Street to 18th Avenue S.W., and turn right (west). Proceed west on 18th Avenue to the Anderson Apartments' recessed entrance.

Anderson Apartments
Address: 804–18th Avenue S.W.
Style: Baroque, with Classical features
Architect: Roscoe B. Whitten
Date: 1913

The H-shaped plan of the Anderson Apartments allows for outdoor windows in each of its high-class apartments. An automatic brass cage elevator adds an extra touch of style. Musician Jann Arden's Insensitive *video was filmed here the mid-1990s.* KAREN OLSON

Businessman Alexander Victor Anderson (1863–1920) left his native Quebec in 1882. By the 1890s, he had established a successful machinery business in Calgary. Victor's wife Laura died in 1908; as a rich widower, he had this massive building designed as a bachelor hotel (although it always operated as luxury apartments). Victor lived in the building, managed it personally, and died in his suite after a year's illness. Other notable occupants included pioneer oilman Archibald W. Dingman and pioneer bookseller James C. Linton, who served on the Town Council in 1888–89.

Built in 1912–13, this six story brick building follows an H-shaped pattern, forming window wells to provide all rooms with natural lighting. The Anderson boasted a marble rotunda and main stairway, twelve-foot ceilings, all-night elevator and telephone service, and a serving window between the pantry and dining room in every suite. The birdcage elevator—a brass 1928 Otis model, reportedly the first automatic elevator in the city—remains in working order.

Anderson's heirs sold the building in 1977. In 2000, its suites were upgraded and sold as condominiums.

Route: Return east along 18th Avenue to 7th Street S.W., turn left (north), proceed north on 7th Street to 17th Avenue S.W., and cross. Tomkins Gardens occupies the whole of this narrow block. Turn left (west), and proceed west along 17th Avenue through Tomkins Gardens, which among its trees and benches contains a dedication plaque and a bandstand.

Tomkins Gardens

Tomkins Gardens provides a respite in the midst of a bustling avenue, but its patron had puritanical expectations for its use. SHANNON LEE RAE

Before he died just before Christmas 1914, Henry William Tomkins told his wife Eleanor he wanted to donate some of his land to the city for use as a public park. The city initially approved the name "Tomkins Square," but eventually developed the park as Tomkins Gardens. Tomkins' will reportedly placed limitations on the park's use, including ". . .for the discussion of political, religious, trade, or social questions or otherwise to be held, or religious services to be conducted, or lectures or addresses or any games or recreation of any kind whatsoever to be played by children or adults on any part of the said lots . . ."[4] Have fun.

In 1919, Imperial Oil proposed building a service station at the west end of the park, but at the city's request (along with thousands of dollars for purchase of the property), it was never completed.

Route: Continue west on 17th Avenue to 8th Street S.W. Cross 8th Street.

Devenish Apartments (Devenish Design Centre)

Address: 908–17th Avenue S.W.
Style: Gothic
Architect: Alexander Pirie
Date: 1911

Stylized parapets along its 17th Avenue façade, and crenellate turrets at the building's four corners, contributed to the castle-like appearance of the Devenish Apartments as seen in this circa 1912 photograph. The crenellation has been removed. GLENBOW ARCHIVES NA-4385-2

Indiana-born real estate developer and oilman Oscar Grant Devenish (circa 1867–1951) moved to Calgary around 1902 and built this luxury apartment building in 1911. Devenish lived in a fine mansion in Mount Royal. However, by the 1940s, he had moved into the Devenish Apartments.

To maximize the number of suites (57), the building originally had no bedrooms. A Murphy bed pulled down from the living room wall, and a double bed slid out from the bottom drawer of the dining room china cabinet. Tenants could use the building's sunrooms, steam laundry, and "odorless" garbage incinerator. The high-class nature of the building eventually declined. In 1980 it was sold, renovated, and transformed into the Devenish Design Centre, a retail complex of specialty shops that opened in 1981. It became a Provincial Historic Resource in 1982.

Route: Continue west on 17th Avenue S.W. As you pass, note the Wood-Roberts Block at 926–17th Avenue S.W., built by grocer William Wood-Roberts in 1910 as the home of his namesake grocery.

Calhoun Block (Megatunes)

Address: 934–17th Avenue S.W.
Style: Simplified Edwardian Classical (with Romanesque influence in the round-headed windows)
Architect: Unknown
Date: 1912

George J. Calhoun (circa 1870–1942), a building contractor and onetime High River rancher, built this eponymous three-story residential/commercial block. Early storefront occupants included the Velvet Delicatessen and Henry Levant's grocery store. One of the early residential tenants was Thomas Scrivens, who worked as a gardener at Eugene Coste's sprawling estate in Mount Royal.

Within a few years, the building became city property, presumably through non-payment of taxes, and its stores and suites were administered by the city land department. At one point, it was down to a single tenant, and the city considered closing it up. Plumber John H. Hillier bought the property in 1939 and renamed it Goderich Lodge, after his hometown of Goderich, Ontario. In 1988, the building was converted into a strictly retail property. Megatunes, a popular independent music shop, has occupied the main storefront since it was established in 1988.

Up-to-the-minute popular music pounds out of Megatunes' speakers, in juxtaposition to the Edwardian-era building it occupies. SHANNON LEE RAE

Route: Continue west along 17th Avenue to 9th Street S.W. Cross 17th Avenue, and continue south along 9th Street to 18th Avenue, and cross. Turn left and proceed east along 18th Avenue.

John Snow House

Address: 915–18th Avenue S.W.
Style: Homestead
Architect: Maxwell Bates (studio addition)
Date: 1912 (addition circa 1960)

The original occupant of this house was Charles McCallum, a Nova Scotian attracted by Calgary's pre-World War I real estate boom, who left the city with the Canadian Expeditionary Force when war began in August 1914. His fate remains a mystery.

As the home of artist John Snow, this humble Homestead house was a gathering place for Calgary's artistic elite. As the John Snow House for writers-in-residence, it has become a centre for literati. SHANNON LEE RAE

Another notable personality associated with this house is Mrs. Mary Luck, who owned it from 1923–51. Before she married her boss, Connaught School principal L. Henry Luck, Miss Mary Willetts had helped found the Connaught Mothers' Club and Art League, forerunner to the Connaught Home and School Association, the first parent-teacher association in western Canada.

The building's chief distinction, however, is its half-century occupancy by the internationally acclaimed artist and lithographer John Harold Thomas Snow (1911–2004). Born in Vancouver, Snow grew up in England, where he started painting at the age of two, and then on a farm near Innisfail, Alberta. As a teenager, Snow decided he would become an artist or a banker. He joined the Bowden, Alberta, branch of the Royal Bank of Canada in 1928, then served as an air force navigator during World War II. After the war, he settled in Calgary, re-joined the bank's service, and took an evening art course from Maxwell Bates. The two became fast friends, and Bates, who was also an architect, designed a studio addition to the house Snow had purchased in 1951. Snow acquired two lithographic presses that had been discarded by the Western Printing and Lithography Company in 1953, and together Bates and Snow became experts in color lithography. In 1972, Snow retired as assistant manager of Calgary's main Royal Bank branch and spent the next twenty years as a full-time artist. The elite of Calgary's artistic community gathered at Snow's house for meetings and informal exhibitions. Snow moved to a retirement home in 2000, and, the following year—at the suggestion of art historian Nancy Townshend—publisher Jackie Flanagan purchased the property and created the John Snow House for use by the Markin-Flanagan Distinguished Writers Programme. Participants have included Robert Kroetsch (author of *Lines Written in the John Snow House*) and Timothy Findley.

Route: Return to 9th Street S.W., turn left (south) and proceed south to 19th Avenue S.W. Cross both roads and proceed west along Cameron Avenue S.W., as 19th Avenue becomes on the west side of 9th Street.

Braeside Lodge

Address: 1023 Cameron Avenue S.W.
Style: Eclectic (Colonial Revival influence)
Architect: Unknown
Year: 1912

With its symmetrical design, central front portico and classic Greek Doric columns, Braeside Lodge still dominates Cameron Avenue far below, despite the construction of larger apartment blocks on both its sides. Dr. Betty Mitchell, a longtime occupant, likely appreciated its dramatic position with respect to the street. SHANNON LEE RAE

A daunting concrete stairway leads high above Cameron Avenue to Braeside Lodge, an imposing presence that still seems to dominate the street below, even though it is no taller than the 1960s apartment blocks that flank both its sides. It was originally the home of Thomas Heeney, assistant manager of the CPR's Department of Natural Resources, who enlisted when World War I broke out and whose fate is unknown. It remained a private residence until about 1920, when it became Braeside Lodge apartments. The most distinguished resident was Dr. Betty Mitchell (1896–1976), the Virginia-born teacher who inspired generations of drama students at Western Canada High School. Mitchell's 1942 production of Thornton Wilder's *Our Town* won her a university fellowship from the Rockefeller Foundation in the United States; it also won a scholarship for Mitchell's best-known student protégé, Conrad Bain (the future star of television's *Maude* and *Diff'rent Strokes*). In 1946, Mitchell and her students founded Workshop 14, a theatre company later known as MAC 14 and the precursor to Theatre Calgary. After retiring from Western in 1961, Mitchell taught drama at the University of Alberta in Edmonton for three years. Apart from that time, she lived in Braeside Lodge for the last three decades of her life. She never married. Two theatres have been named for her, but neither still exists. But each year, the local theatre world remembers her when its annual awards—the Bettys—are presented.

Late in the 1970s, Braeside Lodge was converted into offices and lost its original charm. Richard Lindseth Architecture Inc. took over the building as its office in 1988 and incrementally restored both the building and its grounds.

Route: Continue west on Cameron Avenue to 10th Street S.W., and cross Cameron Avenue.

Stanley House

Address: 1740–10th Street S.W.
Style: Simplified Queen Anne style, with Tudor half-timbered
detailing
Architect: T. E. A. Stanley
Date: 1911

*Educator T. E. A. Stanley, who later became principal of Western Canada High
School, was also an amateur architect and designed this Lower Mount Royal
home. Stanley's wig inspired the nickname his students bestowed on him: Mat.*
SHANNON LEE RAE

Besides his day job as a mathematics teacher at Central Collegiate
Institute—and later its principal, and eventually principal of
Western Canada High School—Thomas Edwin Adelbert Stanley
(1869–1947) was also an amateur architect. He bought this property
in 1911 from former mayor Daniel Webster Marsh, designed and

built this house, then sold it to David S. McCutcheon. Like Stanley, McCutcheon hailed originally from Ontario, and, like Stanley, he went into the real estate business, abandoning his career as a pharmacist. With his brother Gordon in Winnipeg, McCutcheon established a successful real estate agency with nine Canadian offices and one in London, England. McCutcheon lived here from 1912–15. Another notable occupant was alderman and brick manufacturer Edward Henry Crandell (1859–1944), whose company had manufactured the bricks used to construct this house, and who lived here briefly in 1920. In 1983, the house was converted into the law office of Pittman and Newcombe, who researched the building's history and named it for its architect and developer. Stanley House has been the office of Singleton Associated Engineering Ltd. since 1991.

Route: Cross 10th Street S.W., and continue west on Cameron Avenue to 12th Street. Cross both roads, and proceed south (uphill) on 12th Street S.W.

Brydon house and stable

Address: 1915–12th Street S.W.
Style: Homestead
Architect: Unknown
Year: 1908

Ontario-born dairyman George Brydon settled in Calgary in 1901 with his schoolteacher wife Katherine and their six children. He built this two-story frame house and stable in 1908 and later added a two-and-a-half story "tower" that was demolished in 1951. George kept a horse and cow on the property and delivered milk door-to-door with his horse and cart. (The stable still stands but was long ago converted into a garage.) He was widowed in 1928 and died in the house in 1935. The three Brydon daughters continued living in the house for decades, and none ever married. Lucy became a public school principal, Shirley a nurse and confectioner, and Florence a stenographer and cashier.

Dairyman George Brydon built this Homestead house in 1908, and his original horse stable still stands at the rear of the property. SHANNON LEE RAE

Route: Proceed west through the public lane immediately north of the Brydon house. Emerge from the lane at 13th Street S.W., cross, and continue west on Bagot Avenue S.W. to 14th Street S.W. Turn left (south), cross Bagot Avenue S.W., and proceed south on 14th Street to the T-intersection with 21st Avenue S.W. Cross 14th Street to the northwest corner of 14th Street and 21st Avenue, turn right (north), and proceed north on 14th Street, downhill. Continue north to the next stop after crossing 19th Avenue S.W.

Nimmons house

Address: 1827–14th Street S.W.
Style: Queen Anne
Architect: Unknown
Date: 1898

When William Nimmons (1824–1919) built this brick house in 1898, the Bankview hill from which it held a commanding view of the city was all his. Born in Ireland, Nimmons first settled in England with his parents, then emigrated to Guelph, Ontario, where he set up a woolen mill. In 1869, he moved west to Fort Garry, Manitoba, where he was taken prisoner when the first Riel Rebellion broke out that year. Nimmons escaped and eventually made his way to Calgary, where he had purchased a hillside ranch from the Hudson's Bay Company for eight dollars an acre. Natives who camped west of Calgary (in what is now the Scarboro district) to collect their treaty money often called at the Nimmons home, where they found hospitality.

The sweeping veranda and northeast-facing tower gave the Nimmons family a dramatic city view from their hillside farm. It remained the family's home for generations after the city spread around it. Shannon Lee Rae

Nimmons had already begun to subdivide and sell his land by the time it was annexed to the city in 1907. As in downtown Calgary, some of the streets and avenues in Bankview once had names; Nimmons named 19th Avenue for his son Albert, and called other streets after his children George, Isabella, and Kate. Nimmons' sandstone quarry near present-day Crowchild Trail supplied many of Calgary's building projects prior to World War I, including his own house. While the city sprawled around it to the south and west, this stately residence remained the Nimmons family home for decades. Nimmons' grandson' John McCloy, who was born in the house in 1909, still lived there when the house became a Provincial Historic Resource in 1978. It has been converted into apartments.

Route: Proceed north on 14th Street to 17th Avenue S.W.

Isabella Block (Nimmons Corner)

Address: 1431–17th Avenue S.W.
Style: Edwardian Commercial
Architect: Unknown
Date: 1911

*William Nimmons replaced his suburban commercial greenhouse with a two-story
residential/commercial block. It was far from the city centre in 1912, but attracted
the Bank of Nova Scotia as a tenant.* SHANNON LEE RAE

Four years before William Nimmons built this structure in 1911, its
site was kitty corner from the city limits and the location of
Nimmons' commercial greenhouse. He named the two-story building for his daughter Isabella. Son Albert Nimmons lived in the
apartments upstairs, and William's widow, also named Isabella
(1850–1936), spent her final years there, dying in Albert's apartment
on her 85th birthday.

This was an early commercial building far from the city center;
the Bank of Nova Scotia kept its West End branch in the Isabella
Block's corner storefront from 1912 until the late 1920s, when it
moved to a purpose-built bank that still stands directly across 14th

Street. The building was upgraded in the early 1980s and renamed Nimmons Corner. Since 1987, the Chocolate Bar dessert café has occupied the corner storefront.

Route: Cross both 14th Street S.W. and 17th Avenue S.W.

Crooks Drugs (The Medicine Shoppe)
Address: 1426–17th Avenue S.W.
Style: Edwardian Commercial
Architect: Unknown
Year: 1910

Photographer William J. Oliver took a dramatic series of well-known photographs when South Calgary streetcar no. 68 crashed into Crooks' Drugs in December 1919. GLENBOW ARCHIVES NB-16-467

Nine years after Ivan Holmes Crooks (1883–1969) established his eponymous pharmacy and built the Mount Royal Block[5] to house it, Crooks' Drugs formed the backdrop to one of the most famous photographs taken in Calgary and the tragedy that lay behind it. On Monday morning, December 15, 1919, motorman William J. Walker lost control of northbound South Calgary streetcar no. 68 as it descended the 14th Street hill. Hoar frost had made the tracks slippery, and the only hope to avoid catastrophe was the position of the 17th Avenue switch at the bottom of the hill. The neutral position was straight north-south, which would allow the car to coast safely along 14th Street. If a waiting passenger, anticipating a 17th Avenue car, had turned the switch as a favor to the conductor—as sometimes happened—then disaster awaited. The switch had been turned, the car made a violent turn, then jumped the tracks and crashed through the corner entrance of the drugstore. Thirteen passengers were injured, and Robert D. McWilliam, a postal carrier and returned veteran, was killed. Crooks' Drugs was not yet open and no one was inside. The city paid $3000 to repair Crooks' store, and did so under the city engineer's direction—without admitting responsibility, and on condition that Crooks did not sue. Car no. 68 was also repaired and remained in service until the 1940s. The switch was set permanently in the north-south position, and the 17th Avenue turnoff was relocated to the level 12th Avenue intersection.

Ivan Crooks retired in 1951, and the business remained under family ownership until 1993. It was renamed The Medicine Shoppe a few years later.

Route: Cross 14th Street S.W., turn right (north), and proceed north along 14th Street to 15th Avenue S.W.

Sacred Heart Church
Address: 1307–14th Street S.W.
Style: Gothic Revival
Architect: William Stanley Bates
Date: 1931

Calgary's growth in the years before World War I led to the creation of a Roman Catholic mission in the city's west end. A temporary frame church was constructed on this block in 1910, and Sacred Heart Parish was incorporated the following year. World War I and the depressed conditions that followed delayed construction of a permanent church and rectory, which were finally completed in 1931. The steeple and carillon were installed in 1957, providing a striking new landmark as seen from Bankview, with distant Nose Hill as its backdrop.

The spire on Sacred Heart Church provides a delightful landmark at the west end of downtown. SHANNON LEE RAE

Route: Continue north on 14th Street to 12th Avenue S.W.

Sunalta Block (Wheel Covers Unlimited)

Address: 1504–12th Avenue S.W.
Style: Edwardian Commercial
Architect: Unknown
Date: 1912

This typical Edwardian commercial/residential building was constructed in 1912, but metal cladding disguises its original appearance. It now houses Wheel Covers Unlimited, the Surveillance Shop, and Ossie's Office Equipment.

This 1960s photograph shows one of Norman Libin's Shoprite Stores in the corner storefront that once housed his Sunalta Grocery. Metal cladding now obscures the original appearance. CALGARY HERITAGE AUTHORITY

One longtime occupant was the Sunalta Grocery, whose owner, Norman Libin (1895–1975), later ran the Palace Bakery and established a grocery store chain known as Shoprite Stores. In the fall of 1920, a burglar broke into Libin's home and stole his .23 Colt revolver. The following week, an eighteen-year-old former employee of Libin's, whom the *Albertan* termed a "clumsy excuse for a gun man," held up the store—with Libin's gun.[6] The young man demanded fifty dollars. After he left, Libin drove to police headquarters, where two detectives jumped into Libin's vehicle, and they drove in search of the thief—whom they found within minutes. He got three months' hard labor.

Route: Continue north along 14th Street, and cross 11th Avenue S.W.

Kennedy's Garage (Globe Steering Clinic)

Address: 1504–11th Avenue S.W.
Style: Industrial
Architect: Pattern book design
Date: 1927

The clear span arched roof in the Globe Steering Clinic is a rare remaining example for a wooden building of its type. With its false front, it evokes a small-town feel at the edge of a bustling downtown. SHANNON LEE RAE

Many Calgarians recall historian and broadcaster Jack Peach (1913–1993), but few are aware that his father, Reginald H. Peach (1881–1940), was a notable Calgary building contractor. Peach built this service garage and White Rose filling station in 1927 for Robert Kennedy, who operated it for nearly thirty years. Edward Pargee (circa 1915–1987) took it over as the Globe Steering Clinic in 1955. Pargee had become a self-taught mechanic during World War II, when he served with the Calgary Highlanders and ended up in the motor pool after suffering an injury. This delightful building keeps a small-town charm in the midst of a metropolis.

Route: Continue north along 14th Street S.W. and through
the subway that passes under 9th Avenue. As you do,
note the utility cover plates on the sidewalk underfoot.
Their markings demonstrate their antiquity: they include
Calgary Electric Light (long since changed to ENMAX),
AGT (the former Alberta Government Telephones, now
TELUS), and Riverside Iron and Engineering Works, a
large-scale local industry that closed in 1987.

Continue north on 14th Street to the Mewata
Bridge. Be cautious—this is a busy traffic area, and
crossings are uncontrolled and sometimes confusing. Do
not follow the bridge all the way across the river. Turn
left (west) on the footpath that leads from the bridge to
the Bow River pathway along the south side of the river.
Follow the pathway to the Pumphouse Theatres.

Pumphouse Theatres

Address: 2140–9th Avenue S.W. (Pumphouse Road)
Style: Utilitarian (Classical influence)
Architect: Unknown
Year: 1913 (addition 1945)

Calgary's original, privately owned waterworks system was inaugurated in 1889 but ultimately proved inadequate. The city took over
the company in 1900. By 1907, the city had replaced it with a gravity-fed system that drew water from the Elbow River a dozen miles
west of town, then channeled it through a thirty-inch wood stave
pipe on a downward slope. The gravity system could not keep up
with the city's growth, so Pumphouse No. 2 was constructed in 1913
to supplement the system with water pumped from the Bow. The
completion of the massive Glenmore dam, reservoir, and water
treatment plant in 1933 shifted the city's water source back to the
Elbow, and Pumphouse No. 2 became a booster station, pumping
water from Glenmore to the North Hill. An addition was built to
the north in 1945 to service waterworks vehicles. The building was

decommissioned in 1967 and soon fell into disrepair. In 1969, University of Calgary drama professor Joyce Doolittle "discovered" the classically detailed utilitarian building, and, through her efforts and those of others, it was spared from demolition and converted into a live theatre venue in 1972. It was designated a Registered Historic Resource in 1975. In 1980, the American Waterworks Association declared it an Official Water Landmark, the third such designation in Canada.

The efforts of drama professor Joyce Doolittle and others tranformed an abandoned pumphouse into a beloved venue for the live theatre. COURTESY OF PUMPHOUSE THEATRES

Tour ends.

Notes
1 Jennifer Bobrovitz, "Huge bash hailed Corral opening," *Calgary Herald* 5 Jul. 1998: D2.
2 "M. Ross Wallace Victim of Gas," *Calgary Daily Herald* 28 Jan. 1929: 11.
3 "Apartments En Fete," *Calgary Daily Herald* 27 Nov. 1913: 18.
4 Jack Peach, "Eclectic 17th Avenue," *Calgary Real Estate News* 1 Oct. 1993: 2.

5 From 1911–2005, another building known as the Mount Royal Block stood at 801–17th Avenue S.W., opposite Tomkins Gardens and directly north of the Anderson Apartments.

6 "Held Up Grocery Store; Arrested in Quarter of an Hour," *Weekly Albertan* 6 Oct. 1920: 6.

17 Ave. S.W.

Cameron Ave. S.W.

Royal Ave. S.W.

Prospect Ave. S.W.

Hillcrest Ave. S.W.

Cliff-Bungalow–Mission

This tour covers the neighborhood of Cliff Bungalow–Mission, formed from two districts with widely different origins, and separated by 4th Street S.W.

From Calgary's incorporation as a town in 1884 until its massive annexation of surrounding land in 1907, 17th Avenue formed the southern city limit. Across that boundary lay Rouleauville, a Roman Catholic settlement established in 1883, officially incorporated on June 2, 1899, and absorbed into Calgary eight years later as the Mission district.

Calgary and Rouleauville had somewhat parallel origins. The year 1875 might be considered their common birth date: that year the North-West Mounted Police (NWMP) founded Fort Calgary at the confluence of the Bow and Elbow rivers, and the Roman Catholic Church—which already had a presence in the Calgary area—built a new mission a little further south, in what is now called the Mission district.

Another seminal year in the development of both communities was 1883. For Calgary, the arrival that summer of the Canadian Pacific Railway (CPR) ensured the tiny community's future and contributed materially to its growth. That same year, the future site of Rouleauville was acquired from the federal government by Father Albert Lacombe (the namesake for Lacombe, Alberta, 1827–1916) and Father Hippolyte Leduc (for whom Leduc, Alberta, was named, 1842–1918). Both men belonged to the order of Oblates of Mary Immaculate, which originated in France and became active in the missionary field of what is now western Canada by the middle of the nineteenth century. The two priests acquired the property as homestead land, but their intention was to subdivide and sell it as building lots. The future development of a Roman Catholic community had been established.

Calgary, always the larger of the two communities, developed much more swiftly. Rouleauville still remained unincorporated at the time Calgary was declared a city in 1894. Finally proclaimed a village in 1899, Rouleauville stretched from 4th Street S.W. (known in Rouleauville as Broadway) to the exhibition grounds (today's

Stampede Park), and from 17th Avenue (Notre Dame Road) to 26th Avenue S.W. (Legal Street). Many of Rouleauville's street names reflected the village's Roman Catholic heritage.

The village name came from two of its prominent Quebec-born residents: Judge Charles Borromée Rouleau, who was one of three stipendiary magistrates of the North-West Territories (NWT), and his brother Dr. Edouard-Hector Rouleau, who headed the Holy Cross Hospital and served as Belgian Consul for the NWT. Charles Rouleau died in 1901; Edouard lived a decade longer—long enough to see Rouleauville disappear.

The village population included Catholics of both Irish and French-speaking origin, but its first overseer (a position equivalent to mayor or reeve) was the Protestant, Cambridge-educated J. P. J. Jephson. Rouleauville was no match for Calgary's phenomenal growth after the turn of the century, and, by 1905, talks were under way for the community's eventual annexation to the city.

Fourth Street S.W. forms the section line between the one-time Oblate property to the east (Section 10, Township 24, Range 1 west of the Fifth Meridian) and the CPR section to the west (Section 9). The railway company acquired its property as part of a twenty-five million acre grant of land from the Dominion government, and it maximized its profit by developing much of the section as the exclusive Mount Royal district. But the Mount Royal hill drops off abruptly at an escarpment a little more than two blocks west of 4th Street. The CPR developed this narrow strip with the unimaginative name "Addition to the City of Calgary," later called "An Extension Of Mount Royal," and named some of its streets for Canadian governors general. The street furthest west, at the foot of the escarpment, was descriptively named Cliff Street. In 1909, a streetcar line was built along 4th Street between 17th Avenue and the Mission Bridge, contributing to 4th Street's development as a mixed commercial-residential strip. Western Canada College (a boys' school that operated from 1903–26 on the present site of Western Canada High School) added to the CPR Addition by subdividing part of its campus in 1912 as building lots. The district's present name originated in 1927, when the bungalow-style 22nd Avenue School was renamed, using elements of its street name and its building type— Cliff Bungalow. The area originated as an upper-middle-class subdivision, but in later decades some of its larger homes were later converted into apartments. As in neighboring Mission, many older homes have been demolished to make way for apartment buildings and office blocks. Both districts were "discovered" and gentrified by the 1990s, creating renewed development pressure. The community associations amalgamated in 1990 as the Cliff Bungalow–Mission Community Association.

Rouleauville Square, developed in 1995 with funds from the Calgary Parks Foundation, interprets the history of the former village. First Street S.W. was closed between 17th and 18th avenues to create the park. AUTHOR PHOTO

Start: Begin the tour in Rouleauville Square, where interpretive panels tell the story of the former village. Exit the park onto 18th Avenue S.W. (originally known as St. Joseph Street), and turn left. Proceed east on 18th Avenue to the McHugh House (110–18th Avenue S.W.).

McHugh House (Elizabeth House)

Address: 110–18th Avenue S.W.
Style: Queen Anne Free Classic
Architect: Unknown
Date: 1902

With its asymmetric design, turret, and steep roofline, the McHugh house reflects popular design elements of Victorian Calgary. KAREN OLSON

The original occupants of this property were Deputy Sheriff J. G. Fitzgerald—a rancher who advertised himself as a land, mining, and general agent; auctioneer and valuator; notary public; and conveyancer—and his wife Mary. The Fitzgeralds built their house in 1885 and sold the property in 1896.

The next owners were perhaps the most prominent Irish Catholics in Rouleauville—rancher John Joseph (J. J.) McHugh (1885–1928) and his wife Frances. The McHughs had come from Ottawa, where Frances' brother, James R. Bowes, worked as an architect. (Bowes was the architect of Senator James A. Lougheed's Calgary mansion, Beaulieu.) J. J. McHugh first came west in 1873 as part of a government survey party and later served the government in the west as a farm instructor to the Blackfoot, as assistant inspector of Indian reserves, and as the first land agent in the district of Assinniboia (now part of Saskatchewan) in the 1880s. In 1883, in partnership with brothers Felix and Thomas, he established the JJ Ranch (later renamed the H2) near the Blackfoot Reserve. As McHugh Bros., J. J. and Felix operated a railway construction business. Frances McHugh was active with the Holy Cross Hospital and with a variety of Roman Catholic societies. Frances and her children spent much of their time in Europe.

This Queen Anne-style house was built in stages and was finally completed in 1902. It is unknown whether it was enlarged from the Fitzgerald house or was a completely new structure. The McHughs retired to Braemar Lodge, a downtown residential hotel, and sold the house in 1921. In the 1930s, it became a residence for the Basilian Fathers who operated St. Mary's Boys' High School across the street. Around 1960, it was sold to a Roman Catholic order for use as Don Bosco House, a pioneer group home for troubled teenage boys. By the 1980s, it housed the Calgary Catholic Immigration Society and was renamed Cabrini House. After a 1999 fire, the house was repaired and reopened as Elizabeth House, a residence for teenage mothers and mothers-to-be.

Route: Proceed east along 18th Avenue, and cross Centre Street (originally McTavish Street).

House of Israel Building (Lindsay Park Place)

Address: 102–18th Avenue S.W.
Style: Art Deco influence
Architect: Ernest T. Brown
Date: 1949

For nearly half a century, Calgary's Jewish community made its collective home at the House of Israel, a purpose-built structure in the Mission district.

Art Deco elements of the House of Israel Building include simplified Classical details, symmetry, and an oculet (a disk containing a design motif; in this case, a Star of David). This pre-1949 view shows the original round-headed windows, squared off when the building was finally completed in 1949. GLENBOW ARCHIVES PA-3538-15

By the 1920s, more than 1,000 Jews lived in Calgary, comprising two percent of the population. New organizations and a youthful generation required a common gathering place, and, in 1926, a building fund was established. The House of Israel Association was incorporated in 1929. In 1930, it acquired six lots along Centre Street and commenced building. But the Great Depression intervened and only the basement was finished, housing the Beth Israel Synagogue and the Calgary Hebrew School.

In 1936, the association hired architect Ernest T. Brown and contractors Bennett and White to complete the building. Unemployed Jewish men found themselves doing construction work. But a contract dispute shut down construction in 1942; above ground, the building remained a shell, where Jewish children—when not in classes—played amid the unfinished walls and bare beams.

Finally dedicated in 1949, the building quickly fulfilled its mandate as the centre of Jewish life. By the 1950s, growing suburbanization led two anchor tenants—the synagogue and the school—to vacate. Most Jewish organizations remained, and the new Shaarey

Tzedec Synagogue was built next door in 1960. But the building's age and the flight to the suburbs eventually took their toll. A new Jewish centre in southwest Palliser opened in 1979, and the House of Israel was sold in 1985. After many years of vacancy, it was expanded and transformed into condominiums in 1998.

Route: Cross to the south side of 18th Avenue, turn right (west), and proceed west along 18th Avenue to 1st Street S.W. (originally St. Jean Baptiste Street).

St. Mary's Parish Hall / Canadian Northern Railway Station (Nat Christie Centre)

Address: 141–18th Avenue S.W.
Style: Classically influenced, with French-style mansard roof
Architect: James J. O'Gara
Date: 1905

The former St. Mary's Parish Hall is seen here as a "temporary" railway station around 1916–18. The station remained in service until 1971. Glenbow Archives ND-8-307

In 1905, the Oblate Fathers built St. Mary's Parish Hall to serve parishioners of nearby St. Mary's Church. It also housed boys' classes for St. Mary's School. Before long, the building was also used for secular purposes, in effect becoming Rouleauville's community centre. In 1911, the parish sold the hall to the Canadian Northern Railway (CNoR), whose right-of-way into downtown Calgary included this property. By 1916, the CNoR had converted the building into a "temporary" station and built a bridge connecting it to the railway yards on the opposite bank of the Elbow River. The financially troubled railway was nationalized in 1918, and it was incorporated into the government-owned Canadian National Railways (CNR) a few years later. The CNR never exercised the right-of-way, and the line's abrupt terminus at 18th Avenue—and its "temporary" station in the former parish hall—became permanent. This made for a complex procedure, using a Y-formation in the tracks, to reverse the locomotive's position in readying trains for departure.

The CNR ended its service on July 5, 1971, when the last train departed for Edmonton. The city acquired the building and railway yards in 1979, and the yards were redeveloped as Lindsay Park, after the property's earlier owner, Dr. Neville James Lindsay. The former station remained vacant until the mid-1980s, when it was remade into the Nat Christie Centre, a dance studio and headquarters for Alberta Ballet. The building was damaged by fire in 1984 while under restoration.

Route: Cross 1st Street S.W.

St. Mary's Cathedral
Address: 219–18th Avenue S.W.
Style: Modernist interpretation of Gothic
Architect: Maxwell Bates
Date: 1956

Calgary's Roman Catholic cathedral originated with *Notre Dame de la Paix*, a log mission church constructed on the Elbow River bank

Edward McCoskrie designed the original sandstone St. Mary's Church in 1899, and William M. Dodd designed the domes that were added to the towers in 1902. The church was consecrated as a cathedral in 1913, but structural problems required its demolition in 1955. GLENBOW ARCHIVES ND-8-289

in 1882. A new sandstone edifice, which had two domed towers, was constructed on this site in 1889 and dedicated as St. Mary's Church. But delays during construction reportedly led to structural weaknesses; by 1955, St. Mary's Cathedral (as it had been consecrated in 1913) had to be demolished. The present brick structure, a Modernist interpretation of Gothic style, was completed in 1956. Architect Maxwell Bates was also an artist, and the building's artistic features are steeped in church symbolism. The landmark Madonna sculpture above the main entrance was sculpted by Alberta artist Luke Lindoe. Before the 1990s, when it was obscured by the new CPR pavilion next to the Palliser Hotel, the cathedral enjoyed a sight line along 1st Street S.W. that stretched across downtown Calgary.

The broken cornerstone of the original cathedral, inscribed "O.M.I. 1889," is embedded in a cairn to the west of the modern building. The abbreviation stands for Oblates of Mary Immaculate, the order that first established the mission and built the original church.

Route: Cross 1st Street S.W. again, turn right (south) and proceed south along 1st Street to the Rouleau House, located at the rear of the former railway station. Although it faces 1st Street, the house has an 18th Avenue address.

Rouleau House
Address: 141–18th Avenue S.W.
Style: Queen Anne Free Classic
Architect: Pattern book design
Date: 1885

When Ontario-born hardware merchant Edwin Robert Rogers (1859–1926) built this Victorian house in the autumn of 1885, it stood on the north side of what was then St. Joseph Street (now 18th Avenue S.W.), at what is now the location of the parking lot behind La Chaumiere restaurant. Two years later, Rogers sold the house to Dr. Edouard-Hector Rouleau (1843–1912), who lived in it until about 1903. Dr. Rouleau then built a larger home in its place, and the original 1885 house was moved a few lots to the east. For the next century, the original house stood immediately west of the McHugh house, where it functioned variously as a private residence and as a boarding house. It survived a 1950 fire, but, in 2003, it came under threat of demolition to make way for a parking lot. Concerned citizens formed a support group, *Les amis de la maison Rouleau*/Friends of the Rouleau House, to save what was by then one of the ten oldest homes in the city (outside of Heritage Park Historical Village). The city paid to move the house to city-owned property south of 18th Avenue in 2005.

Dr. E. H. Rouleau and his family pose in front of their house in this circa 1900 photograph. Victorian characteristics of the house include tall, narrow windows that create a vertical emphasis, and fretwork in the gable. GLENBOW ARCHIVES NA-5222-2

Edwin R. Rogers had worked for the J. H. Ashdown & Co. hardware firm in Winnipeg before moving to Calgary in 1884 and forming the pioneer Rogers & Grant hardware store. (The Ashdown firm eventually took over Rogers & Grant.) Rogers also became clerk of the Supreme Court of the NWT, and in that capacity he came to know Justice Charles B. Rouleau, who was appointed to the court in February 1887. The following month, Rogers sold his house to Justice Rouleau's brother, Dr. Edouard-Hector Rouleau. Rogers later moved to Toronto, where he served as Ontario's provincial inspector of prisons and public charities.

Dr. Rouleau was born in Ile Verte, Canada East (now Quebec), and studied medicine at Laval university. He married Catherine O'Meara in 1883. In 1884, he followed his brother Charles to Battleford, NWT. After returning to Quebec following the 1885 North-West Rebellion, Dr. Rouleau returned west, this time to Calgary where Charles had been transferred. Dr. Rouleau set up a medical practice. In time, he took charge of the Holy Cross Hospital, served as NWMP surgeon in the city, and became founding president of the local St. Jean Baptiste Society, Belgian consul for the NWT, and chairman of the separate school board.

From about 1903–11, the Rouleaus lived in a new, larger home on the original site of the 1885 house. But the property lay in the Canadian Northern Railway's new right-of-way to downtown Calgary, and, in 1911, the family sold the house to the railway and moved to what is now Elbow Park. Although the Rouleaus' second house was demolished, the right-of-way was never exercised and 18th Avenue became the railway's terminus. (Dr. Rouleau's final home before his death in 1912 still stands at 3041 Elbow Drive S.W.).

Route: Cross 1st Street S.W. and 19th Avenue (originally known as St. Mary Street), and proceed west along 19th Avenue.

Sacred Heart Convent

Address: 225–19th Avenue S.W.
Style: Second Empire
Architect: William Stanley Bates (existing 1924 additions)
Date: 1882 (original structure demolished, existing wings date from 1893 and 1924)

In 1882, *Notre Dame de la Paix*—a frame mission church and rectory—was constructed on this site. When the 1885 North-West Rebellion broke out in what is now Saskatchewan, the Sisters of the Faithful Companions of Jesus (FCJ) fled to Calgary, where they took over the mission building as a convent, which they named

Sacred Heart. The Catholic school they established here—named St. Mary's School in 1893—became the first of its type in the NWT. A new west wing was constructed in 1893, and, in 1924, the original 1882 building was demolished and replaced by an east wing that duplicated the 1893 structure. William Stanley Bates (whose son Maxwell later designed St. Mary's Cathedral) designed the new east wing, as well as a new south chapel also built in 1924.

William Stanley Bates' 1924 additions were entirely sympathetic with the 1893 wing. KAREN OLSON

In 1909, a new building was constructed to the west, fronting 2nd Street S.W., to house St. Mary's School. Sacred Heart provided residences for its out-of-town female students, and the Sisters served as educators. The FCJ sisters continue to operate the convent as a retreat centre.

Route: Proceed west to 2nd Street S.W. (formerly Hamilton Street)and turn left (south). Note that Our Lady of Lourdes School, built in 2005 on the former site of St. Mary's School, reflects the earlier building's design and incorporates the original front entry and tower. Proceed south on 2nd Street to the Holy Cross Centre.

Holy Cross Hospital (Holy Cross Centre)

Address: 2210–2nd Street S.W.
Style: Simplified Modern Classical (what remains)
Architect: William Stanley Bates (1928 wing)
Date: 1892 (original structure demolished, many additions since)

This 1940s photograph of the Holy Cross Hospital shows an early sandstone wing with a mansard roof (right) and part of the 1928 addition designed by William Stanley Bates (left). The oldest remaining portion of the complex is the outside wall of the 1928 wing. GLENBOW ARCHIVES PA-3538-17

Like nearby St. Mary's Church, St. Mary's School, and Sacred Heart Convent, the Holy Cross Hospital formed a key institutional focus for the Roman Catholic settlement incorporated as the village of Rouleauville in 1899. The hospital began in 1891 with the arrival of four Sisters of Charity, part of the Montreal-based Order of the

Grey Nuns. A small wood-frame building was ready within months, and the Oblate Fathers donated land for the three-story, mansard roofed, brick and sandstone hospital built in 1892. Incremental additions meant the demolition of older wings, and the oldest remaining portion is the exterior of a 1928 addition along 2nd Street. The Grey Nuns sold the hospital in 1969, and it became a locally operated public institution. The Holy became known for its cardiac and mental health facilities, as well as for the school of nursing that operated from 1907–79. The hospital closed in 1996 and became a privately owned health, professional, and office complex.

Route: Continue south to 24th Avenue, cross 2nd Street, and proceed west on 14th Avenue to 4th Street S.W. (formerly Broadway). Turn right, and proceed north on 4th Street.

Bannerman Block

Address: 2306–4th Street S.W.
Style: Edwardian Commercial
Architect: Unknown
Date: 1912

Businessman Lloyd Bannerman (1877–1956) hailed from Springfield, Ontario, and came to Calgary after seeking wealth in the Yukon during the Klondike gold rush. Long-term occupants of his eponymous residential/commercial building have included the wonderfully named Super Cream ice cream shop (1937–57) and the Sun Grow Grocery, which occupied the same store front from 1943–2003. Nellie's on 4th, a popular breakfast restaurant, opened here in 1996.

Route: Continue north along 4th Street S.W. to the next block.

A large identification block still identifies this building as the Bannerman Block.
SHANNON LEE RAE

Aberdeen Apartments (Sushi Kawa/Antonio's Garlic Clove/Aida's Mediterranean Bistro/Gallery of Canadian Folk Art/Mortal Coil)

Address: 2204–4th Street S.W.
Style: Edwardian Commercial
Architect: Unknown
Date: 1912

Dr. Harry P. Wright (1874–1921), a dentist from Prince Edward Island, built this two-story residential/commercial building as the Wright Block shortly after moving to Calgary with his wife Emma around 1910. By 1917, for reasons now unknown, it was called the Aberdeen Apartments. Wright died in his forties, and his widow later lived in the building, which she continued to own for decades. Jimmie Condon (1889–1981), a well-known merchant, developer, sports promoter, and restaurateur, owned the Mission Grocery in the corner storefront at 4th Street and 22nd Avenue between 1925 and 1945. Older Calgarians remember Condon through his landmark Jimmie's restaurant in the Alberta Corner building, across 8th Avenue from the downtown Hudson's Bay Company store. University alumni are familiar with the statues of Greek philosophers on the campus of the University of Calgary that the Turkish-born, ethnic Greek Condon donated.

In the 1970s, restaurateur Marv Segal introduced a generation of Calgarians to Kosher-style deli food in the former Aberdeen Apartments. Shannon Lee Rae

In the 1970s, this was the home of My Marvin's, a well-remembered restaurant that introduced a generation of Calgarians to Kosher-style deli food. The similarly styled Sam's Original Deli took over the same space by the 1980s.

Route: Cross 22nd Avenue S.W. (formerly Doucet Street) to the northeast corner with 4th Street.

Young Block (Original Joe's)
Address: 2120–4th Street S.W.
Style: Edwardian Commercial
Architect: Unknown
Date: 1912

In 1912, printer James W. Young demolished his family home and built this two-story corner block—distinguished by its west-and south-facing oriel windows—in its place. The Young family moved into a large second-floor apartment, and the J. W. Young Printing Company remained in the Aberdeen Apartments across 22nd Avenue. Young moved to Oregon in 1918, and a variety of longtime businesses operated here, among them the Crown Meat Market (circa 1924–52) and La Moderne Mode Beauty Parlor (circa 1938–56). From 1940–46, the corner storefront housed Rusty's Confectionery, an ice cream parlor operated by Jimmie Condon's brother Orestes ("Rusty"). Alice Louie-Byne owned the building from 1946–75, and she lived here with her husband, Louie Byne, and children while they operated the corner Dandee Confectionery from 1946–57. A series of restaurants later occupied the corner, including Pasta Frenzy, the Bread Line, and, since 2001, Original Joe's.

The Young Block's timber cornice is a rare feature in Calgary. Most buildings of its era had a pressed metal cornice, which could be ordered from a catalog and easily applied. SHANNON LEE RAE

Route: Cross 4th Street, turn right (north), and proceed north on 4th Street to 21st Avenue. S.W. Cross 21st Avenue.

Tivoli Theatre (Tivoli Shops)

Address: 2015–4th Street S.W.

Style: Moderne

Architect: John Russell, head of the University of Manitoba
Architecture Department; Cecil Blankstein (supervising
architect, also of Winnipeg)

Date: 1936

*A strong horizontal line on the Tivoli Theatre's plain 4th Street façade formed a
juxtaposition with the dramatic vertical tower. The wall was cut up into storefronts
when the building became the Tivoli Shops.* KAREN OLSON

While the 1920s had been the era of lavish downtown movie palaces, the 1930s saw construction of modest, neighborhood cinemas. Built for the Odeon theatre chain, the Tivoli opened October 7, 1936, with *Rose Marie*, a musical set in Canada and starring Nelson Eddy as a Mountie and Jeannette Macdonald as an opera singer. The building's Moderne style, complete with a "Buck Rogers" tower and south-facing glass block wall (the first recorded use in the city), enlivened the appearance of 4th Street and delighted neighborhood cinema-goers for generations. During the 1940s, manager Joe Brager made British films the Tivoli's specialty and had staff walk up and down the aisles selling ice cream. By the 1970s, it became an adult theatre; in the 1980s, it showed Chinese and Kung Fu movies. The theatre closed in 1990 and was converted into the Tivoli Shops in 1992.

Route: Proceed north along 4th Street to 18th Avenue S.W. Cross 18th Avenue, turn left (west), and proceed west to about the middle of the block.

Red Cross Children's Hospital #1

Address: 522–18th Avenue S.W.
Style: American Foursquare
Architect: Unknown
Date: 1912

In 1922, the Alberta Division of the Canadian Red Cross Society rented this ten-year-old two-and-a-half-story brick duplex for use as the Red Cross Crippled Children's Hospital, the first of its kind in Canada and only the third in North America. Officially opened by the Lieutenant-Governor, R. H. Brett, it offered beds for thirty-eight children whose parents could not afford orthopedic care. The facility moved to larger quarters in a converted Mount Royal mansion in 1929; in 1952, it relocated to a purpose-built hospital in the Richmond district, where it was later renamed the Alberta Children's Hospital. The original hospital in Mission was converted into the Walter Murray Apartments in 1929 and remains an apartment building.

The former hospital's full-width veranda and central dormer are common features of its American Foursquare style. SHANNON LEE RAE

Route: Continue west along 18th Avenue, and cross 5th Street S.W. Turn left, and proceed south along 5th Street to the corner of Royal Avenue S.W.

Treend residence

Address: 1933–5th Street S.W.
Style: Prairie
Architect: Unknown
Date: 1922

This Prairie-style brick house, built in 1922, might well reflect the preferences of its original owner, retired rancher William R. Treend (pronounced "trend," 1865–1940). London-born "Doggie Bill" Treend homesteaded in the Wintering Hills near Hussar, Alberta, in 1901 and established a massive cattle and horse operation. During World War I, he sold horses to the French government.

Frank Lloyd Wright originated the Prairie style, reflected in this 1922 home with its horizontal emphasis. Architect Harold Hanen grew up in the house and later studied under Wright. KAREN OLSON

Treend retired to this spacious Calgary home with his third wife, Leona, and became active with the Calgary Exhibition and Stampede board. After their 1931 divorce, he moved to California; during the 1930s, the house was occupied by Spence's Shoes owner Robert M. Spence, who was also a rancher and horse breeder. Merchants Samuel and Lena Hanen lived in the house from 1941 until their deaths in 1972 and 1979, respectively. Samuel left his native Russia at the age of nine and settled with his parents at a Jewish bloc farming settlement near Rumsey, Alberta. He left the farm at seventeen, but years later purchased a large ranch, the V Bar V. In 1959, Lena established a women's clothing store, the Betty Shop, which eventually expanded to include forty outlets.

Their son Harold Hanen (1935–2000) grew up in the house and later studied architecture under Frank Lloyd Wright, who had originated the house's Prairie style. Hanen developed Calgary's Plus-15 system, a set of pedestrian walkways linking downtown buildings fifteen feet above grade, as well as the pedestrian mall on Stephen Avenue.

Route: Cross Royal Avenue S.W., turn right (west), and proceed west along Royal Avenue to Cliff Street S.W. Cross Cliff Street.

Holy Angels School (Rundle College Primary School)

Address: 2105 Cliff Street S.W.

Style: Bungalow school (no identifiable style)

Architect: Burrell and McDonnell (original building); William Stanley Bates (1929 addition)

Date: 1919 (addition 1929)

In this school's original design, the cupola, flagpole, and prominent round-headed pediment over the entrance were centrally placed. The 1929 addition to the south threw off the symmetry. The dark, rough-faced bricks reflect a preference of the Arts and Crafts movement. KAREN OLSON

This small brick school, built on land donated by the CPR, relieved accommodation pressure at St. Mary's Roman Catholic school in Mission. A sympathetic addition in 1929, designed by William Stanley Bates, provided needed space but disrupted the school's original symmetrical design. Sister Magdalen Poland served as principal for a quarter-century, and teaching staff came from the ranks of the Ursuline Sisters, whose convent was located in a converted mansion in nearby Mount Royal. The school closed in 1965, but a land exchange with the city saved it from demolition. It housed the Louise Dean School for single mothers (1981–90) and later became a Montessori school. It is now Rundle College Primary School, with a Montessori pre-school program.

Route: Proceed south along Cliff Street.

Cliff Bungalow School (Montessori School of Calgary)

Address: 2201 Cliff Street S.W.
Style: Bungalow school
Architect: William Branton
Date: 1920

The Cliff Bungalow district took its name from this school, which was named descriptively for its building style and the nearby geographic feature. KAREN OLSON

Following the Catholic school board's construction of Holy Angels School in 1919, the public board brought educational services to Mount Royal Extension (as this district was commonly known) in 1920. This style of building was called a bungalow school, and it proved a cost-effective alternative to the large pre-World War I sandstone variety. Originally called the 22nd Avenue Cottage School, this institution was renamed in 1927; "Cliff Bungalow" combined the name of the street—itself named for the cliff separating the district from Mount Royal to the east—and the building type. The name quickly caught on to describe the district, replacing "Mount Royal Extension." The school was repaired after a 1967 arson and was closed as a public school in 1988. The building is now shared between the Cliff Bungalow–Mission Community Association and the Montessori School of Calgary.

Route: Cross to the southeast corner of Cliff Street and 22nd Avenue S.W. (formerly Lansdowne Avenue, marked by dual signage). Proceed east along 22nd Avenue to 5th Street S.W., and turn right (south). Go south along 5th Street to 25th Avenue S.W. Cross 25th Avenue, turn right (west), and proceed west on 25th Avenue.

Twin Gables

Address: 611–25th Avenue S.W.
Style: Craftsman influence
Architect: Unknown
Date: 1914

The symmetrically placed twin gables of this stately hillside residence had bestowed its name as early as the 1950s. Relatively unadorned, the three-story wood, brick, and stucco house manifests the simplicity embodied in the Craftsman movement, which championed pre-industrial skills, trades, and materials over modern mass production. It was designated a Registered Historic Resource in 1984.

Twin Gables' low-pitched, overhanging roof is consistent with its Craftsman Bungalow influence. KAREN OLSON

Ontario-born barrister Albert E. Millican (circa 1878–1946) built this house just as Calgary's pre-World War I real estate boom was ending, and it remained his family's home until it was lost in a mortgage foreclosure in 1931. Albert and his brother William were partners in Millican and Millican, a law firm located on the present site of the Glenbow Museum. The next owner was sign writer Wellington P. Walker (1874–1965), a one-time Ontario schoolmaster and High River hotelier who moved to Calgary in 1911 and established the Globe Sign Works. The original attached garage—possibly built as a carriage house—sheltered Walker's vintage 1927 Reo and 1930 Ford, which he still drove on the city's streets in the 1950s. In a 1958 feature, the *Herald* described him as "a marvelous raconteur with a remarkable memory, a colorful and educated flow of English, and a tremendous sense of humor."[1]

Walker's housekeeper, Rose Rogers, inherited Twin Gables in 1965 and converted it into a boarding house. One notable later owner was Norris Bick, a popular CBC Radio announcer. Another was Jack Rogers (better known locally as the artist Tzak), who with his wife Marjorie bought Twin Gables in 1979 and restored it as a private residence. New owners converted it into a bed and breakfast in 2003.

Route: Return to 5th Street, turn right (south), and continue to the next house.

Aberhart Residence
Address: 2505–5th Street S.W.
Style: Craftsman
Architect: Unknown
Date: 1927 (addition 1990s)

Future Social Credit premier William "Bible Bill" Aberhart lived in this hillside Craftsman house with his wife Jessie, their parrot Polly, and two notable, successive tenants: journalist Eva Reid and Aberhart's political disciple and successor, Ernest C. Manning. In the 1990s, a rear addition and partial enclosure of the veranda altered the house's appearance. KAREN OLSON

Future Alberta premier William Aberhart built this two-story house in 1927, the same year his Calgary Prophetic Bible Institute opened its new downtown headquarters on 8th Avenue S.W. (now the site of Sears). Aberhart was the principal of Crescent Heights High School and was also an evangelical lay preacher with his own radio program, *Back to the Bible Hour*. During the Great Depression, Aberhart adopted the unorthodox economic theories of a British thinker, Major C. H. Douglas, who had labeled his program "Social Credit." Aberhart organized the Alberta Social Credit party and swept to victory in 1935. The new premier and his wife Jessie moved into the Hotel Macdonald in Edmonton but retained ownership of this house until Aberhart's premature death in office in 1943. Ernest Manning, who had boarded at the Aberhart home in the 1930s while studying at Aberhart's institute, succeeded his mentor as premier and held the office until 1968.

Tour ends.

Note

1 "High River History Holds Memories For Hotelman," *Herald Magazine* 24 May 1958: 6.

17 Ave. S.W.

Ave. S.W.

Royal Ave. S.W.

Tour Ends

Tour Begins

Prospect Ave. S.W.

Hillcrest Ave. S.W.

Mount Royal

In June 1904, an article in the *Herald* described a treeless hill south of the city's west end as "a pretty area."[1] The story featured a hilltop sanitarium that Dr. Ernest Wills was about to open. After practicing in South Africa and Colorado, the English-born physician (and specialist in "Lunacy") settled in Calgary, where he believed the climate and high altitude were ideal for the treatment of tuberculosis. Dr. Wills' sanatorium was the second institution built on a sprawling, undeveloped property outside the municipal boundaries and owned by the Canadian Pacific Railway (CPR). The first was Western Canada College, a boys' school on what is now the south side of 17th Avenue S.W., just outside the city limits.[2]

Both institutions were carved from a parcel of land that the CPR had owned since 1885. It was part of a twenty-five million acre land grant from the Dominion government, an incentive given the CPR for building the transcontinental railway. This parcel comprised three quarters of Section 9, Township 24, Range 1 west of the Fifth Meridian—a section that stretches from what is now 17th Avenue south to 34th Avenue S.W., and from 4th Street to 14th Street S.W. The southeast quarter, which did not belong to the CPR, developed separately as Rideau Park and the northern portion of Elbow Park.

Apart from the college and sanatorium, the property lay undeveloped for twenty years. In 1905, the railway company subdivided the northeast corner of the parcel as the virtually nameless "Addition to Calgary." There was nothing unusual about the grid street pattern and narrow uniform lots of the flat areas north of Royal Avenue (now part of Lower Mount Royal) and east of Western Canada College (now within Cliff Bungalow). But the hill south of Royal Avenue and west of what is now Cliff Street was a different matter. To attract the wealthy and maximize its profit, the CPR established massive "through lots" that stretched an entire block and encouraged development of mansions with enormous setbacks and rear coach houses. Before long, seven beautiful homes were constructed along Royal Avenue and Hope Street. Because the district lay outside the city limits until 1907, these homes had their own generators and water supply.

Most of these dwellings were built for wealthy American businessmen and their families. Some of them had been business partners in North Dakota before moving to Calgary on the eve of the city's great boom. Their presence created a popular conception that this was "American Hill," and city directories began using the name. This rankled patriotic and Imperial sentiments, notably those of William Toole, the CPR's District Agent in Charge of Railways and Land Affairs in Alberta, and his friend R. B. Bennett, a lawyer, Conservative politician, and future Canadian prime minister. Bennett complained to CPR Assistant Land Commissioner J. Lonsdale Doupe, a key player in the design and development of the company's suburb in Calgary. Doupe renamed it Mount Royal after an exclusive district in Montreal, and the name appeared on the subdivision plan registered in November 1906. With this subdivision plan, and subsequent additions in 1910 and 1911, street names took on a distinctly Canadian character. Names like Amherst, Durham, Sydenham, and Wolfe all figure in Canadian history.[3] The addition of French-Canadian street names, like Frontenac, Joliet, and Vercheres, completed the transformation of American Hill into Mount Royal. Bennett's biographer, James H. Gray, notes Doupe's satisfaction: "'There,' he chortled, 'let them damn Yankees try to pronounce those names when they tell their friends where they live!'"[4]

In its 1911 subdivision, the CPR introduced elements of the "City Beautiful" movement then current in North American city planning, involving irregular lots and curvilinear streets that conformed to topography and maximized beauty and scenic views. Caveats in the early subdivisions, and a restrictive covenant in the 1911 plan, established a high minimum value for any house built and prevented subdivision of lots. There is one notable exception. At the top of the hill—between Prospect and Dorchester avenues, from 10th Street to Carleton—there is a grid-like development that was exempt from the restrictive covenant, and bears no resemblance to the curvilinear streetscapes around it. This is the ten-acre site of Dr. Wills' sanitarium, which the CPR sold before Mount Royal began. Dr. Wills was killed in a fall from his bicycle shortly after the sanitarium opened; a later owner, Dr. Richard L. Morrison, subdivided and sold the property in 1909. Morrison Street bisects this part of Mount Royal.

Mount Royal became the abode of Calgary's *nouveau riche*, but not of the established millionaires like James A. Lougheed, Patrick Burns, A. E. Cross, and William Roper Hull, who kept to their mansions in older districts. Many in Mount Royal lost their fortunes in the crash of 1913, and the phenomenon was repeated during the Great Depression. In the finest homes, families laid off their domestic servants, took in boarders, and rented out coach houses as dwellings. Two great mansions—the Skinner and Coste houses—became city property through non-payment of taxes. Several houses were converted for institutional use, particularly during World War II, and a wartime housing shortage encouraged the use of mansions as boarding houses and apartments. The sustained oil boom that began in 1947, and the new wealthy elite that it created, revived Mount Royal's exclusive status and saw its surviving mansions returned to their early prestige. In recent decades, subdivision of lots and construction of large infill houses has created higher density, but it has not changed the overall character of the neighborhood.

Start: Begin the tour at the southwest corner of Royal
     Avenue and 7th Street S.W.

Davidson Residence and Coach House
Address: 801 Royal Avenue S.W.
Style: Tudor Revival
Architect: Unknown
Date: 1908

Minnesota-born James Wheeler Davidson (1872–1933) was one of the wealthy Americans whose mansions on Mount Royal gave it the early characterization as American Hill. He built this two-and-a-half story house at the northern base of Mount Royal just as the district was beginning to develop, and it remained his family home for the last quarter-century of his life. The prominent gables and mock half-timbering—exposed wooden beams, with stucco filling the space between them—is a signature feature of Tudor Revival style, inspired by the buildings of sixteenth-century Tudor England. The house features a triple-arched open stucco veranda with a balcony above.

The triple-arched entrance is a defining feature of James Wheeler Davidson's Tudor Revival house, one of the first built on "American Hill". SHANNON LEE RAE

Davidson led an exciting life before moving to Alberta in 1905. Following his military training, he was selected for the Peary Arctic expedition to the North Pole in 1893–94. He later worked as a war correspondent in Asia and served as a U.S. diplomat in Formosa (now Taiwan), Manchuria, and Shanghai. Davidson wrote several histories of the Far East, for which the Emperor of Japan awarded him the Order of the Rising Sun. Davidson moved to Alberta in 1905 and managed the Crown Lumber Company for a decade. He later became active in land development, forming a partnership with Thomas L. Beiseker to colonize the Beiseker district.

After two brief occupancies in the 1930s, this house became the longtime residence of novelist and playwright Winnifred Eaton Reeve (1887–1954) and her husband, businessman Francis F. Reeve

(1879–1956). The Reeves lived here from 1938 until their respective deaths. Winnifred wrote under the pseudonym Onoto Watana. In 1977, the charitable Reeve Foundation that they established donated one million dollars toward the establishment of the Reeve Theatre at the University of Calgary.

Route: Cross 7th Street S.W., and proceed east a short distance on Royal Avenue. The Sayre house is behind a row of tall spruce trees and an iron fence with brick gateposts.

Sayre Residence

Address: 717 Royal Avenue S.W.
Style: Eclectic, with Tudor Revival influence
Architects: Wilson, Hodgson and Bates
Date: 1906

This postcard view features four original homes on Royal Avenue, among the first built in what was once known as "American Hill." Only the Sayre Residence (right) remains. The Strong Residence (centre right) burned in 1998. The Linton Residence (centre left) and Honens Residence (far left) were demolished in the late 1960s for apartment development. The Linton home became the Calgary Old Folks' Home in the 1930s, which it remained for decades. Its fieldstone fence remains. GLENBOW ARCHIVES NA-2022-2

Like the contemporary Strong house that once stood directly to the east, this two-and-a-half-story mansion is situated on a massive "through lot" that extends from Royal south to Durham Avenue. Both were among the first seven homes built in American Hill, and were situated on the first rise of the hill's northern slope. They were set back some fifty feet from the curb, with long walkways from the sidewalk to the front door. Both had a coach house at the rear, accessible from Durham. While the Strong estate was subdivided, and the main house destroyed by fire in 1998, the Sayre property survives as a rare example of an intact estate with a through lot and coach house. The Sayre house is built of Cochrane brick, half-timbering, and stucco over a sandstone foundation. Its hipped roof features a cornice line, and the front façade is defined by an open front veranda and second floor balcony framed by symmetrically placed bay windows.

Born in Iowa, Absalom Judson Sayre (1859–1941) earned his wealth in North Dakota, where he and fellow businessman Louis P. Strong invested in land and grain. The two were among a group of North Dakota businessmen who settled in Calgary in 1905 and established the Calgary Colonization Company. (Another associate was Thomas L. Beiseker, the North Dakota banker for whom Beiseker, Alberta, was named.) Sayre and Strong acquired and subdivided farmlands from the CPR and facilitated settlement by American immigrants. Sayre's investments also included mining, timber, and petroleum, and he served as president of Archibald Dingman's Petroleum Products Company during the 1914 Turner Valley oil boom. But economic decline on the eve of World War I eroded Sayre's fortunes, and he moved to Los Angeles after the war. Sayre's house became the residence of U.S. consul Samuel C. Reat from 1919–21 (when Reat moved in with the Strongs next door). As a tax recovery measure, the city lodged a caveat against the property in 1923. The Roman Catholic diocese bought Strong's house that year for use as the Convent of the Ursuline Sisters. The sisters, who taught at nearby Sacred Heart and Holy Angels schools, named the house Villa Angela for their order's sixteenth-century founder, Sister Angela. They taught music in the coach house, which became known as "The Music House." The convent closed in 1975, and the house again became a private residence.

Route: Continue east on Royal Avenue to Hope Street. Turn
right (south), and proceed south on Hope Street to
Durham Avenue. Turn right (west), and proceed west on
Durham. Be aware that there is no sidewalk on this block.

Strong Coach House
Address: 708 Durham Avenue S.W.
Style: Tudor Revival
Architect: Unknown
Date: 1911

*When his fortunes ebbed, Louis P. Strong started renting out the suite over his coach
house (left), pictured here circa 1925. From 1937–44, it was home to Calgary Herald
janitor Robert Warner and his family. Warner did gardening work for the Strongs
and other Mount Royal families. The building was converted into a house after
World War II. The Strong Residence, visible to the right, was destroyed in a 1998 fire
that killed its owners, Kevin and Dorothy Murphy, who had been planning to turn
it into a bed and breakfast.* GLENBOW ARCHIVES NA-5585-12

This coach house is all that remains of the Strong estate, another of
the original pre-annexation mansions on American Hill. New York-
born Louis P. Strong (circa 1867–1952) settled in Calgary in 1905,

where he established the Alberta Pacific Grain Elevator Company, continued the business partnership he had formed with A. Judson Sayre in North Dakota, and built a mansion next door to Sayre's own. Strong built this coach house at the rear of his property in 1911, adding living quarters upstairs for his family's chauffeur. Like Sayre, Strong saw his fortunes ebb when the boom ended in 1913. He subdivided and sold part of the property, rented out the living quarters over the coach house, and even took in roomers and boarders in the main family house. In the late 1920s, Strong divided the house into apartments, while continuing to live there with his wife Julia. One of their tenants, lawyer Joseph Greenan (died 1969), bought the coach house from them in 1945 and converted it into a house. From 1948–74, it was the home of gas station owner Ted Hornoi (1906–1974) and his wife Helen.

The two-story Strong Coach House was designed as a modest, symmetrical outbuilding with a central front gable. The half-timbering details, filled in with rough cast stucco, reflect Tudor Revival influence.

Route: Continue west on Durham Avenue, and cross 7th Street S.W. Turn left (south), and proceed south, uphill, on 7th Street.

Dick Residence
Address: 2211–7th Street S.W.
Style: Tudor Revival
Architects: Holman and Gotch
Date: 1912

Only months before they built this secluded hillside mansion, businessman Albert Adrian "Bert" Dick (1880–1970) and his musician bride, Vera Gillespie (1894–1973), honeymooned in Europe and Britain, where they bought paintings, carpets and other furnishings for their matrimonial home. The Dicks returned first class on the *Titanic*, which struck an iceberg in the North Atlantic and sank on its maiden voyage in April 1912.

Bert Dick made a fortune in real estate, logging, mining, and petroleum, and married seventeen-year-old musician Vera Gillespie. This mansion became their matrimonial home, but the Dicks' voyage on the ill-fated Titanic *marred their honeymoon.* SHANNON LEE RAE

The Dicks met with financial difficulty after the boom collapsed in 1913. To save money, they moved into the downtown Alexandra Hotel, which Bert owned (on the present site of the EPCOR Centre for the Performing Arts), and later lived in the Palliser Hotel, the Lorraine Apartments, and a series of modest homes before returning to this mansion in the early 1930s. In 1956, they sold the house to Robert A. Brown Jr., the president of Home Oil. Brown lived here with his family until his death in 1972.

This substantial home is set on a large estate lot with an outdoor fountain, located on a prominent hillside and shielded from the street by foliage. At the ground floor, the gray sandstone façade features a full-width open front veranda. The gables above are a Tudor Revival influence, with half timbering and stucco. Large additions have been constructed at the side and rear.

Route: Continue north on 7th Street S.W. to Prospect
Avenue, and turn right (west). Proceed west on Prospect.

R. B. Bennett House

Address: 802 Prospect Avenue S.W.
Style: Georgian Revival
Architect: Unknown
Date: 1912

Calgary lawyer and future prime minister R. B. Bennett owned this two-and-a-half-story brick house from 1917–39 but never lived in it. The house inspired the myth of a broken engagement for the bachelor politician. SHANNON LEE RAE

Calgarian Richard Bedford Bennett (1870–1947) is best remembered as Canada's twelfth prime minister, a Conservative who held the office during the worst years of the Great Depression (1930–35). The New Brunswick-born lawyer moved to Calgary in 1897 and formed a law partnership with Senator James A. Lougheed, who was also a Conservative. Bennett remained a lifelong bachelor and made his home variously in a downtown boarding house, the Ranchmen's Club, and the Alberta and Palliser hotels. Bennett's ownership of this twelve-room brick house, in which he never lived, created a myth: that he had intended it as a matrimonial home, but that his sweetheart had turned down Bennett's proposal of marriage.

The truth is less romantic. Malcolm E. Davis, managing director of the Alliance Investment Company Ltd., built the house in 1912 and lived in for two years. From 1914–22, it was the home of Louis Melville Roberts (1879–1958), a lawyer with Lougheed and Bennett. Unlike the firm's principals, Roberts was a Liberal and sat as the member for High River in Alberta's second legislature (1909–13). For some now-forgotten reason, title to the house passed from Roberts to Bennett in 1917, and it remained Bennett's property until he retired to England as Viscount Bennett of Mickleham, Calgary and Hopewell in 1939. Bennett biographer James H. Gray speculates that Roberts might have turned the title over to Bennett to settle a debt. Roberts later moved to Arkansas and eventually settled in Erskine, Alberta.

Typical of Georgian Revival style, the design features a central front entrance (in this case, an enclosed porch with a balcony on top) and a front-sloping pitched roof. Sandstone quoins (from the French for "corner") highlight the corners of the house, its chimneys, and front porch, and together with the sandstone lintels and windowsills, they provide contrast with the red Medicine Hat brick walls. At the rear is a rounded corner tower with an octagonal roof, not typical of Georgian Revival style.

Route: Continue west on Prospect Avenue to Amherst Street. Note the Dower House, a Tudor Revival-style home at 2226 Prospect Avenue S.W., as you turn right onto Amherst. Both the Dower House and the Coste House (next stop) were originally part of the Coste Estate. Continue northwest on Amherst to the gatepost marked "Coste House." En route you will notice a sympathetic infill house at 2224 Amherst Street, built in the 1990s and modeled after the Coste House.

Coste House

Address: 2208 Amherst Street S.W.
Style: Tudor Revival
Architect: Eugene Coste (presumed)
Date: 1913

Many Calgarians remember going to the Coste House for lectures, classes, art exhibits, and theatrical performances during its tenure as the Calgary Allied Arts Centre (1946–60). In 1993, actors Brad Pitt and Aidan Quinn spent a week on location at the Coste House filming Legends of the Fall, *but the scene was cut from the film's final version.* GLENBOW ARCHIVES NA-5093-249

This elaborate home reflects the lavish tastes of Eugene Coste (1859–1940), the "father" of Canada's natural gas industry. Coste spent more than $10,000 on this sprawling property, which comprised ten lots, in 1911. He augmented its hilltop prominence by raising its elevation with landfill. Coste himself is believed to have designed the landscaped estate, which included a 28-room mansion, a garden, greenhouse, and automobile driveways. The brick and sandstone mansion features a red clay tiled roof, tall corbelled brick chimneys, Tudor-detailed gables and gabled dormers, and, most prominently, a centrally placed two-story sandstone *porte-cochère* with Tudor arches and a stepped parapet. A large entrance hall greeted guests in this most grandiose of Mount Royal's estate homes, which architectural historian Bryan Melnyk has described as "visible symbols of achievement which publicized the wealth and power of their owners".[5] Coste also built two outbuildings designed to compliment the main house: a coach house, and—rare for Calgary—a "Dower House" for his widowed mother-in-law.

Born in Ontario and educated in France, engineer Eugene Marius Antoine Coste drilled successfully for natural gas in Essex County, Ontario, in 1889. He came west in 1908 as a consultant for the CPR, and in that capacity he discovered natural gas at Bow Island, Alberta, the following year. Coste secured the rights to the field in 1912 and established the Canadian Western Natural Gas, Light, Heat and Power Company, which distributed gas to Calgary and Lethbridge through a 360-kilometer pipeline. Coste's firm continued to provide home heating until the 1990s, when it was acquired by the ATCO group of companies and renamed ATCO Gas.

In 1922, following his son Dillon's death a couple of years earlier, Coste and his family left Calgary permanently for Toronto. Unable to sell the estate, Coste proposed giving it to the city provided that it become a children's hospital. The city declined the offer, and the house remained vacant until 1935, when it became city property through non-payment of taxes. One suggested use for the house, though never realized, was as the mayor's official residence. It became storage for artifacts from the defunct Calgary Public Museum when that institution closed in 1935. During World War II, when the military took over the campus of the Provincial Institute of Technology and Art (later renamed SAIT), its arts students were relocated to the Coste House, where they used the old museum's natural history specimens for models. In 1946 the house became the newly formed Calgary Allied Arts Centre, a nationally renowned cultural facility managed by director Archibald F. Key (1894–1986). The house faced possible demolition when the centre moved in 1960, but it returned to private ownership and has been beautifully maintained.

Though termed the estate's "coach house," the 1912 Tudor Revival-style brick building to the southeast (which is not visible from the street) was designed and used as "auto sheds," and housed a grease pit and gas pumps in its automobile bay. It also included a residence, possibly used by the driver or gardener, and eventually became a guest house. It was severed from the estate in 1975 and became a separate private residence with an Amherst Street address. A wide setback separated the coach house from Amherst, and, in the 1990s, that space was filled by a large new infill modeled after the Coste House.

Landscaping separated the Dower House (2226 Amherst Street) from the main residence, offering privacy for Coste's mother-in-law Louisa Tims (died 1925), for whom he built this Tudor Revival home in 1912. Lawyer Maurice Groberman (circa 1884–1958), a pillar of the local Jewish community, lived here with his family from 1924–37. The house was separated from the estate in 1938, when it was sold to lawyer John James Saucier (1903–1986) and his wife Lillian (died 1973). Among his other accomplishments, J. J. Saucier served as executive assistant to Prime Minister R. B. Bennett and as president of the Calgary Chamber of Commerce and the Canadian Bar Association. The Sauciers lived here until Lillian's death.

Route: Continue northwest on Amherst to the Blow residence, which is well hidden behind mature foliage.

Blow Residence

Address: 2104–8th Street S.W.
Style: Italianate
Architect: Unknown
Date: 1912

With its west-facing tower and its commanding hilltop position, this 1912 mansion dominates its streetscape, and its residents enjoy a panoramic view. Its style is modeled after Italian villas and is expressed through the square brick tower, rounded windows and archways, and tile-clad hipped roof. Dr. Thomas Henry Blow (1862–1932), who was born in humble circumstances, built this mansion less than a decade after moving to Calgary in 1903, and it remained his home until his death. The Ontario-born physician was the sole eye, ear, nose, and throat doctor in southern Alberta in his day.

Dr. Blow's Italianate mansion dominates the hill as seen from 8th Street S.W. The outdoor fire escape, visible on the west side of the three-story tower, dates from its 1944–48 use as a veterans' convalescent home. SHANNON LEE RAE

The province of Alberta was created two years after Blow's arrival, and when Edmonton became its capital, many Calgarians expected that the provincial university would be located in the southern city. But Alexander Rutherford's provincial Liberal government placed the University of Alberta in the premier's political seat, the city of Strathcona—which before long was annexed to Edmonton. A group of outraged Calgarians, including Dr. Blow, decided to establish a separate, privately endowed University of Calgary. The joint-stock institution was chartered as Calgary College, and classes began in 1912 in the Carnegie Library (now the Memorial Park Library) while Blow and his group laid out plans to develop a proper campus. By 1915, three circumstances led to the college's demise. The provincial government refused to grant degree-conferring power, reserving this right to the government university. Finances evaporated when Calgary's overheated real estate boom (in which Dr. Blow himself had invested) collapsed in 1913. Military enlistment during World War I diminished the potential student body.

Blow fought for higher education in Calgary as a Conservative member of the Alberta legislature from 1913–23. In part through his efforts, the Provincial Institute of Technology and Art—later renamed SAIT—was created in 1916. It took until 1946 before Calgary's future university began in earnest, when the University of Alberta took over the Calgary Normal School (the teaching college that shared the technology institute's campus) as the Calgary branch of the Faculty of Education. As more faculties added their branches in the city, Calgary developed a branch university that became autonomous in 1966.

Blow's family sold the house in 1937, and in 1944 the federal government bought the property and turned it into a convalescent home for World War II veterans. Coincidentally, Blow was an in-law of Senator James A. Lougheed, who chaired the Military Hospitals Commission that established convalescent facilities for returned veterans of World War I. (Blow's daughter Marion married Lougheed's son Douglas.) The house returned to private ownership in 1948, and the estate was eventually subdivided.

Route: Proceed along Amherst to 8th Street S.W., and keep right along 8th Street to Durham Avenue. Cross 8th Street.

Young Residence
Address: 2101–8th Street S.W.
Style: Tudor Revival influenced
Architect: J. Llewellyn Wilson
Date: 1909

Businessman and onetime Calgary Herald *city editor D. J. Young built this Tudor Revival influenced home atop a prominent hillside overlooking downtown Calgary.*
SHANNON LEE RAE

It's a long way from narrow, one-way Maggie Street in Calgary's Ramsay district with its blue-collar origins to posh Mount Royal, but it passes right through this house. Margaret Jean Beattie (1865–1949), who lived here with her husband John (1868–1943) from 1930 until their respective deaths, was the daughter of nineteenth-century mayor Wesley Fletcher Orr (1831–1898), who subdivided Ramsay and named Maggie Street for her.

The house was built for David Jackson Young (1875–1961), an English-born businessman who had moved to Calgary in 1896 to become city editor of the *Calgary Herald*. Young's older brother, John Jackson Young, had purchased the newspaper in 1894. D. J. interrupted his *Herald* career to search for gold in British Columbia, then returned briefly as the *Herald*'s business manager. He then quit for good and opened a stationery shop, which doubled as a lending library and a book and music shop, and remained in business until 1935. D. J. also invested in real estate and oil, served as governor of Western Canada College, and became president of the Calgary Golf and Country Club, the Calgary Horticultural Society, and both the city and provincial Liberal associations. He lived here with his family until 1930, then converted the stable house into a residence, and lived there for many years.

John and Margaret Beattie moved into the house in 1930, and they brought another *Calgary Herald* connection to the house. Besides serving as Calgary's mayor from 1894–96 and 1897–98, Margaret's father was also a onetime manager and editor of the *Herald.* After the Beatties' deaths in the 1940s, their widowed daughter Mary operated a rooming house here in the 1950s and 1960s, and her tenants included the city solicitor of the day, Edward M. Bredin. By 1967 the house was again a private residence.

From its setting atop a steep hillside, this two-and-a-half story house offers its residents a commanding downtown view. Its features include wood shingle siding with half-timbering and stucco on the upper floor, a wrap-around veranda, and a prominent cross gable. The original estate has been subdivided.

Route: Turn left (south) on 8th Street S.W., and continue south to Prospect Avenue. Cross 8th Street.

Price Residence

Address: 930 Prospect Avenue S.W.
Style: Eclectic, with Tudor Revival influence
Architect: W. D. Chown
Date: 1912

In 1907, the same year Mount Royal was annexed to Calgary, Toronto-born Alfred Price moved to Calgary as the CPR's General Superintendent for its Alberta division. Five years later, Price built this two-and-a-half-story house in this CPR-developed subdivision, built to a square plan and clad in sandstone, brick, and Tudor Revival-style half-timbering and stucco. Its gambrel roof is covered in red tile and is interrupted by two low shed dormers on the front façade. The *Herald* published the architectural plans, which featured a unique four-car basement garage.[6] Price moved to Montreal the following year when the company promoted him. Later occupants included merchant and alderman George T. C. Robinson and his wife Alberta (from

1913–23), and James T. Dee, owner of the Silver Spray Brewing Company (who lived here from 1924–26).

Owner John Burns developed a Japanese sunken garden behind his house in 1929. The lot has been subdivided, and only traces of the garden remain. SHANNON LEE RAE

The house was probably best known for the sunken Japanese garden developed on its grounds in 1929 and for the owner who created them—John Burns (1883–1953), who lived here with his wife Alma from 1926–45. In a feature page on the garden in 1929, the *Herald* noted it was "intended by Mr. Burns to be the Bucharts Garden [sic] of the prairies", referring to the famous gardens in Victoria, B.C.[7]

John Burns was, in turn, general manager, president, and chairman of the board of P. Burns & Co., the international corporation founded in Calgary by his uncle, Senator Patrick Burns. Born in Ontario, John moved to Calgary in 1901 to work in his uncle's meatpacking plant, where he started as an office boy; he became general manager in 1918 and president in 1934. John was also chairman of the separate school board, Honorary Colonel of the King's Own Calgary Regiment, and head of the Navy League of Alberta. He became a Member of the Order of the British Empire in 1945 in recognition of his war-related work during World War II.

In 1945, Robert J. Dinning (1884–1969) replaced Burns both as president of P. Burns & Co. and as owner and resident of this house. (The Burns family moved to the Bow Valley Ranch, in what is now Fish Creek Provincial Park.) Dinning came west from Ontario to work for the Merchants Bank of Canada, and by 1924 he had become a Bank of Montreal executive in Lethbridge. That year, the provincial government tapped him to head the new Alberta Liquor Control Board, formed when Alberta ended an eight-year experiment in prohibition. Dinning held the high profile post until 1937, when he joined the Burns company. Dinning and his wife Sidney sold the house in 1959 and retired to Edmonton. Their grandson, politician Jim Dinning, served as provincial treasurer from 1992–97 and is often named as a possible future successor to Premier Ralph Klein.

Route: Cross 8th Street S.W., and proceed west on Prospect Avenue to Morrison Street.

Wetmore Residence
Address: 1128 Prospect Avenue S.W.
Style: American Foursquare
Architect: None (likely a pattern-book design)
Year: 1912

Plumbing and heating contractor William R. Wetmore built this two-and-a-half-story red brick house but lived in it only a year. The house is typical of its style, featuring a large central dormer and full-width veranda.

Perhaps its most prominent occupant was Francis Mollison Black (1871–1941), who was secretary-treasurer of P. Burns & Co. at the time he lived here (1913–18). Black later moved to Manitoba, where he served as provincial treasurer from 1922–26 in Premier John Bracken's United Farmers of Manitoba government. From 1919–21, this was the home of Loran A. Tupper (circa 1871–1963), secretary-treasurer of the Rose Deer Coal Mining Company, one of dozens of mining companies that operated in the Drumheller valley northeast of Calgary before petroleum superseded coal as Alberta's primary energy industry. From 1925–29, this house was home to silk merchant Najeeb Mitri Hashim (circa 1870–1940).

William Wetmore's 1912 house is a typical example of American Foursquare style.
SHANNON LEE RAE

From 1930 until his death nearly four decades later, this was the home of geologist and mining engineer Stanley J. Davies (1893–1967). While serving overseas with the Canadian Expeditionary Force during World War I, Davies escorted the Prince of Wales—the future King Edward VIII, who later abdicated and became the Duke of Windsor—to the front. He was reprimanded for endangering the prince, but the heir to the throne reportedly appreciated the opportunity. During World War II, Davies served at home as a militia organizer and as an officer with the Royal Canadian Engineers.

Route: Cross Prospect Avenue, turn right (west), and continue west on Prospect past Carlton Street to the Traunweiser residence.

Traunweiser Residence

Address: 1213 Prospect Avenue S.W.
Style: Eclectic, with Georgian Revival influence
Architect: Unknown
Date: 1912

Hotelier Charles Traunweiser built this brick house in 1912. Its pale yellow bricks are oversized and laid in an unusual pattern. SHANNON LEE RAE

The brick walls of this beautiful two-and-a-half story residence boast several unusual features. The bricks are oversized, and their pale yellow color is rare for the city. The mortar is thin and beaded, and the bricks are set in a pattern rarely seen in Calgary. In an A-B-A-B repetition, rows of bricks overlap by one-third the length of a brick, instead of the usual one-half, forming an H-pattern in the mortar. The front elevation features a centrally placed portico-like entrance, with large open verandas on either side, and surmounted by an enclosed central bay with open decks on either side. Together, these form a powerful symmetrical façade.

Hotelier Charles Traunweiser (1873–1954) built this house, and it remained his family home until 1927. Born in Ogdensburg, New York, Traunweiser moved to Calgary in 1893, first opening a barbershop and then the Hub Cigar Store. Traunweiser later bought the Commercial Hotel on 9th Avenue S.W. (on the present site of the Marriott Hotel) and changed its name to the Yale. From 1927–45, Traunweiser served as president of the Alberta Hotel Association.

The next occupant was Welsh-born Chris J. Yorath (circa 1880–1932), president of the Canadian Western Natural Gas, Light, Heat and Power Company founded by Eugene Coste. Yorath had earlier been city commissioner of Saskatoon and commissioner of public works and finance in Edmonton. After Yorath's death, his widow continued to live here until about 1937. In 1941, it became the home of Jewish immigrants Abraham Singer (1880–1942) and his wife Bella (1880–1984). As a result of Bella's efforts, some 200–300 Russian Jewish immigrants were able to come to Canada. Calgary's Jack Singer Concert Hall is named for the Singers' son Jack, a real estate magnate who lived here with his family from about 1950–53. Rick Orman, the provincial minister of energy from 1989–92, lived here with his wife Susan from 1995–2002. The house was extensively renovated in 2004.

Route: Continue west along Prospect Avenue.

Colgrove Residence
Address: 1227 Prospect Avenue S.W.
Style: Eclectic, with Tudor Revival influence
Architect: None (pattern-book design)
Date: 1912

Robert J. (Jack) Colgrove and his brother Mark hailed from London, Ontario, and came to Calgary during its phenomenal real estate boom that preceded World War I. Through their Colgrove Land Company, they built and operated apartment buildings—among them the extant Colgrove Apartments in Victoria Park (129–15th Avenue S.E.). Jack and his wife Florence, a musician, built this house and lived here with their children until they moved to California in the early 1940s. The Colgroves modeled the house on a Vancouver home they admired and included a sixty-foot ballroom in its design. Jack and Florence are buried in Forest Lawn Cemetery in Los Angeles.

The Colgrove Residence is characterized by its large half-timbered front gable and large veranda. A circular front driveway once bridged Prospect Avenue and 12th Street, but it was removed when the 12th Street side of the lot was subdivided in 1979. SHANNON LEE RAE

Jack's father, Robert D. Colgrove, had been killed in a train wreck in 1893 on his way to Chicago to see the Columbian Exposition. Had he survived to attend that World's Fair, the elder Colgrove might have thrilled at the marvels of technology on display and the future wonders they promised. But he could never have imagined the guest who would some day visit the house his son built in Calgary—astronaut Edwin A. "Buzz" Aldrin, the second man ever to walk on the moon. Aldrin gave a lecture at the Canadian Mental Health Association's annual general meeting in Calgary in the early 1970s. During that visit he attended a party hosted by psychiatrist Dr. Patrick Conway, who lived here with his family from 1966–76.

The front elevation is dominated by a large gable with Tudor half-timbering and a large veranda with hexagonally cut granite stones at the base of its columns. The original coach house still stands at the rear.

Route: Continue west along Prospect to 12 Street S.W., and
cross Prospect.

Patrick Residence

Address: 1228 Prospect Avenue S.W.
Style: English Revival
Architect: Unknown
Date: Circa 1926

*The simulated thatched roof on the Patrick Residence typifies the English Revival
style brought across the Atlantic by soldiers who returned from World War I.* SHANNON
LEE RAE

This house was a late addition to Mount Royal, and its design can
be understood in the context of its time. World War I veterans who
had been stationed in England returned with a taste for English
styles, reflected in the cottage-style two-story home with its rough
cast stucco finish and imitation thatched roof.

This was the second home in Mount Royal for Dr. Omer H.
Patrick (1869–1947) and his wife Lulu (died 1957), who built the
house and lived in it for the rest of their lives. Dr. Patrick earned his

medical degree in 1892 at the University of Western Ontario and practiced medicine in Port Huron, Michigan, until the family moved to Calgary in 1912. He gave up medicine and went into business, becoming the controlling investor in the Atlas Coal Mine at East Coulee, near Drumheller. He became the founding president of the Calgary Zoological Society in 1928 and remained in that position for sixteen years. Patrick also headed the Board of Trade and Calgary Civic Government Association, managed two of R. B. Bennett's election campaigns in the 1920s, and served as a school board trustee. Patrick built the Beltline apartment building that he named for his son: the Lorraine (620–12th Avenue S.W.) The Patricks' daughter Lenore and her husband George Eaton lived next door at 2222–12th Street S.W., and the two yards were joined.

Edmonton-born Frank Swanson (1917–1990), publisher of the *Calgary Herald* from 1962–82, lived here with his wife Vera from 1962–66.

Route: Proceed north on 12th Street S.W. to Colborne Crescent. Turn right (east) on Colborne, and continue east on Colborne to Carlton Street. Cross Carlton Street.

Skaken Residence
Address: 1131 Colborne Crescent S.W.
Style: Moderne
Architect: Designed by owner Colin Skaken
Date: 1947

Calgary architect Jeremy Sturgess has termed the two-story Skaken Residence "a heroic example of the Modern Movement located amid Mount Royal's older mansions."[8] This prominent hillside property was a treeless knoll until 1947, when the city sold it at a reduce price—$1,800—to naturopathic physician Colin Skaken (born Dmitri Scakun, 1900–83), on the promise that he build a house within eight months. Inspired by buildings he had seen in Romania as a soldier after World War I, Skaken helped the contractor design this two-story house, which Sturgess describes as the city's "best remaining example of early modernism."[9] The cubic-formed house boasts typical features of its style, including a flat roof, corner windows, projecting canopy, use of glass block, and a simple white stucco finish.

The Skaken Residence gives the impression of interlocking or overlapping boxes.
AUTHOR PHOTO

Skaken was born in Bukovina, in what is now Ukraine. According to family lore, his grandmother's reputation as a midwife who never lost a baby reached the Emperor Franz Joseph. The Austro-Hungarian monarch gave her a commission to study in Vienna, where she became a naturopath. Colin followed his grandmother's footsteps, and, after moving to Calgary in 1943, he took over the Swedish Massage Institute and transformed it into the Naturopathic Health Institute, which he later renamed Vienna Clinics. Son Ross Skaken later joined his practice, and, when Colin moved to Edmonton in 1956, this house became Ross' longtime residence. Both father and son were active in getting provincial legislation passed to govern their medical field.

Route: Continue east on Colborne Crescent.

Connacher Residence

Address: 1111 Colborne Crescent S.W.
Style: Tudor Revival
Architect: Lawson and Fordyce
Date: 1911

The Connacher Residence rises above the street on a sloping hillside behind a massive stone wall. Fine hand-painted patterns grace the library and living room ceilings. AUTHOR PHOTO

About ten kilometers east of Calgary lies the hamlet of Conrich, where the Grand Trunk Pacific Railway established a flag station by that name in 1913. Conrich is an amalgam of the names Connacher and Richardson, who, according to lore, were real estate men who promoted Conrich during the pre-World War I boom. (In another version, the two men used the land for horse breeding.) While Richardson remains an enigma, his partner was New Brunswick-born banker William Murray Connacher (1887–1956), who built this house in 1911 and lived in it for the rest of his life. If the real estate version of the story is true, Connacher and Richardson probably earned little. *Calgary Herald* columnist Ken Liddell described Conrich in 1952: "Wouldn't take any more than four minutes to drive from the service station to the elevators and back again and pause to admire the goats on the way."[10]

Connacher moved to Calgary in 1903 to open the city's first Bank of Nova Scotia branch, which he managed until 1917. He then became president of the Security Trust Company, a position he held until his death. Connacher's two-story house is set behind a massive stone wall, on a sloping hillside high above the street. Tudor half-timbers form a diamond pattern at the corners of the upper floor.

Route: Continue east on Colborne Crescent, which becomes 10th Street S.W. as you keep to the right. Continue to the corner and the next stop, the Simmons Residence.

Simmons Residence

Address: 2101–10th Street S.W.
Style: Classical influence
Architect: Francis J. Lawson
Date: 1911

This large two-and-a-half-story brick house, with its prominent balcony fronting a large, curved corner lot, dominates its surroundings. Carved wooden Ionic columns frame its central portico and veranda, which surmount a massive sandstone base with stairs on either side. A semicircular driveway passes in front.

Two prominent public figures, both born in Ontario and both Liberal politicians, have lived in this house: the Honourable Justice William Charles Simmons (from 1911–36) and Alderman Ernest Arlinton McCullough (from 1936–65).

Justice Simmons (1865–1956) moved to Calgary in 1899 to article with R. B. Bennett, then practiced law in Cardston and Lethbridge. He was elected to Alberta's first legislature in 1906 as the Liberal member for Lethbridge but lost his 1908 bid for a federal

seat to former Lethbridge Mayor Charles A. Magrath, for whom
that city's Mayor Magrath Drive was named. Simmons moved back
to Calgary in 1910, when he was elevated to the bench. He served as
Chief Justice of the Trial Division of the Alberta Supreme Court
from 1924–36, when he retired to Victoria.

With its rounded corner lot, semicircular driveway and central portico surmount-
ing a massive sandstone base, the Simmons Residence dominates its surroundings.
AUTHOR PHOTO

Ernie McCullough (1891–1965) settled in Calgary in 1908. In
1915, he joined the Ford Motor Company, quickly becoming its top
salesman in the country. McCullough joined the Royal Flying Corps
during World War I. After the war, he co-founded (with T. W. Lines
of Edmonton) one of the city's original Ford dealerships, Maclin
Motors, which continues to operate in 2004 as Maclin Ford. The
name is an amalgam of the partners' surnames. McCullough spent
eight years on City Council before his unsuccessful bid for the mayoralty in 1945. Among his other accomplishments, McCullough was
the first president of the Glencoe Club, headed the Calgary Liberal
Association, and was a founding member of the Canadian Council
of Christians and Jews. McCullough's widow, Dorothea, continued
to live here for a quarter century after his death.

Route: Cross 10th Street S.W., and proceed east along Durham Avenue.

Devenish Residence

Address: 1035 Durham Avenue S.W.
Style: Eclectic, with strong Colonial Revival detailing
Architect: Alexander Pirie (presumed)
Date: 1911

Oscar G. Devenish, who built this large home in 1912, is best remembered in the city as the owner and namesake of the Devenish Apartments (now the Devenish Design Centre) on 17th Avenue S.W. AUTHOR PHOTO

Best known for constructing the luxurious Devenish Apartments (now the Devenish Design Centre) in 1911, Indiana-born Oscar Grant Devenish (1867–1951) built this two-and-a-half story brick home, with its downtown view, the same year. After settling in Calgary with his wife Lena around 1903, Devenish prospered in the real estate business, then entered the petroleum industry during the Turner Valley oil boom in 1914. He sojourned in Texas from about 1914–26, but kept the house and moved back in when he returned to the city. During one of his visits in 1918, the house was gutted by fire. Devenish established Devenish Petroleum in the 1920s, but financial problems evidently motivated him to sell the house in 1929 and buy a smaller one nearby at 837 Royal Avenue.

The second owner was William Stewart Herron (1870–1939), the self-taught petroleum geologist whose observations and deductions along Sheep Creek south of Calgary set off the Turner Valley oil boom and launched Alberta's oil industry. Though his fortunes rose and fell sharply, Herron's refusal to sell any of his interests earned him the moniker "Won't Sell Herron." This was Herron's last home, where he died at the peak of his prosperity. The Alberta Petroleum Association sent a five-foot high floral arrangement, shaped like an oil derrick, to his funeral.

The next owner also belonged to the oil industry. Minnesota-born rancher Albert H. Mayland (1874–1947), who also died in the house, had settled in Calgary around 1907. He owned the Union Packing Company and helped establish the city's public stockyards. Mayland's early involvement in the Turner Valley field was the start of a long career in the petroleum business. His ranch became the Mayland Heights subdivision in 1962. Texas-born oilman William A. Friley, who became Chancellor of the University of Calgary in 1970, bought the house from the Mayland family in 1958 and lived here until 1975.

The house has a massive appearance, and features an open front veranda, twin corbelled chimneys, and a central gable dormer. Of particular note is the prominent balustrade over the open veranda, executed in terra cotta. Terra cotta shields on each of the veranda's columns reinforce the prestigious character of the overall composition. Architect Alexander Pirie, whom Devenish hired to design the Devenish Apartments, probably designed this house for him as well.

Route: Proceed a short distance east on Durham Avenue to its T-intersection with 9th Street S.W. Cross Durham on the east side of 9th Street, and proceed north on 9th Street, downhill, to Royal Avenue.

Rae Residence

Address: 927 Royal Avenue S.W.
Style: American Foursquare
Architect: None (Probably a catalog design)
Date: 1912

This brick house with its wrap-around veranda rises high above the street, from which it is shielded by thick foliage. The original coach house still stands at the rear of the property. AUTHOR PHOTO

In 1912, at the peak of Calgary's pre-World War I building boom, contractor George W. Rae (1869–1923) had probably never been busier in his life. Nonetheless, he probably built this two-and-a-half story brick house himself, and it remained his family residence for over a decade. That same year, he built the extant Vendome Block in Sunnyside (938–2nd Avenue N.W.), which many Calgarians know as the home of the popular Heartland Café. Rae retired in 1923 and held an auction in the house in preparation for moving to Vancouver with his family. A week later he was dead of appendicitis.

The next long-term occupant, from 1936–49, was Quebec-born James S. Ingram (1865–1949). Ingram moved to Alberta around 1888 and became a rancher, butcher, real estate agent, car and farm implement dealer, hotelkeeper, and department store owner. He bought the Brooks Hotel in Brooks, Alberta, in 1910, and, during Prohibition (1916–24), Ingram converted its bar into a general store. He later expanded the shop into larger quarters as Ingram's Department Store.

The home's best-known resident, from 1949–52, was Charles Vernon Myers (1912–1990), an oil reporter, novelist, and publisher best known for an epic tax battle with Revenue Canada. Vern Myers grew up on a farm near Vulcan, Alberta, studied at Regina College, and worked on the CANOL (Canadian Oil) pipeline from Norman Wells, NWT, to Alaska during World War II. He then wrote and self-published a booklet, *Oil to Alaska*, which helped him land a job as the *Calgary Herald*'s oil editor in 1944. Myers' CANOL experience formed the basis of his 1955 novel, *Through Hell to Alaska*.

Myers lived here with his wife Muriel and their young family, a time he described as an "idyllic life" in his 1989 biography, *Fifty Years in the Furnace*.[11] Myers dedicated a paragraph to the house:

> By some break we were able to purchase this twelve room brick house perched on the hill overlooking the whole city for $10,000. It was in bad repair but we fixed it up with new wallpaper throughout and some other more expansive contributions and inside six months we were offered $27,000 for the house. We didn't take it. I often thought afterwards that's what my dad would have described as "the day when two fools met." The one fool who was crazy enough to offer the price and the other fool who was crazy enough to turn it down.[11]

In 1952, Myers founded the influential *Oilweek* magazine, which he later sold to Maclean Hunter. He then published *Myers Finance and Energy Newsletter* for nearly a quarter-century. Myers distrusted currency and advised his readers to buy precious metals. Americans were not permitted to buy gold at that time, and Myers offered to buy gold for American clients and safeguard it for them. In 1974, Revenue Canada seized $4-million worth of gold from Myers; he refused to name the owners, and he was assessed for nearly $900,000 in taxes owing. That same year, the U.S. government legalized ownership of bullion, and his clients suddenly wanted their gold—which Revenue Canada possessed. Myers and his wife fled to Spokane. In 1977, he was convicted in Canada in absentia of tax evasion and sentenced to two years. In 1979, he returned to Calgary and turned himself in, but hated prison and fled after eight months while on a weekend pass. "Two days later, he appeared on the Merv Griffin Show," *Alberta Report* magazine later noted, "and jeered at the Canadian authorities."[13] But his story ended tragically. Muriel returned to Calgary in 1987 to undergo a kidney stone operation, but was not expected to survive. Myers sneaked back into Canada and came to her hospital bedside, where he was arrested. Muriel died the next day. Myers was pardoned within a month and returned to Spokane, where his health soon failed.

Route: Proceed east on Royal Avenue to 8th Street S.W.

Stringer Residence
Address: 2003–8th Street S.W.
Style: Queen Anne Free Classic, with Craftsman influence
Architect: Unknown
Date: 1909

Before he settled in Calgary, Ontario-born engineer Bert Stringer (1880–1934) had conducted trade missions to central and South America and worked for the U.S. government in Havana, Cuba. In 1909, Stringer built this brick and sandstone house, with its distinctive corner turret topped by a silver bell-shaped roof. He developed the northwest district of Mount Pleasant during Calgary's pre-World War I boom and was one of the investors in

From its hillside position at an important point of entry into Mount Royal, Bert Stringer's 1909 house is a local landmark, distinguished by its corner turret with its bell-shaped roof. A fieldstone fence borders its extensive grounds. SHANNON LEE RAE

the original, privately owned Centre Street Bridge. Stringer's finances suffered with the 1913 crash, and he rented out rooms in the house for the rest of his life. Arthur Stringer (1874–1950), Bert's brother, was a prolific novelist, poet, and screenwriter—he penned the script for *The Perils of Pauline* (1914)—and the namesake of a public school in the brothers' native Chatham.

Alberta's "cowboy judge," Mr. Justice William Carlos Ives (1873–1950), lived in the house from 1934–45. Ives' parents were Pincher Creek ranchers, and he worked as a cowhand before attending law school at McGill. Known for his dry humor and poker face, Ives presided over the 1930 trials of Isaac Solloway and Harvey Mills, Calgary brokers who were convicted in a stock manipulation scheme just before the Great Depression. Another of Judge Ives' notable cases was the seduction trial of Alberta Premier John E. Brownlee in 1934. The jury convicted Brownlee of seducing a young government employee, Vivian Macmillan, but Ives reversed Macmillan's $15,000 award, noting she suffered no damages. The award was restored on appeal. Ives became Chief Justice of the Trial Division of the provincial Supreme Court in 1942 and held the post until he retired two years later. He rented an upstairs apartment to Louise Riley, the well-known librarian and children's author for whom a library branch in northwest Calgary was named.

After a series of short-term occupancies, this became the home of professional football running back M. L. (Fritz) Hanson from 1957–66. Hanson played for the Calgary Stampeders when the team first won the Grey Cup in 1948. Coming only a year after the Leduc oil discovery that spawned an oil boom, the 1948 win instilled enormous civic pride and boosted Calgary's profile in the national consciousness. From 1966–2003, this was the home of Peter Fitzgerald-Moore (1919–2004), an English-born geologist who served as mayor of Bowness before Calgary annexed that town in 1964. During his 1958–60 tenure, Fitzgerald-Moore modernized the town's infrastructure and practiced grassroots democracy. Each Sunday, he strolled through the town, stopping to chat with citizens and listen to their complaints—everything from potholes and sidewalk construction to wild dogs and loose chickens. The Cambridge graduate and World War II veteran is the namesake for a trilobite species, *Pseudodechenella petermoorei ormiston.*

Tour ends.

Notes

1 "Sanatorium will Soon be Ready," *Daily Herald* 24 June 1904: 6.
2 Western Canada College closed in 1926, and Western Canada High School opened in its place in 1929.
3 University of Calgary historian Donald B. Smith has pointed out that Carlton and Dorchester streets honor the same person: Sir Guy Carleton (1724–1808), the Quebec governor who became the 1st Baron Dorchester.
4 James H. Gray, *R. B. Bennett: The Calgary Years* (Toronto: University of Toronto Press, 1991) 120.
5 Bryan P. Melnyk, *Calgary Builds: The Emergence of an Urban Landscape, 1905–1914* (Edmonton: Alberta Culture/Canadian Plains Research Center, 1985) 56.
6 "Plans of the New Home of A. Price, Superintendent of the C.P.R. Now Being Erected in Mount Royal," *Calgary Daily Herald* 17 June 1912: 18.
7 "Setting a Scenic Gem on a Hillside," *Calgary Daily Herald Magazine* 5 Oct. 1929: 1.
8 Jeremy Sturgess, "Home," in *Calgary Modern* (Calgary: The Nickle Arts Museum, University of Calgary, 2000) 41.
9 *Ibid.*
10 Ken Liddell, "Conrich was Busy in its Quiet Way," *Calgary Herald* 13 Aug. 1952: 12.
11 C. V. Myers, *Fifty Years in the Furnace: Autobiography of a nonconformist* (Spokane: C. V. Myers, 1989) 169.
12 *Ibid* 168.
13 "The passing of a legend," *Alberta Report* 12 Mar. 1990: 33.

SAIT

Jubilee

5 Ave. N.W.

3 Ave. N.W.

14 St. N.W.

10 St. N.W.

Kensington Rd. N.W.

Memorial Drive N.W.

Tour Begins

Hillhurst-Sunnyside

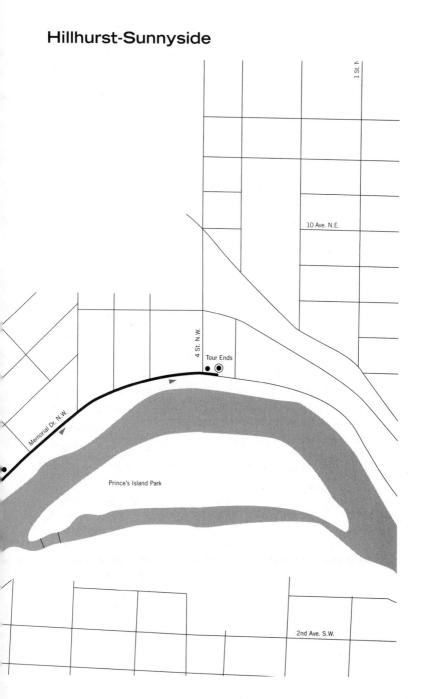

1 St. N.

10 Ave. N.E.

4 St. N.W.

Tour Ends

Memorial Dr. N.W.

Prince's Island Park

2nd Ave. S.W.

Annexed from the surrounding countryside in 1907, Hillhurst-Sunnyside is one of Calgary's earliest suburbs, and, in many ways, it has retained a separate, village-like character. It extends from 4th Street to 14th Street N.W., between the Bow River and the North Hill. (Unlike Sunnyside, Hillhurst extends north to the top of the hill, encompassing the Southern Alberta Institute of Technology [SAIT] campus.) Tenth Street N.W. bisects Hillhurst (to the west) and Sunnyside (to the east). It was originally known as Morleyville Trail and functioned as the pioneer road to Morleyville, where Methodist minister George McDougall established a mission on what is now the Stoney Reserve west of the city. After Calgary annexed the district, 10th Street developed as a commercial area known as "The Bridge."

The northwest districts of Hillhurst, West Hillhurst, and Hounsfield Heights were once part of the sprawling property of the Riley family. English-born farmer Thomas E. Riley (1842–1909) settled in Quebec before homesteading near Calgary in 1888. Riley's sons acquired additional farmlands, and, in 1904, son Ezra H. Riley (1866–1936)—who later represented the area in the provincial legislature as a Liberal from 1907–10—subdivided and began selling lots in what he named Hillhurst. He drew the name from Hillhurst Farm at Compton, Quebec, owned by Senator Matthew Henry Cochrane (for whom Cochrane, Alberta, was named). Ezra Riley supplied British-sounding street names, perhaps signaling the ethnic demographic Hillhurst was expected to cultivate. In a 1907 feature titled "Suburbs North of the Bow River," the *Morning Albertan* observed:

A great feature of the Hillhurst settlement is the fine class of people who are making homes there. They are mostly Canadians or people from the British Isles and great care is exercised in the choice of people to whom to sell lots for building purposes. As a result there is no foreign settlement in Hillhurst and all the new-comers speak the English language and are of Anglo-Saxon origin. This is a guarantee that the public institutions and private homes will be built up on the high plan of Anglo-Saxon and Canadian ideals.[1]

Albertan readers would have understood the distinction between Anglo-Saxon Hillhurst and the ethnic enclave that was developing further east in Bridgeland-Riverside. The city soon changed Hillhurst's street names to numbers, leaving only Kensington and Gladstone roads as a reminder. Dual signage placed in the 1990s revived the memory of the original names.

Like 16th Avenue (the Trans-Canada Highway) to the north and 17th Avenue to the south, Kensington Road once occupied an important geographical position as a section road. Ezra Riley called it Kensington Avenue, but the city soon renamed it Centre Avenue and made it the boundary between the quadrants now designated as "N.W." and "S.W." The quadrant line shifted south to the Bow River in 1925, and Centre Avenue was renamed Kensington Road. The streetcar line built in 1911 transformed the street into a commercial strip that eventually made the name Kensington synonymous with Hillhurst-Sunnyside in the minds of Calgarians. The area south of Kensington Road originally lay outside Hillhurst proper, in a small subdivision originally called Broadview.

East of 10th Street lies Sunnyside, which was homesteaded in 1883 by Ottawa-born rancher Felix Alexander McHugh (1851–1912). McHugh Bluff—the escarpment north of the Bow River, between 10th Street N.W. and Centre Street—was named for him in 1990. Sunnyside was subdivided in 1906–07, and, like Hillhurst, it developed as a working-class neighborhood connected to the rest of the city by streetcar. Its position on the flood plain left its residents vulnerable to periodic floods until remediation took place in the form of dikes, deepening the river channel, and construction of the Bearspaw Dam in 1953.

Between 9A Street and 5A Street N.W., Sunnyside's streets and avenues are laid out at an angle with respect to adjacent areas, following the contour of the riverbank. The roads return to the compass-oriented grid pattern east from 5A Street to 3rd Street N.W., where the district ends. Most of that compass-oriented area (between 5A Street and 4th Street N.W.) was originally called New Edinburgh. The easternmost block of modern Sunnyside, where the tour concludes, was considered part of Crescent Heights when it was subdivided in 1907.[2]

Between Hillhurst-Sunnyside and the Bow River lies Memorial Drive, a thoroughfare that began as a quiet street with a confused identity. It was once known simply as "Boulevard" or as Boulevard Road, but early city maps show it, from west to east, as: Westmount Boulevard (between 24th Street and 14th Street); Broadview Boulevard (14th Street to 10th Street); and Sunnyside Boulevard (east from 10th Street). East of the Langevin Bridge that leads to Bridgeland-Riverside, it was known as Riverside Boulevard. In 1922, that portion between Sunnyside and Riverside was renamed Memorial Drive, and Mayor Samuel H. Adams planted the first of hundreds of trees that eventually lined the boulevard, each of which reportedly once had a plaque memorializing a soldier killed in World War I. In 1963, the entire road as far west as Crowchild Trail was renamed Memorial Drive. Many of the aging trees were later removed, and alternative memorials were dedicated.

Age, development pressure, and Light Rail Transit (LRT) construction took their toll on Hillhurst-Sunnyside in recent decades. Commerce shifted to the nearby North Hill Shopping Centre, Calgary's first suburban mall, which opened in 1959. Apartment blocks replaced many family homes, and the LRT cut through Sunnyside in the mid-1980s despite local opposition. Salvation took the form of gentrification and yuppification; inner-city hipness reversed inner-city decay, making Hillhurst-Sunnyside a vital "urban suburb."

Route: Begin at the Hillhurst (Louise) Bridge, which connects Hillhurst-Sunnyside with downtown Calgary at 10th Street S.W.

Hillhurst (Louise) Bridge

The Hillhurst Bridge (left) was still new when this photograph was taken in the early 1920s. The adjacent Louise Bridge (right) was dismantled in 1927. Ever since, Calgarians have called the newer bridge the Louise Bridge, so the city finally renamed it the Hillhurst (Louise) Bridge. It was extensively repaired in 1978 and again in the 1990s. GLENBOW ARCHIVES NA-2365-25

The original timber bridge at this location (from 1888–1906) was the Bow Marsh Bridge, built by the Eau Claire and Bow River Lumber Company. It was apparently named for both the river and real estate agent George C. Marsh, who had petitioned for its construction. The second bridge (from 1906–27) was a steel truss structure, located a short distance downstream from the first. It was built under the aegis of provincial Public Works Minister William H. Cushing, who had been Calgary's mayor from 1900–01. The bridge was named for his daughter Louise (1878–1906), who had died following an emergency appendectomy, and whom the *Calgary Herald* termed "one of the best known young ladies of the city".[3] The third bridge—the present concrete structure—was built in 1920–21, a short distance downstream from the 1906 bridge, and named the Hillhurst Bridge. Both the Louise and Hillhurst bridges coexisted until 1927, when the older structure was dismantled and its spans reused elsewhere in the province. Its name endured, however, and, decades after the Louise Bridge was gone, Calgarians still referred to the Hillhurst Bridge as the Louise Bridge. Accordingly, in 1970 the city officially renamed it the Hillhurst (Louise) Bridge.

Route: Proceed north toward Memorial Drive and Fire Hall No. 6.

Fire Hall No. 6 (Calgary Parks Outdoor Resource Centre)
Address: 1101 Memorial Drive N.W.
Style: Utilitarian (simplified Classical influence)
Architect: City Engineer
Year: 1910

A decade after it was retired from service, this former fire hall was gutted by fire. It now houses the city parks department's Outdoor Resource Centre. Kirsten Olson

File this one under irony. A decade after its long service (1910–64) as a satellite fire station ended, this small brick building was gutted by fire. Like its No. 4 counterpart in Bridgeland-Riverside, Fire Hall No. 6 was designed and built just as the fire department was converting from horse-drawn wagons to motor vehicles. After the 1974 fire, it was used for storing city parks equipment. The building was repaired and renovated in 1980, and became the headquarters of the Calgary Area Outdoor Council. After an historic restoration in 2002, the city turned the old fire hall into its Outdoor Resource Centre, a parks information facility located right on the Bow River bicycle and pedestrian pathway. The main floor also houses Angel's Cappuccino and Ice Cream Café.

Route: Cross Memorial Drive, turn left, and proceed west toward the intersection with 10A Street N.W. (originally called Norfolk Street). Note the Edwardian Commercial-style brick façade of the Kensington Gate parkade, which evokes the Kerr Block that stood on the site from 1912–89. Cross 10A Street, turn right (north), proceed to Kensington Road, and cross it.

Hillhurst Block (Starbucks)
Address: 1122 Kensington Road N.W.
Style: Edwardian Commercial
Architect: Unknown
Year: 1911

In 1909, the streetcar system's Red Line was built across the Louise Bridge and entered Hillhurst-Sunnyside via 10th Street N.W. But the cars originally traveled only a few blocks; at 5th Avenue N.W., the base of the North Hill, they turned around at a loop in the tracks and returned downtown. In 1911, the new Hillhurst loop circled the district along 10th Street, 5th Avenue, 14th Street, and Kensington Road. Kensington quickly developed as a commercial strip, and the Smith Block—as its builder, Yorkshire-born John Smith, originally named this two-story brick edifice—helped define the street's new character. Smith died the same year, leaving the Smith Block as his legacy. His widow Alma sold it in the 1920s, and new owner Salvatore Cozzubbo renamed it the Hillhurst Block.

Decades before Starbucks opened its Kensington Road location in this building, Calgarians found refreshment at the Hillhurst Confectionery and Ice Cream Parlor.
SHANNON LEE RAE

Cozzubbo and his wife Rosaria were among Hillhurst's first Italian residents. They operated the Hillhurst Confectionery and Ice Cream Parlor on the main floor for over a decade (1921–32), long before Starbucks took over the same space in 2002. In the 1950s, new owners Arnold and Ellie McArthur called it the Arnell Block (from the first syllables of their first names), and it housed McArthur's Refrigeration Service from 1953–73. Perhaps the best-known residential tenant was Walt Healy, who lived upstairs briefly in 1934–35 and later operated a landmark motorcycle business on 10th Street N.W.

Route: Walk north along 10A Street N.W. to the rear of the Hillhurst Block.

Kensington Pub

Address: 205-209–10A Street N.W.

Style: Tudor duplex and brick bungalow; no strong stylistic references

Architect: None

Date: 1911 (brick residence to the north); 1912 (duplex to the south)

The Kensington Pub comprises two vintage buildings, a 1911 brick bungalow (right) and a 1912 duplex (left). Shannon Lee Rae

Two structures comprise the Kensington Pub. The northern building, a small brick residence, was constructed in 1911 by the same John Smith who built the Hillhurst Block that year. Carpenter John H. Bathgate became the first in a series of blue-collar tenants before Salvatore and Rosaria Cozzubbo bought the house in the 1920s. The Cozzubbos lived here while they operated their ice cream shop in the Hillhurst Block, and it remained Rosaria's home for twenty years after Salvatore's death in 1932. Along with the 1912 duplex to the south, it was renovated to become the Kensington Pub in 1982.

Route: Return to Kensington Road, turn right (west) on Kensington, and proceed west.

King George Lodge No. 59 A.F. & A.M. (Higher Ground)

Address: 1126 Kensington Road N.W.
Style: No discernible style
Architect: D. S. McIlroy
Year: 1926

Architect D. S. McIlroy, who designed this building as a Masonic Lodge, was also a longtime lodge member. The building was converted into retail space in 1985 and heavily renovated a decade later. Its original appearance has been altered. Shannon Lee Rae

King George Lodge No. 59, of the Ancient Free & Accepted Masons, dates back to 1911, when it began meeting in the nearby Ross Block (a landmark destroyed by fire in 1988 and now the site of the Kensington Gate complex). Whist drives and other fundraising efforts yielded the $12,785 needed to build this hall in 1926, and the Sunnyside Construction Company won the building contract. The design of this single-story, stucco building was the work of a lodge member, architect David S. McIlroy. The cornerstone was laid August 21, 1926, and the King George Masonic Lodge met here for nearly sixty years. Lodge chairmen—known as "Worshipful Master"—included pharmacist W. C. Black, whose eponymous drug store was a 10th Street landmark from 1910–82, and Andrew Davison, mayor of Calgary from 1929–45. The lodge sold the hall in 1984 and moved to the southwest Richmond district, taking original interior fittings and even the cornerstone with them. This building was then converted into the Higher Ground coffeehouse and was heavily renovated a decade later.

Route: Continue west along Kensington Road.

Hayden Block (The Yardhouse)
Address: 1134–1136 Kensington Road N.W.
Style: Edwardian Commercial
Architect: Unknown
Year: 1912

Finials at both ends of the pressed metal cornice provide ornament to the Hayden Block's façade. The storefronts have been heavily modified but remain compatible with the building's appearance. SHANNON LEE RAE

Born in Lockport, Nova Scotia, contractor Edward Augustus Hayden (circa 1852–1923) spent twenty years in Boston before settling in Calgary in 1906. He built this two-story residential/commercial block in 1912 and lived in it until his death. James Smalley, an early Sunnyside developer, bought the building after Hayden's death and operated his Radio Exchange business here in the 1920s. Other business occupants included the Model Meat Market (1929–48), grocery stores (including the delightfully named Big and Little Confectionery in the 1920s), and a dressmaking shop. Proximity to the Plaza Theatre has made its series of restaurant tenants favorite after-movie destinations, beginning perhaps with Strand's Coffee Shop in 1948. Diners remember this building as the site of La Fleur (1978–82), one of the first upscale restaurants that helped gentrify the Kensington area. It later housed Razz Barry's (1988–97), Bass Bros. Beerhouse & Grill (2002–04), and, since 2005, The Yardhouse.

Route: Cross Kensington Road.

Plaza Theatre

Address: 1133 Kensington Road N.W.
Style: Art Deco influence
Architect: Unknown
Date: 1929

While operating an automobile garage in the 1920s, mechanic John A. MacLeod—known to all as "Mac"—conceived the notion of a "fix-it-yourself" garage. Rather than hire a crew of mechanics, Mac imagined a garage where people could fix their own cars. Mac's Garage, which he built in 1929, had bays on all sides; Mac rented tools to customers and walked around from one car bay to the next, offering his expertise. An admirable experiment, but Mac's Garage closed within a few years, and, in 1934–35, it was converted into the Spanish-style, Art Deco-influenced Plaza Theatre. The opening presentation on January 10, 1935, was *Mr. Skitch*, a Will Rogers comedy. The Plaza's "wholesome pictures" offered Hillhurst residents escape from the hardships of the Great Depression, and some attended each time the Plaza changed its picture—as often as three times per week.

A do-it-yourself garage was converted into the Art Deco-influenced Plaza Theatre in 1934–35. Finished in stucco, it features a central pediment and articulated parapets on both sides of the central pediment. CALGARY HERITAGE AUTHORITY 11-140

Many Calgarians remember the Plaza as Calgary's first repertory cinema, inaugurated on September 6, 1977, when new owners Fleming Nielsen and Don Carroll showed *The Maltese Falcon*. But decades earlier, under the ownership of Harry Cohen from 1946–50 and Sam and Bessie Slutker from 1950–66, the Plaza had added British, foreign, and intellectual films to its program of second-run Hollywood pictures. Manager Joe Brager, whom the Slutkers had hired away from the Tivoli Theatre in the Mission district, introduced the British tradition of selling ice cream from the aisles during intermission.

While they owned the Plaza, the Slutkers lived in a large suite upstairs. Years after she retired, Bessie was still recognized around town as "Mrs. Plaza" by grown-ups who, as children, had attended Saturday matinees. Boys who watched the exciting weekly serials had chewed nervously on the backs of the wooden seats in front of them, and, week by week, there would be less and less of those seat backs remaining.

In 1975, the Austrian Canadian Club proposed to convert the theatre into its new home. Instead, it began a twenty-year incarnation as a repertory house, and its program flyer evolved into the *Cinemascope* magazine, later renamed *Cityscope*, and eventually *Calgary* magazine.

Route: Proceed west along Kensington Crescent, originally known as 1st Avenue S.W. and later as Bowness Road.

Hillhurst Presbyterian Church (Hillhurst United Church)

Address: 1227 Bowness Road N.W.
Style: Gothic Revival, with Tudor detailing in the two towers
Architect: G. G. Irvine
Date: 1913 (addition 1965)

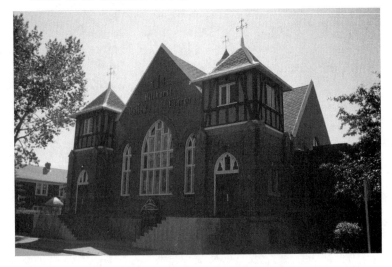

Hillhurst Presbyterian (now Hillhurst United) built this church in 1913 to replace its original 1908 edifice on Kensington Road. Shannon Lee Rae

As with so many historic United churches, Hillhurst has its antecedents in both a Methodist and a Presbyterian congregation. Both denominations established themselves in Hillhurst in 1907, and both first held services in nearby Riley Hall (which still stands at 429–11th Street N.W.). Both built their original church buildings in 1908.

By 1912, Hillhurst Presbyterian had outgrown its edifice at 1127 Kensington Road N.W.; the cornerstone of the present red brick church was laid on September 21, 1912, and the opening services were held on January 19, 1913. The economic downturn later that year resulted in a crushing debt that was not paid off until 1948. Congregants had to do volunteer janitor service and turn off the boiler whenever the building was not in use. As early as 1915, members discussed union with nearby St. Paul's Methodist Church, but the amalgamation of the two congregations as Hillhurst United Church took place only a decade later, when both joined the newly formed United Church of Canada.

In 1965, Hillhurst United built a large addition on the east side of the church. The addition contains the cornerstone of the original 1908 church, which became the Salvation Army Hall after it was sold in 1913, and was demolished in 1963. The congregation recovered the cornerstone at that time and re-laid it in the new addition. It contains coins, stamps, and publications from 1965.

Route: Cross Bowness Road on the west side of 12th Street N.W. (originally known as Oxford Street). Proceed north along 12th Street to Kensington Road, and turn left (west). Proceed west along Kensington Road.

St. John's School (St. John's Fine Arts Elementary School)
Address: 15–12th Street N.W.
Style: Bungalow school
Architect: Burrell and McDonnell
Date: 1917 (additions 1954, 1967)

Hillhurst's Roman Catholic Elementary school had already been established for some time when this four-classroom brick structure—similar in scale to the public school board's contemporary bungalow schools—was completed in 1917. It was the first Catholic institutional building in the district, and, for many years, parishioners had to travel some distance to attend mass at the nearest Catholic church. In 1929, Bishop Kidd approved a temporary chapel in St. John's School. St. John's Parish was created the following year, and, in 1931, a basement church, St. John's Church, opened nearby at 411–10th Street N.W. (The church was rebuilt of brick in 1953; it closed in 2001 and was destroyed by fire in 2003.)

Like all schools in the city, St. John's was closed during the worldwide Spanish Influenza epidemic at the end of World War I. An outbreak of smallpox forced the school's brief closure in 1926.

Route: Proceed west along Kensington Road, to 14th Street S.W. and cross both roads.

Alberta Government Telephones Sub-station/Louise Exchange (Boucock Craig Wong Architects)

Address: 1510 Kensington Road N.W.
Style: Simplified Edwardian Classical, with Romanesque influence
Architect: Unknown
Date: 1922

At 11:45 p.m. on September 30, 1922, Alberta Government Telephones staff began pulling hundreds of toothpick wedges out of the equipment rack at the brand new Louise Exchange, allowing the contact that would transfer 1500 telephone lines (that would now be preceded by 'H', for Hillhurst, rather than 'M' for Main). In a two-minute flawless operation—combined with the simultaneous work of counterparts at the main exchange downtown and cable men at outdoor manholes—staff switched all calls in Hillhurst, Sunnyside,

Parkdale, and Grand Trunk over to this new northwest sub-station with no interruption of service. The official party and forty-two staff members then celebrated with a midnight supper complete with speeches. AGT disposed of this single-story brick building around 1981, and it now houses an architectural office.

An identification block over the main entrance identifies the original occupant of this architectural office: Alberta Government Telephones, the communications company now known as TELUS. Rounded windows add a Romanesque touch to this simplified Edwardian Classical building. KIRSTEN OLSON

Route: Cross 14th Street, turn left (north), and proceed north along 14th Street to Gladstone Road. Cross Gladstone Road, turn right, and follow it to 12th Street N.W. Turn left on 12th Street, and proceed north.

Hillhurst Cottage School (Alberta Wilderness Association)

Address: 455–12th Street N.W.
Style: Homestead House
Architect: Unknown
Date: 1910

During Calgary's rapid growth period before World War I, the public school board built low-cost cottage schools designed for current needs and eventual conversion and sale as residences. Hillhurst Cottage School was the first of two institutions in the city built to this design. The board bought this property from Ezra Riley in the spring of 1910, and the wood frame, two-story school was completed in the fall. It is extremely simplified in appearance and gives maximum floor space under a single roof. Despite original intentions, the building remained in use as a school until the late 1950s. It became the North Hill Optimist clubhouse from 1963–75, followed by the Canadian Youth Hostel Association and, since 1981, the Alberta Wilderness Association. It was designated a Provincial Historic Resource in 1986.

The public school board designed schools like Hillhurst Cottage for temporary use, but they served their original purpose for decades. SHANNON LEE RAE

Route: Continue north along 12th Street, and turn left at 7th Avenue N.W. (originally Church Avenue).

St. Barnabas Church tower

Address: 1407–7th Avenue N.W.
Style: Gothic Revival
Architects: Leo Dowler and James Stevenson (1912 church); J. K. Shedden (1957 church)
Date: 1912 (rebuilt 1957)

The original St. Barnabas Church was destroyed by fire in 1957, but its sandstone and brick tower survived. It was incorporated into the modern St. Barnabas built that same year. KIRSTEN OLSON

When the original church on this property opened in 1906, it housed the city's first Anglican congregation north of the Bow River. Hillhurst developer Ezra H. Riley endowed the church in 1912, making it possible for a new stone and brick edifice to be built. Bishop William Cyprian Pinkham laid the cornerstone on June 12, 1912, for a church dedicated to the memory of Ezra's parents and his infant daughter, who are buried in the churchyard. Fire destroyed the church on January 11, 1957, and only the tower survived. It was incorporated into the new edifice that was dedicated on March 7, 1958.

Route: Cross 7th Avenue N.W., turn left (west), and proceed west.

Hillhurst Elementary School

Address: 1418–7th Avenue N.W.
Style: Free Classical
Architects: Lang and Dowler
Date: 1911 (additions 1912, 1963)

Hillhurst Elementary School is a simplified version of Connaught School in the Beltline. It features a two-story sandstone porch and a stylized central pediment.
AUTHOR PHOTO

Between 1892 and 1913, the public school board built some eighteen sandstone schools throughout the city. These imposing structures illustrated the great value placed on public education. They also impressed on students and their parents—whether Anglo-Saxon or not—that these were British institutions, and that, as residents of Canada, they were part of the British Empire. Like Colonel Walker School in Inglewood, Hillhurst Elementary was built as a simplified variation of Connaught School in the Beltline. It is a two-story, rusticated sandstone structure with a centred third story topped by a stylized pediment and tall flagpole. During the 1920s, militia soldiers used the basement for rifle drill, and student teachers from the nearby Calgary Normal School (the teacher training college on the present SAIT campus) taught at Hillhurst.

Route: Return east along 7th Avenue N.W., and cross 12th Street N.W.

Riley Park

Women playing cricket at Riley Park, 1921. GLENBOW ARCHIVES NA-2393-1.

Ezra Riley, who subdivided the Hillhurst district from his family's rural property, donated Riley Park to the city in 1910. Although it was not mentioned in Riley's formal agreement with the city, he expressed his wish that cricket be forever played in the namesake park that he donated. The Calgary and District Cricket League has played on the Riley Park pitches since 1910.

In 1967, Riley's nephew, Mr. Justice Harold W. Riley, threatened he would try to take the park back unless hippie demonstrations and "love-ins" were stopped.

Route: Optional detour. Exit the park at 10th Street N.W., proceed north on 10th Avenue to SAIT Avenue N.W., and follow the path south of SAIT Avenue to the left. Follow the path to the crosswalk, traverse SAIT Avenue, and continue north along the narrow asphalt path uphill. The path is steep and winding, and is not maintained in inclement weather. But the beauty of Heritage Hall, and the stunning skyline view, are worth it.

Main Building, Provincial Institute of Technology and Art (Heritage Hall, Southern Alberta Institute of Technology)

Address: 1301–16th Avenue N.W.

Style: Modern Gothic

Architect: Richard P. Blakely, Provincial Department of Public Works Architect

Date: 1922 (additions 1926, 1928, 1950, 2002)

Calgary's technical and arts college, the first of its kind in Canada, came as something of a consolation prize. In 1905, the provinces of Alberta and Saskatchewan were created from what had been the North-West Territories. Both new provinces had two major urban centres, and, when Regina became Saskatchewan's capital, Saskatoon was named the university city. Albertans expected the same model, and, when Edmonton became the capital, Calgarians rightly expected the university. But, in 1908, the government located the University of Alberta in Strathcona, a city later absorbed into Edmonton and at that time the political constituency of Liberal premier Alexander Rutherford. An outraged group of Calgary professionals and businessmen endowed a private institution, the University of Calgary, and commenced classes in 1912 in the Calgary Public Library (later renamed the Memorial Park Branch) until a permanent campus could be developed. Arguing that resources could not be divided between two universities in a sparsely populated province, the provincial government refused to confer degree-granting power and chartered the institution as Calgary College. This handicap, combined with the city's economic reversal in 1913 and the outbreak of World War I the following year, sapped away funds and prospective students. The college folded, but a royal commission recommended the establishment of a technology and arts college in Calgary.

Heritage Hall's Modern Gothic design was popular for schools, colleges, and universities when it was built in 1922. Shannon Lee Rae

In 1916, the new Provincial Institute of Technology and Art began classes in Colonel Walker School and Fire Hall No. 8, both in Inglewood, but wartime conditions soon interrupted the school's operations. In July 1919, one month after the official end of the war, the province bought a this campus from Ezra Riley. On June 22, 1921, provincial Education Minister George P. Smith laid the cornerstone for the Main Building, the largest of three original buildings on the campus. Its hilltop position offered a stunning view of the city and, in return, provided the city with a stunning view of the building. When it opened in 1922, its east wing was dedicated to the "Tech" while the west wing became the new home of the Calgary Normal School, a teacher-training college founded in 1906 and originally housed in a downtown sandstone edifice. Built in Modern Gothic style, the brick, sandstone, and Tyndall stone building evokes a medieval appearance, complete with towers, battlements, and stone carvings.

During World War II, the Royal Canadian Air Force took over the Tech campus as the No. 2 Wireless School, part of the wartime British Commonwealth Air Training Plan. Tech students were displaced to the Stampede grandstand and the Coste House, and Normal School students to King Edward School. By 1946, when the two institutions returned, the campus had been filled in with "temporary" wartime buildings that remained in use for decades. The normal school became part of the University of Alberta's faculty of education in 1946, making it the nucleus of what eventually grew into a southern branch of the provincial university. Renamed the University of Alberta, Calgary in the 1950s, the institution moved to its present campus in 1960 and became the autonomous University of Calgary in 1966. In 1963, the "Tech" was renamed the Southern Alberta Institute of Technology when its northern counterpart opened in Edmonton.

In 1985, the Main Building was designated a Provincial Historic Resource and renamed Heritage Hall. It was rehabilitated as part of a new, larger structure to the north in 2002.

Route: Return to Riley Park, and exit at 12th Street N.W. Proceed south along 12th Street, and cross 5th Avenue N.W. Turn left (east), and proceed east along 5th Avenue.

The International-style Southern Alberta Jubilee Auditorium was built in 1955-57 on a portion of the Tech campus. This performing arts centre was the province's gift to southern Alberta in commemoration of Alberta's golden jubilee in 1955. The building's counterpart in Edmonton was built to an identical design. SHANNON LEE RAE

Riley Park Grocery & Confectionery (Pushing Petals)

Address: 1209–5th Avenue N.W.
Style: Edwardian Commercial
Architect: Unknown
Date: 1908

This two-story, wood frame building dates back almost as far as Hillhurst's annexation to Calgary, and its longtime owner had the delightful name of Theodophilus Thompson. After a period of vacancy during World War I, the building became a neighborhood grocery store, known for years as Riley Park Grocery & Confectionery.

Early in World War II, soldiers from Mewata Armouries trained at nearby Hillhurst Athletic Park (now the site of the Hillhurst-Sunnyside Community Association). Military police prevented the soldiers from leaving the grounds, so they gave schoolchildren tips to buy them candy, cigarettes, and pop from Riley Park

Grocery. Bob Walker, who later became Calgary's fire chief, was one of those kids. "They gave us the money in advance, and we provided change," Bob remembers. "The soldiers didn't pay us, they paid us tips after giving change. I was making more money than my dad was."[4] The storefront now houses a flower shop, Pushing Petals.

This former grocery store dates back to Hillhurst's early days as part of the city. Riley Park Grocery was one of many corner stores in the district. SHANNON LEE RAE

Route: Continue east along 5th Street to 11th Street N.W.
(originally Beverley Street). Cross 11th Street, turn right
(south), and proceed south to Gladstone Road. Turn left
(east), and proceed east along Gladstone Road.

Hillhurst Baptist Church (Lifesport)
Address: 1110 Gladstone Road N.W.
Style: Simplified Gothic Revival
Architect: Unknown
Date: 1908 (enlarged 1914, 1957)

*This frame building has long outlived its original occupant, Hillhurst Baptist
Church.* SHANNON LEE RAE

Originally known as Morleyville Road Baptist Church, this church
was constructed shortly after Hillhurst's annexation to the city. The
small building was often overcrowded, so it was ventilated to relieve
discomfort. But the proximity of a nearby manhole sometimes
brought unwelcome odors through the ventilation system. To cover
the ventilating shaft when needed, the church caretaker set up a
pulley that could raise or lower a sheet of cardboard that blocked
the intake. When it was closed, the cardboard advertised to all
assembled: "Quaker Oats is a choice breakfast food."[5]

Declining membership led the congregation to disband in 1972, and the building later housed Factory Theatre, a Tae Kwan-Do school, a craft gallery, food store, and, since 2001, a cycling and cross country ski shop.

Route: Continue east along Gladstone Road, and cross 10th Street N.W. Turn right, and continue south along 10th Street.

Lido Café

144–10th Avenue N.W.
Style: Edwardian Commercial
Architect: Unknown
Date: 1912

This space has satisfied Sunnysiders' appetites since its days as Minnie Hewitt's fish and chips shop in 1935, and through its later incarnations as May's Fish & Chips (1941–44), Harry's Coffee Shop (1946–50), Lucas Coffee Shop (1951–52), Mac's Coffee Shop (1953), and Roy's Coffee Shop (1954–61). It became the Lido around 1962, when Henry Fong, Len Hong, and Ken Lee took over. With its round stools, booths with wall-mounted juke boxes, and Chinese and Western cuisine, the Lido has remained an island of period charm amid the gentrification that has gone on around it. It is typical for a commercial building of its era, distinguished only by its period neon sign. This single-story brick edifice was originally called the Union Building, and its original tenants included Bernard Kurland's confectionery and Albert E. Sharman's harness shop. From 1936–46, one storefront housed the Green Lantern Library and Gift Shop, one of a handful of privately owned circulating libraries in the city. The Wall Street Art Gallery now occupies the second storefront.

Route: Continue south along 10th Street N.W.

The Lido Café's neon sign has been a 10th Street landmark since the 1960s. SHANNON
LEE RAE

Carscallen Block (Kismet Clothing/Quinn's Of Kensington Hair)

Address: 116–10th Street N.W.
Style: Edwardian Commercial
Architect: Unknown
Date: 1911

Its highly visible location, at the T-intersection of Kensington Road and 10th Street, has made the Carscallen Block a local landmark. KIRSTEN OLSON

Brothers Shibley G. and Phillip H. Carscallen moved to Calgary from Smith Falls, Ontario, and built this two-story commercial/residential building in 1911. It housed the brothers' Carscallen Realty & Building Company, as well as Carscallen Hardware & Heating, which their brother Harry owned. For nearly a decade (1911–20), it housed Black's Drug Store, which operated for more than seventy years and went on to become the city's longest surviving business north of the Bow River. Many older Calgarians recall Black's, with its soda fountain, ice cream counter, and glass candy jars, but their memories are of Black's other location a few doors south at 106a–10th Street N.W., where it operated from 1920–82.

As an alderman from 1912–14, Shibley Carscallen (circa 1880–1944) chaired City Council's finance committee. He sold the building in 1927 and moved to Okotoks. The building's original appearance was lost in a 1966 renovation, but it was restored in 2001.

Route: Continue south along 10th Street N.W.

Irwin Block (Hot Wax Records/Grass Roots/Oo Long Tea House)

Address: 110–10th Street N.W.
Style: Edwardian Commercial
Architect: Unknown
Date: 1911

The Irwin Block's original appearance was lost in a 1966 makeover but was restored in 2001. Kirsten Olson

A fading painted sign on the south face of this two-story brick building, peeking out over its neighbors, recalls the Irwin Block's best-remembered commercial tenant: the Uneeda Bakery, which Reginald W. Long operated here between 1914 and 1939. Long sold the bakery in the early 1920s but bought it back a few years later. The good-hearted baker gave loaves away to families in need, but Long's generosity left him unable to pay his bills and drove him from business.

Other longtime tenants included Martin's Jewellery (1931–67), the Brown Derby Meat Market (1934–60), and the Star Confectionery (1952–74). The building is named for contractor John R. Irwin, its builder and original owner. It was city property from 1924–41, likely because of tax default. Hot Wax Records, a second-hand music shop, has been a landmark tenant since 1978.

Route: Continue south along 10th Avenue to Memorial Drive N.W. Turn left (east), and proceed east along Memorial to 9A Street N.W.

Brower House (DSA Baron Communications)

Address: 1052 Memorial Drive N.W.
Style: American Foursquare
Architect: Unknown
Date: 1908

The yellow brick Brower House remains a vintage landmark on Memorial Drive. It is one of Sunnyside's oldest remaining buildings. KIRSTEN OLSON

Luckily for posterity, this delightful two-story yellow brick house—one of the oldest in the district—was spared from demolition when the LRT was constructed nearby in the mid-1980s. Carpenter James Tennant was its original owner, but he lived here only a year before renting to a series of tenants. In 1919, it became the longtime home of Iowa-born Archibald Brock Brower (1876–1952), his wife Sarah, and their children. Archibald worked as a steam engineer for the Allis-Chalmers Company until 1925, when he began a two-year stint as a steam engineering instructor at the Tech. After Archibald's death in the house in 1952, it remained the home of his daughter, Eva Davidson, for decades. From 1949–65, Archibald's brother Frank C. Brower (1878–1965) also lived in the house. Frank published the *Olds Gazette* at Olds, Alberta, from 1909–36; of his retirement from the newspaper business, Frank wrote, "I decided I had butted into other people's business long enough".[6] The house was eventually converted into offices; it has housed a media buying company, DSA Baron Communications, since 2002.

Route: Turn left (north) on 9A Street N.W. (originally Merchiston Avenue), and proceed north to 2nd Avenue N.W. Turn right (east), and cross 9A Street. Continue east along 2nd Avenue N.W. to the Vendome Block.

Vendome Block

Address: 938–2nd Avenue N.W.
Style: Edwardian Commercial
Architect: Unknown
Date: 1912

Contractor George W. Rae (1869–1923) built and originally owned this typical two-story brick building with an atypical name. Why Rae chose this French name—which belongs to a town in northern France and to the Place de la Vendome district in Paris—remains a mystery.

For about seventy-five years before the Vendome Block's corner storefront became the Heartland Café in 1988, the space housed the North Star Grocery. Corner stores were everywhere in their heyday, and Morris Austin, who owned the business from the 1940s to the 1970s, distinguished the North Star from its competitors by specializing in fruit by the crate. Though widowed young and handicapped from being hit by a truck, Austin ran a successful business and raised three children in their home behind the store. Son Jack Austin later attended Harvard and was called to the Senate in 1975. He became the federal cabinet minister for British Columbia (1981–84) and in 2003 was named government leader in the upper house. Another notable personality who grew up in the building was Sid Finney, who played professional hockey for the Chicago Black Hawks in the 1950s.

Chicago Black Hawk Sid Finney and Senator Jack Austin grew up in the Vendome Block, long before it became the Heartland Café. KIRSTEN OLSON

The second storefront, which variously housed a meat market, candy store, and shoe repair shop, was converted into apartments before it was later returned to commercial use. It became Child at Heart, a children's clothing store, in 1999.

Route: Cross 2nd Avenue N.W., and proceed south along 9th Street to Memorial Drive. Turn left (east), and continue east on Memorial to Glenwood Manor.

Glenwood Manor

Address: 904–908 Memorial Drive N.W.
Style: Eclectic, with reference to then-popular Spanish Revival
Architect: Andrew Murdoch
Date: 1928

Glenwood Manor has the appearance of being two separate apartment blocks, each with its own entrance. The pressed-metal roof suggests clay tiles, a reference to Spanish Revival style. SHANNON LEE RAE

This luxury three-story brick apartment block was constructed during a brief building boom in the city that ended with the onset of the Great Depression. Andrew Murdoch designed and built Glenwood Manor, and he owned it until 1948. Murdoch had worked for the Canadian Pacific Railway's Engineering Department in Vancouver before moving to Calgary to work for the Dominion government's survey department. In a feature page on the building, the *Calgary Albertan* praised its location "in a quiet and beautiful residential district far enough removed from the bustle and clang of street cars and throngs to be peaceful."[7] The reporter lauded each of its twelve suites as "the equivalent of a modern bungalow, having a private garage, back veranda, halls and a southern front view of the river and city."[8] The building had a freight elevator, an unusual feature in an apartment block, and was designed to include a basement billiard room with a fireplace. Besides Murdoch, two of the building's most notable tenants have been Samuel C. Nickle, Sr. (1889–1971) and Pansy L. Pugh (circa 1889–1980). Sam Nickle and his wife Olga lived here from 1938–41, just as he began building a fortune in the oil industry. The Nickles later donated $1-million to the University of Calgary to establish the Nickle Arts Museum. Pugh lived in Glenwood Manor from 1968–75, long after her election in 1929 as one of Calgary's first female alderman. Glenwood Manor became a co-op in the early 1980s and was designated a Provincial Historic Resource in 1997.

Route: Cross 8th Street N.W., and continue east along Memorial Drive.

Donegal Mansions

Address: 830 Memorial Drive N.W.
Style: Italianate, with reference to then-popular Spanish Revival
Architect: Andrew Murdoch (presumed)
Date: 1930

Two years after he built nearby Glenwood Manor, Andrew Murdoch erected another luxury brick apartment block, the four-story Donegal Mansions. Its completion coincided with the Great Depression. The building's most notable tenant, from 1946–61, was former Alberta premier John E. Brownlee (1883–1961). Long after scandal drove him from office in 1934 (he was convicted of seducing a young government employee), Brownlee served as president and general manager of the United Grain Growers during the time he lived in this stately apartment building with his wife Florence.

The Brownlees enjoyed walking along the banks of the Bow, and, when the city proposed cutting down the trees to widen Memorial Drive, the former premier reportedly put in one call to the mayor and had the project stopped.

Donegal Mansions was damaged by fire in 1991 and repaired. It became a Provincial Historic Resource in 1997.

Stone quoins at the corners, and a stone central arch, accent the appearance of Donegal Mansions. As with nearby Glenwood Manor, the pressed-metal roof gives the appearance of clay tiles, a dominant feature of Spanish style. SHANNON LEE RAE

Route: Continue east on Memorial Drive to 4th Street N.W. Cross 4th Street.

Smalley Residence

Address: 440 Memorial Drive N.W.
Style: Spanish/Mission Eclectic, with Craftsman influence
Architect: Unknown
Date: 1908

With its rough-cast stucco finish, bell-shaped roof, and round-headed windows, James Smalley's house reflects Craftsman influences and might have reflected his British tastes. The Spanish/Mission-style bell tower is the dominant feature and reflects a separate, Spanish influence. SHANNON LEE RAE

This landmark two-story home originally belonged to English-born businessman James Smalley (1876–1949), who, with his brother Thomas (circa 1882–1971), built many Sunnyside homes through their Calgary Home Building Company. A photograph of this house illustrated James Smalley's feature page in a 1911 booster publication titled *Calgary, Sunny Alberta: The Industrial Prodigy of the Great West.* Smalley likely intended this house to serve as a model to fuel the imagination of potential Sunnyside homebuyers. James lived in this house during his tenure on City Council in 1909–10, and it remained his home until 1923. That year, he quit the real estate business and opened a radio shop. The house was converted into a duplex in 1937 in the midst of a housing shortage in the city but has since returned to single-family occupancy. It remains a tangible link to the district's origins.

Route: Continue east on Memorial Drive to the next house.

"Cappy" Smart House

Address: 436 Memorial Drive N.W.
Style: Craftsman
Architect: Pattern book design
Date: 1914 (addition 1991)

This two-story, shingled Craftsman home features a full-width veranda and central dormer. CPR accountant John A. McBurney was its original occupant. A caveat on the original land title prohibits the property from use "for the sale of intoxicating liquors, or as a house of ill fame." SHANNON LEE RAE

James Smart (1865–1939) was born in Arbroath, Scotland, the son of a ship captain who was lost at sea. The son's nickname, "Cappy," was a tribute to his father and not the legacy of his one-time rank as hose captain in Calgary's fire department. Smart emigrated as a young man and made his way to Winnipeg to work for his uncle, mortician Thomas Swan. The two came to Calgary in 1883, where Smart became an undertaker in his own right. He joined the volunteer fire brigade on its formation in 1885, became its chief in 1898, and held the post until he retired in 1933. Smart loved firefighting and led his men from the front, which for him meant repeated injuries and lung damage from smoke inhalation. He oversaw the modernization and professionalization of his department and also cultivated a profile that made him one of Calgary's most memorable characters. Each year from 1904–39, "Cappy" led the Stampede parade as its marshal.[9] He kept two boxing bears at Fire Headquarters and enjoyed boxing with them for demonstration—until one killed a child in 1911 and both bears had to be destroyed.

"Cappy" and his wife Agnes moved into this house in 1926, and he had a fire alarm bell installed to alert him to any emergency. It remained in place after "Cappy" retired in 1933—to keep him abreast of the department's work—but was switched off every night to let the Smarts sleep. On his retirement, he reportedly planned to build an extension to his home as a museum for the thousands of relics he had collected. There is no evidence he did so. Later owners Maggie and Patrick Hawes built a rear addition in 1991, twenty years after Smart's collection had been donated to the Glenbow Museum.

Tour ends.

Notes

1 "Hillhurst, the Residential Suburb of Calgary City," *Morning Albertan* 16 Nov. 1907: 9, 10.

2 This southern portion of Crescent Heights, now part of Sunnyside, came within the city limits in 1907. That portion of Crescent Heights north of 8th Avenue, atop the North Hill, lay outside Calgary until 1910 and developed separately as the village of Crescent Heights.

3 "Miss Cushing's Death," *Daily Herald* 1 Dec. 1906: 1.

4 Bob Walker, telephone interview, 26 Jan. 2004.

5 Susan McTaggart and Helen Armstrong, "The Story of Hillhurst Baptist Church, Calgary" (Calgary: Hillhurst Baptist Church, 1957) 3. Glenbow Archives, Hillhurst Baptist Church fonds, f. 29.

6 Olds History Committee, *A History of Olds and Area* (Olds, Alta.: Olds History Committee, 1980) 59.

7 "Glenwood Manor, Calgary's Newest Apartment Bldg.," *Calgary Albertan* 18 May 1928: 9.

8 *Ibid.*

9 The parade was part of the Calgary Exhibition until 1923, when the Stampede became a permanent component of the annual fair. Previously, the Stampede had been held in 1912 and 1919, but not as part of the Exhibition.

Tour Ends

18 Ave N

1 St. N.W.

10 Ave. N.E.

4 St. N.W.

Memorial Dr. N.W.

Prince's Island Park

2nd Ave. S.W.

Bridgeland-Riverside, Renfrew, and Crescent Heights

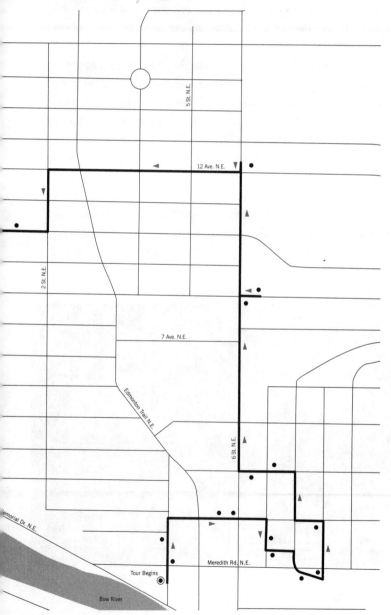

As with all of the city north of the Bow River, the districts covered in this tour originally lay outside Calgary's corporate boundaries. Two massive annexations in 1907 and 1910 brought a wide swath of territory into the city limits, including the North Hill and the river flats below it.

Beginning in the early 1880s, the trail from Calgary to Edmonton—and the mail and stagecoach service along it—passed through what is now Bridgeland-Riverside. To northbound travelers, this was the Edmonton Trail; in the reverse direction, it became the Calgary Trail. Travelers crossed the Bow River by ford or ferry until the completion of the original wood truss Langevin Bridge in 1890. It was named for Sir Hector-Louis Langevin (1826–1906), a Conservative politician, one of the Fathers of Confederation, and minister of public works from 1879–91. The bridge provided convenient access for settlers who chose to live on unserviced lots across the river from Calgary, and to the brothels that were built along Nose Creek, near present-day Deerfoot Trail. The present steel bridge replaced the wooden one in 1910.

The steel truss Langevin Bridge replaced its original wooden counterpart in 1910.
SHANNON LEE RAE

Bridgeland-Riverside, Renfrew, and Crescent Heights

The 1907 annexation extended Calgary's northern boundary to 8th Avenue north, but left out the river flats south of what is now Centre Avenue N.E. (originally called Northcote Avenue) and east of Edmonton Trail. The massive 1910 annexation included the river flats and established distant city limits that remained more or less unaltered until the 1950s.

Two distinct ethnic districts developed north of the Langevin Bridge and east of Edmonton Trail. Riverside, which occupied the river flats annexed in 1910, was largely settled by ethnic Germans from Russia and became known as "Germantown." North of Centre Avenue, in the area annexed in 1907, Italian immigrants formed the dominant character of Bridgeland. Other immigrant groups, including Jews and Ukrainians, also settled in these areas in smaller numbers. A new Calgary General Hospital opened in Riverside in 1910, and the following year streetcar service began along 4th Street N.E. (Edmonton Trail) and 1st Avenue N.E. (originally called Louisa Avenue). Both districts developed as working-class neighborhoods filled with small shops, churches, and single-family houses, with easy access to industrial employers in the district and across the river in east Calgary. That working-class character remains, although proximity to downtown and a massive redevelopment project on the former hospital site (following its 1998 demolition) have contributed to gentrification. One notable element of the district is Tom Campbell's Hill, an undeveloped feature east of 12th Street N.E., opposite the Bow River from the Calgary Zoo on St. George's Island. A massive billboard advertising Tom Campbell's downtown hat shop graced the brow of the hill for years and provided its lasting name. From 1965–85, the zoo grazed its hoofed mammals on Tom Campbell's Hill.

The 1907 annexation also excluded the nascent community of Crescent Heights, west of Edmonton Trail. One of its promoters was Ontario-born businessman Archibald John McArthur (1857–1911), who had acquired a large block of land between the Bow River and the section road to the north (16th Avenue) and registered it as the subdivision of Crescent Heights. He built his home and real estate office in the new subdivision. To attract buyers who might otherwise gravitate toward existing bridges to the east and west, McArthur put together the Bow River Bridge Company, which in 1907 constructed the original Centre Street Bridge. When Calgary's expanded boundaries left out the subdivision, residents organized the short-lived Village of Crescent Heights. (Those same residents helped elect McArthur to the provincial legislature as a Liberal in 1910, but he died in office less than a year later.) The village limits extended beyond McArthur's subdivision, including not only the modern Crescent Heights district but also parts of Mount Pleasant, Tuxedo Park, Winston Heights, and Renfrew. The village of Crescent Heights had its own governing council and school board, collected local taxes, and had a volunteer fire brigade and a village constable. But its residents soon petitioned for annexation to booming Calgary, which absorbed Crescent Heights in 1910 and extended streetcar service the following year. The city bought the private Centre Street Bridge in 1912 and replaced it with the present structure in 1916. Crescent Heights remains a middle class inner city neighborhood, bisected by the Centre Street commercial district and bounded to the north by the Trans-Canada Highway.

East of Crescent Heights, and north of Bridgeland-Riverside, lies the Renfrew district. Its southern portion at the brow of the North Hill developed early as an extension of Bridgeland. The area north of Stanley Jones School—which was originally named Bridgeland School—lay undeveloped until 1929, when it became the site of the Calgary Municipal Airport. It was replaced a decade later by a superior facility that was eventually renamed the Calgary International Airport—McCall Field. (The present terminal, located north of McCall Field, opened in 1978.) After World War II, the old Calgary Municipal Airport's grass-covered runways were replaced by post-war housing, and the Renfrew district was born.

Start: The tour begins at the Armour Block and Reliance Block, two adjoining structures at 15–4th Street N.E. and 27–4th Street N.E.

Reliance Block

Address: 27–4th Street N.E.
Style: Edwardian Commercial
Architect: Burroughs and Richards (1911 addition)
Date: 1910 (third floor addition 1911)

Placement of the title block and cornice line reveal the Reliance Block's original design as a two-story building. SHANNON LEE RAE

Armour Block

Address: 15–4th Street N.E.
Style: Edwardian Commercial
Architects: Burroughs and Richards
Date: 1912

Streetcar service in Bridgeland-Riverside was still a year away when merchants Thomas A. Wiggins and James Lough built the two-story Reliance Block, one of the oldest remaining buildings in the Edmonton Trail commercial district. Its three storefronts originally housed Riverside Hardware, the Reliance Meat Market, and Wiggins & Co., Groceries, Flour & Feed. Wiggins and Lough added a third story in 1911, and the following year they constructed the adjoining Armour Block to the south, forming a block-long, three-story brick complex that housed offices, apartments, a billiard hall, and a Dominion Bank branch. The owners borrowed $40,000 from the city in 1912 to finance the project, and, a decade later, unable to recoup the loan, the city took possession of both buildings. Wiggins' name remained associated with the site in the form of Wiggins' Hall, a social facility in Armour Block's basement. Part of the district's lore is that this space was once a speakeasy. The city's ownership overlapped the Great Depression, when many of the complex's tenants were on relief. The city sold the buildings in 1939 but re-acquired them in the 1980s for possible future widening of Memorial Drive. Since the mid-1970s, an artists' collective has provided apartments and studio space upstairs.

The clerestory windows over the Armour Block's storefronts and main entrance have been covered over. Original architectural drawings show the building's name in the large window over the main entrance. SHANNON LEE RAE

A fading painted sign on the north side of the Reliance Block announces the Riverside Department Store, a longtime business that occupied the main floor from 1950–74. Since then, the space has housed Bud's Used Office Furniture, whose vast inventory includes a special collection that is not for sale at any price. These items are rented to movie studios and have been used in numerous films shot on location in Alberta—including *Superman III, Unforgiven, Honey I Shrunk the Kids, Shanghai Noon, Mystery, Alaska,* and *How The West Was Fun.*

Route: Proceed north along 4th Street N.E. to Meredith
    Road. Cross both roads.

Poffenroth Block (De Waal Apartments)
Address: 608 Meredith Road N.E.
Style: Edwardian Commercial
Architect: Unknown
Date: 1910

Sandstone quoins frame the angled corner of the De Waal Apartments. The store-fronts are typical of Edwardian Commercial style, with recessed entrances and large clerestory windows that allowed maximum natural light to enter. SHANNON LEE RAE

Russian-born dairyman Henry Poffenroth (1884–1960), who operated a dairy farm in what is now the Connaught district, built this two-story brick apartment block and retail complex just before the arrival of the streetcar. He reportedly traded it for a ranch in 1914 and by 1920 the building was in the hands of the Canada Life

Assurance Company. Tenant Theodore de Waal (1887–1981) was hired as manager and caretaker, and within a decade he had saved enough money to buy the building. As Dutch immigrants, Theodore and Mary de Waal reflected the ethnic/immigrant character of the district, and residential tenants included German, Italian, Hungarian, Polish, and Ukrainian immigrants. The de Waals took in Dutch immigrant boarders in their own living quarters in the building along Meredith Road. Notable storefront occupants have included a glass works, a cigar factory, the Bridgeland & Riverside Community Club, the Netherlands Canada Society, and the family-owned de Waal Music Studio, established by Theodore's grandson John de Waal in 1979. John's father (also named Theodore) played big band drums with local acts like Louis Trono in the 1940s. John has become a renowned jazz drummer and has performed with the likes of Rosemary Clooney, the Guy Lombardo Orchestra, and Tommy Banks. John and his wife Mari Jo restored the De Waal Apartments in 2001, retaining the heritage character of the block and each of its upstairs suites. Il Sogno, an Italian restaurant, has been the anchor tenant since 2001.

Route: Return west across 4th Street N.E., and proceed north to Marsh Road (an avenue originally known as Berlin).

Immanuel Lutheran Church (Riverside Christian Fellowship)

Address: 43–4th Street N.E.
Style: Gothic vernacular
Architect: Unknown
Date: 1902

Immanuel Lutheran, one of the city's first Lutheran congregations, was organized in 1901 and built this frame church the following year. By 1913, the congregation had established a school for 175 local students in the church, but the city's medical officer of health ordered it closed, insisting that the students attend public schools. Members clashed over whether to use hymnals rooted in their Volga German origins or in the High German American variation. The congregation split evenly, and the Volga traditionalists started building a new church a few blocks to the north. The project was never completed, and a Catholic church, Our Lady of Perpetual Help (610–2nd Avenue N.E.), now stands on the foundation. The splinter group eventually built nearby Jehovah Lutheran Church (70–6A Street N.E.) around 1920. Immanuel Lutheran disbanded in 1948 and its members joined other congregations. A final dispute, over the proceeds from the sale of the church, reached the Supreme Court of Alberta before it was finally resolved.

The former Immanuel Church's pointed windows are a Gothic influence. The octagonal spire remains, but the original bell tower—a separate structure south of the church—was removed at an unknown date. SHANNON LEE RAE

Rev. John William Lucas (1882–1979), a retired prize-winning Cayley farmer once known as the "Oat King," later entered the ministry and bought the church in 1948. He operated it as the evangelical, trans-denominational Immanuel Church and also ran the Booster Club for area children. Dr. Lucas stuccoed the church and expanded the living quarters on the south side of the building. His son, Dr. John Watson Lucas, eventually succeeded him as Immanuel's pastor, and he moved the congregation to 17th Avenue S.W. in 1969. The congregation later operated this building as Elim House, a halfway house for recovering addicts. Since 1982, it has housed another evangelical group, Riverside Christian Fellowship.

Route: Cross both 4th Street and Marsh Road N.E. Proceed north on 4th Street and cross 1st Avenue N.E. (originally Louisa Avenue). Turn right (east) and proceed east on 1st Avenue. Cross Edmonton Trail and continue east on 1st Avenue.

Morasch Block (Sandlewood Developments' Pontefino Marketing Centre)

Address: 644–1st Avenue N.E.
Style: Edwardian Commercial
Architect: Unknown
Date: 1911

In 1911, a new streetcar route transformed 1st Avenue N.E. into a commercial strip and prompted carpenter Peter Morasch (circa 1861–1947) to build this two-story brick commercial/residential building. More than ninety years later, the Morasch Block became part of another phenomenon that transformed the district—as a sales office for Pontefino, a residential phase of The Bridges, a new "urban village" developed a few blocks away on the former site of the Calgary General Hospital.

Nothing identifies the building as the Morasch Block, which became city property around 1920, presumably for non-payment of taxes. Notable occupants have included Adam Kaiser's Lagora Cigar Factory (in the 1930s), the Beehive Confectionery (1923–65), and the Italia Rinascente grocery store (circa 1972–86).

Unlike many remaining examples of its type, the Morasch Block has no title identifying the building's name. Its façade is unadorned apart from the signband cornice and upper cornice. SHANNON LEE RAE

Route: Continue east along 1st Avenue N.E.

St. Stephen's Ukrainian Catholic Church (Calgary Buddhist Temple)

Address: 207–6th Street N.E.
Style: Gothic Revival
Architect: Unknown
Date: 1912

St. Stephen's Ukrainian Catholic Church was originally built at 23rd Avenue and 1st Street N.E. in Tuxedo Park, where it doubled as a Roman Catholic church until the completion of St. Joseph's in 1915. Discrimination against Ukrainian-Canadians during World War I—many had come from the Austro-Hungarian Empire—led to the closure of St. Stephen's for almost two years. Renewed post-war immigration created a concentrated Ukrainian community in Riverside and what later became East Village, and, in 1926, the church was moved to its present location. Calgary's Roman Catholic Bishop, Most Rev. John T. Kidd, had befriended the city's Ukrainian Catholics and offered financial support for the move. The church was renovated in 1939, badly damaged by fire in 1942, and repaired.

The original twin bell towers, typical of Byzantine churches on the prairie, have been removed since this photograph was taken in 1958. GLENBOW ARCHIVES NA-2864-836

A new wave of immigration after World War II led to the construction of a new Ukrainian Catholic church, the landmark Assumption of the Blessed Virgin Mary (704–6th Street N.E., visible from the brow of the hill to the north). The old building was sold in 1958 and became a Roman Catholic church, Our Lady Queen of Poland. When the Polish congregation moved in 1968, this building became a Croatian church, Our Lady Queen of Mercy. By 1981, it proved too small for the Croatian church, and that year it began a new manifestation as the Calgary Buddhist Temple.

Route: Cross 6th Street N.E., and proceed east on 1st Avenue to 6A Street N.E. (originally Dresden). Cross both roads and proceed south on 6A Street.

Fire Hall No. 4 (Private residence)

Address: 104–6A Street N.E.
Architect: City Engineer
Style: Modern Classical
Date: 1910

Fire Hall No. 4 was built as a satellite sub-station, without a hose tower. SHANNON LEE RAE

Like its surviving contemporary in Hillhurst, Fire Hall No. 6, this was a satellite sub-station built to serve an outlying suburb in a rapidly expanding city. These two stations, along with No. 5 in Scarboro, doubled the number of fire halls in Calgary. Budget cutbacks led to the closure of No. 4 in 1922, and for the next thirty years the nearby Calgary General Hospital doubled as the local fire station. With financial help from the Rotary Club, this building operated as the Riverside YMCA from the 1920s to the 1940s. It proved a blessing during the Great Depression, when many area families were on relief.

The building again served as Fire Hall No. 4 from 1952–78, and it was here that firefighters mended toys as part of the department's annual Christmas toy campaign for needy children. The Unitarian Service Committee rented the building in the late 1970s and early 1980s, and it was later converted into a residence and photograph studio. Fire Hall No. 4 became a Municipal Historic Resource in 1999 and a Provincial Historic Resource in 2002.

Route: Continue south to the corner, and cross Centre Avenue (originally Northcote).

Jehovah Lutheran Church (Private residence)
Address: 70–6A Street N.E.
Style: Gothic Revival
Architect: Unknown
Date: 1920

Built as a Lutheran church, this building later housed Moravian and United Korean congregations before its conversion into a private residence. SHANNON LEE RAE

When the congregation of nearby Immanuel Lutheran Church split over which hymnal to use, ex-members started building a new church on the present site of Our Lady of Perpetual Help but soon abandoned the project. Around 1920, they built Jehovah Lutheran, a wood-frame building that served the congregation until 1945. While its membership grew, that of the nearby Moravian Church declined, and, in April 1945, the two groups exchanged properties. This building served the Moravian Church until 1978, when the congregation (renamed Good Shepherd Community Church) moved to a new building in North Haven. The United Korean Church bought this edifice in 1978, but it was sold around 2004 and converted into a single detached dwelling.

Route: Proceed east on Centre Avenue N.E., and cross 7th Street N.E. (originally Munich). Turn right (south), and proceed south on 7th Street.

Moravian Church (St. Matthew's Lutheran Church)

Address: 60–7th Street N.E.
Style: Gothic Revival
Architect: George Lenschner
Date: 1913

In 1902, the year Lutheran settlers in "Germantown" built Immanuel Lutheran Church, their Moravian counterparts built their own sanctuary, located south of the Bow River in what is now East Village. A decade later the Moravian congregation built a much larger brick edifice just west of the Calgary General Hospital and held the first service in the new church on September 28, 1913. Anti-German sentiments during both world wars, combined with a decline in immigration, created problems for the church and made it an inviting target for vandals. A fire that broke out just days before Christmas 1944 left the sanctuary unusable. The declining Moravian congregation could not afford the upkeep; meanwhile, the nearby Jehovah Lutheran Church was growing beyond the capacity of its small wooden building (70–6A Street N.E.). The two groups swapped properties in April 1945.

This highly visible church was designed for a Moravian congregation but has been a Lutheran church since 1945. SHANNON LEE RAE

From 1945–60, this building was known as Jehovah Lutheran Church, but, to avoid confusion with the Jehovah's Witnesses, the congregation changed its name to St. Matthew's in 1960. The installation of Carillonic bells in 1956, and of a donated neon cross atop the spire in 1958, gave the church a nickname: "The church with the bells and lighted cross." The neon cross provided comfort at night to hospital patients whose rooms faced west. St. Matthew's is a Registered Historic Resource.

Route: Turn left (east) onto the narrow asphalt path south of the church, and walk east. At the end of the path, enter the cul-de-sac at the south end of 7A Street N.E. (not marked). To the east lies the site of the former Calgary General Hospital, which was demolished in 1998. Construction of The Bridges, a mixed-use "urban village" on the hospital's former location, began in 2004.

This 1912 photograph of Mrs. Clif Andrew with a horse and buggy shows the 1910 Calgary General Hospital in the background. The original building was later demolished for hospital expansion. When the Calgary General Hospital opened its new Peter Lougheed Centre in the northeast Sunridge district in 1988, the original complex was renamed the Bow Valley Centre. Closed in 1997, the hospital was imploded in 1998 and redeveloped as The Bridges beginning in 2004. GLENBOW ARCHIVES NA-1341-5

Proceed north along 7A Street, cross to the west side, and continue west along 1st Avenue N.E.

Cannibale Block (Merlo Vinoteca)
Address: 813–1st Avenue N.E.
Style: Edwardian Commercial
Architect: Unknown
Date: 1912

The Cannibale Block's name still appears in the title block below the cornice.
KIRSTEN OLSON

This building's curious name—which translates from Italian as "cannibal"—might be a modified spoonerism of Anniable Corradetti (circa 1868–1952), the Italian-born carpenter who built the two-story, wood frame edifice and remained its owner until his death. Corradetti arrived in Calgary around 1904 and worked for the city for thirty-five years. Perhaps the most notable residential tenant was another Italian immigrant, machinist Antonio Rebaudengo (1892–1980), who briefly lived here with his family around 1931. Rebaudengo became an Italian consular agent in the mid-1930s, and, with his wife Angelina's assistance, he helped many fellow Italians settle in the city. Canada and Italy fought on opposite sides during World War II; while the Rebaudengos' son Mario was drafted into the Canadian army, Antonio was classified an "enemy alien" and spent three years in internment camps. His wartime diary has been placed in the Glenbow Archives.

Proximity to the Calgary General Hospital made the Cannibale Block a good location for a series of flower shops. It now houses a wine shop, Merlo Vinoteca.

Route: Proceed west on 1st Avenue, and cross 7th Street N.E. Turn right (north), cross 1st Avenue, and proceed north on 7th Street to 2nd Avenue N.E. Cross 2nd Avenue, turn left (west), and proceed west to 6A Street N.E.

Gerlitz Block

Address: 728–2nd Avenue N.E.
Style: Edwardian Commercial
Architect: Unknown
Date: 1911

Owner Emma Greenstreet restored the aging Gerlitz Block as a private residence in 2000. SHANNON LEE RAE

Like so many of Bridgeland's early residents, Johannes and Maria Gerlitz were Germans from Russia who settled in Calgary at the beginning of the twentieth century. Johannes bought the corner property in 1911 and built this two-story brick building as both a home and revenue property. The Gerlitzes raised their seven children upstairs and kept a vegetable garden, a Jersey milk cow, and a menagerie of chickens, dogs, and cats on the grounds. Perhaps appropriately, one of the ground-floor retail tenants, Dave Greenfield, called his business the Farmer's Grocery. The second storefront was a butcher shop.

The growing Gerlitz family moved out in the mid-1920s, and, by the 1940s, the Hergert Block (as it was renamed) had become apartments. British immigrant Emma Greenstreet (niece of actor Sydney Greenstreet) bought the decaying building in 2000 and transformed it into a private residence. She brought back the building's original character, stripping exterior paint, exposing the original tin ceiling on the ground floor, and installing windows to illumine the basement.

Route: Cross both 2nd Avenue and 6A Street N.E., and continue west on 2nd Avenue.

Riverside Bungalow School No. 2

Address: 711–2nd Avenue N.E.
Style: Bungalow school
Architect: Unknown
Date: 1920

Before World War I, the public school board constructed wooden cottage schools to supplement classroom space, and designed them for easy conversion and sale as residences when no longer needed. After the war, the four-classroom bungalow school became the "temporary" school design of choice, and some like this one were built of brick. As with the cottage schools, the bungalow schools remained in use long after originally intended. To supplement classes at the sandstone Riverside School south of 1st Avenue N.E., the board built two Riverside Bungalow schools: the now-demolished

No. 1, at the south end of this block, in 1914; and the extant No. 2 in 1920. When the sandstone school became Langevin Junior High School in 1934, the two bungalow schools were designated Riverside Elementary. Fire destroyed the sandstone school in 1966, and the present Langevin Elementary and Junior High School was built to replace it, with an overpass over busy 1st Avenue for children to cross safely to their playground. The Calgary Board of Education now uses Riverside Bungalow School No. 2 as an English as a Second Language facility.

Built in 1920, Riverside Bungalow School No. 2 followed a design identical to its contemporary in Cliff Bungalow. SHANNON LEE RAE

Route: Continue west on 2nd Avenue N.E. to 6th Street. Turn right (north), and proceed north on 6th Street to the base of the North Hill. Five concrete steps, followed by 121 wooden steps, lead to the top of the hill and the Renfrew district to the north. The stairway is terraced, so there is plenty of opportunity to rest, and the beautiful domed Ukrainian church above is always in view. At the top of the stairway, continue north on 6th Street to 8th Avenue N.E.

Stanley Jones Grocery & Deli

Address: 701–8th Avenue N.E.
Style: Converted residence
Architect: Unknown
Date: Circa 1912

A period signband, complete with Coca-Cola buttons, distinguishes this long-time corner store. SHANNON LEE RAE

With its Coca-Cola buttons and ice cream bar, this suburban corner store evokes the 1930s and 1940s era that created it. Built around 1912 as a private residence, it had become a multiple-family dwelling by the time Guido Terzi (1889–1977), the captain waiter at the Palliser Hotel, moved in around 1938. Terzi converted the ground floor into the Stanley Jones Grocery & Deli, which he and his family operated while he continued working at the railway hotel for a few more years. The store was named for the Stanley Jones Elementary School across the street, whose students came in for penny candies, bubble gum, and, beginning in the mid-1950s, soft ice cream. Most Italian families still lived in Bridgeland, but many came up the hill to buy Terzi's cold cuts, gouda cheese, and imported

Italian products. The Terzis sold the store in 1966 to German-born Edwin Ergan, a longtime employee of Jenkins' Groceteria. At Ergang's request, the Coca-Cola Company removed the tin lettering that indicated Terzi's proprietorship and replaced it with "E. Ergang, Prop." Ergang and his wife established a solid rapport with their customers, and, after he sold the business in 1987, the new owners kept Ergang's name on the façade.

Route: Cross 8th Avenue N.E.

Stanley Jones Elementary School

Address: 950–6th Street N.E.
Style: Neo-Classical Revival
Architect: William Branton, public school board architect
Date: 1913 (addition 1958)

With its rich classical features, including detailed pilasters (shallow pillars) and relief ornamentation in its pediments, Stanley Jones School is one of the city's most highly decorated school buildings. SHANNON LEE RAE

This sandstone school was originally, and briefly, known as Bridgeland School. World War I broke out only months after it opened, and the conflict claimed the life of its builder, former alderman Richard Brocklebank (1864–1916). Another prominent Calgarian killed on active service in France that year was Stanley Livingstone Jones, a Nova Scotian who taught school in Manitoba and fought in the South African War before settling in Calgary in 1901. Jones practiced law in the city after his call to the bar, and traveled to Europe as a war correspondent for the *Vancouver Sun* during the Balkan Wars in 1912–13. Jones was reportedly one of the first six Canadians to enlist after the war began. The school was named for Jones only months after his death.

Like all schools in the city, Stanley Jones was closed during the Spanish Influenza epidemic of 1918–19. This was one of four schools used as emergency influenza hospitals. Later in 1919, portraits of Sgt. Brocklebank and Major Jones—which still hang in the school's foyer—were unveiled.

Noted alumni have included William McKnight (the World War II ace for whom McKnight Boulevard was named), Mayor Don Mackay, industrialists Ron and Don Southern, and Police Chief Duke Kent. An addition was constructed in 1958. The building also houses Alice Jamieson Girls' Academy, named for the Calgarian who became the first woman in the British Empire appointed as a police court magistrate.

Route: Continue north along 6th Street N.E. to Regal Crescent, and cross.

Rutledge Hangar (Calgary Boys' and Girls' Club)

Address: 731–13th Avenue N.E.
Style: Industrial
Architect: Unknown
Date: 1929

Military pilots made their debut during World War I, and after the conflict many turned to barnstorming and to commercial air service.

Bridgeland-Riverside, Renfrew, and Crescent Heights

Commercial operators used Calgary's original "flying field" in Bowness from 1919–23 and again, briefly, in 1928. But its unpaved strip proved too rough, and, in 1928, the city acquired land in what is now the Renfrew district to develop the Calgary Municipal Airport. The new airport opened in September 1929, and, two months, later its most substantial building, the hangar constructed for Rutledge Air Services, was finished. It included living quarters for the airport manager. Proximity to Stanley Jones School gave the airport its colloquial name: the Stanley Jones Airport. It was the first such facility in Canada equipped with sufficient lighting for nighttime flights.

This 1930s photograph taken by William Oliver depict an air show over the Rutledge Hangar, later renamed the City Hangar. The building now houses the Renfrew Boys and Girls' Club. GLENBOW ARCHIVES NA-3691-32

Lieutenant Wilfred L. (Bill) Rutledge, the World War I pilot who founded Rutledge Air Services, offered a charter air service and flying school from this building, and leased hangar space to other local carriers. In affiliation with Commercial Airways of Calgary, Rutledge launched scheduled flights between Edmonton, Calgary, and Lethbridge. But the era of air travel had not yet arrived. Scheduled flights remained unreliable, and the Great Depression resulted in airline bankruptcies and the cancellation of prairie airmail service. Rutledge Air Services ceased operations and sold its assets after its financiers, Calgarians Isaac Solloway and Harvey Mills, were convicted of illegal business practices and sentenced to jail terms. The hangar was seized by sheriff's order for arrears, and it became property of the Edmonton Credit Corporation. Since the airport could not function without its main hangar, the city rented and operated it as the City Hangar. This proved a curious arrangement: the city owned the land but had to rent the building from its Edmonton-based owners.

The creation of Trans-Canada Airlines (now Air Canada) in 1937 put Calgary on the national map, but spelled the end of the municipal airport. The new national carrier would not use the facility with its short, grass-covered runways, so, in 1938–39, a new Calgary Municipal Airport (later renamed Calgary International Airport—McCall Field) was developed to the north. The old airport served briefly as the Calgary Aero Club. During World War II, it became a federal government training centre, and after the war it was used as a vocational training school for veterans. The former airstrip was developed as postwar housing in the late 1940s, and, in 1962, the hangar became the Renfrew Boys' Club (now the Renfrew Boys' and Girls' Club).

Route: Cross both 6th Street N.E. and Regal Crescent, or 12th Avenue N.E. as it is called west of 6th Street. Continue west along 12th Avenue, crossing from Renfrew to Crescent Heights at 4th Street N.E. Continue west to 2nd Street N.E., and cross. Turn left (south), and proceed south along 2nd Street to 10th Avenue N.E. Turn right (west) on 10th Avenue, and continue west.

Sharon Evangelical Lutheran Church

Address: 214–10th Avenue N.E.
Style: Gothic Revival (influenced by Art Deco and traditional Danish design)
Architect: Holnne Moller
Date: 1932 (enlarged in the late 1940s)

Both Art Deco and traditional Danish style influenced the design of Sharon Evangelical Lutheran Church. SHANNON LEE RAE

Calgary's Danish Evangelical Lutheran congregation was formed in 1913 and took its name from the biblical Song of Solomon 2:1—"I am the rose of Sharon, and the lily of the valleys", referring to the Sharon Valley near modern Tel Aviv. For a decade, the congregation had no resident pastor, and it had no building before this edifice was constructed in 1930–32. Until then, the Norwegian Lutheran Church (now Trinity Lutheran Church) in Eau Claire provided space to Sharon Lutheran for afternoon services. Stepped parapets are the dominant feature of Sharon Lutheran's stucco façade. The church was built during the Great Depression by unemployed, skilled immigrants, and enlarged in the late 1940s.

Route: Continue west along 10th Avenue N.E., and cross Centre Street, where the N.E. designation becomes N.W. Continue west along 10th Avenue N.W. to 1st Street N.W., and cross 1st Street.

Crescent Heights Senior High School

Address: 1019–1st Street N.W.
Style: Collegiate Gothic
Architect: William Branton
Date: 1929 (later additions)

Crescent Heights was among a group of massive brick schools built by the public school board in the 1920s. The others were Elbow Park, Rideau Park and Western Canada. SHANNON LEE RAE

Crescent Heights Collegiate Institute was established in 1913 as a branch of the city's original public high school, Central Collegiate. Before this three-story brick building was completed in 1929, the branch collegiate institute (renamed Crescent Heights High School around 1918) was housed in other school buildings, including nearby Balmoral from 1915–29. Calgary's sandstone quarries were exhausted by the time this school was built, and Medicine Hat brick proved an affordable alternative. Educator and lay preacher William Aberhart (1878–1943) was principal of Crescent Heights from 1915 until his election as premier of Alberta in 1935. The faculty also included John Laurie (1899–1959), the secretary of the Indian Association of Alberta for whom John Laurie Boulevard is named.

On November 19, 1936, a shrieking wind lifted the roof off the building during school hours, but no one was injured. A series of additions have not compromised the school's stately appearance.

Route: Proceed north on 1st Street N.W. to 13th Avenue N.W.

North Hill Presbyterian Church (Wild Rose United Church)

Address: 1317–1st Street N.W.
Style: Gothic Revival
Architect: Unknown
Date: 1913 (basement), 1930 (superstructure); additions
1952 and 1957

Besides having once had the largest Sunday school enrollment in Calgary (as North Hill United Church), this brick church might be able to boast the largest number of forerunners of any congregation in the city. The first to use this site was North Hill Presbyterian (after 1925 known as North Hill United), which built the existing basement in 1913 and added the superstructure in 1930, the tower and gallery in 1952, and the Education Centre in 1957. Declining enrolment led North Hill United to amalgamate with nearby Crescent Heights United in 1968; the new congregation moved into this building as Rosedale United Church. In 2002, Pleasant Heights United Church—which had roots in two separate Presbyterian congregations—joined Rosedale, and the church was again renamed, as Wild Rose United Church.

Cornerstones on Wild Rose United Church outline its pedigree back to North Hill Presbyterian and Crescent Heights Methodist. Shannon Lee Rae

Route: Cross 13th Avenue N.W.

Duckworth Residence

Address: 1403–1st Street N.W.
Style: Queen Anne
Architect: Unknown
Date: Circa 1914

Although built after the district's annexation to the city, this two-story brick house offers a link to the village of Crescent Heights. Ontario-born real estate agent Norman James Duckworth (circa 1884–1962) moved west in 1907, and, the following year, he was one of three men elected to Crescent Heights' original village council. Duckworth also served on the village school board and was one of the signatories of a 1909 petition seeking annexation to Calgary.

Duckworth built this house for himself and his wife Florence May, and it remained his home until his death. Duckworth's obituary noted that he was the North Hill's longest continuous resident.

The wrap-around verandah on this corner brick house is a typical feature of Queen Anne Revival style. SHANNON LEE RAE

Route: Cross both 1st Street and 13th Avenue N.W., and proceed south along 1st Street to 12th Avenue N.W. Turn left (east) on 12th Avenue, proceed east on 12th Avenue to Centre Street, and cross Centre Street.

Crescent Heights Public Library (Crescent Heights Professional Centre)

Address: 1304 Centre Street N.E.
Style: Moderne
Architect: Unknown
Date: 1939

With its rounded corner and clean white stucco façade, this Moderne building first opened in 1939 as Puckett's Dine and Dance, the ninth in a chain of White Spot restaurants in the city owned by businessman George Puckett and his family. The new café's novelties included a dance hall known as the Rainbow Room and parking space where diners could enjoy tray service in the comfort of their own vehicles. But the short-lived restaurant closed its doors only three years later, just as librarian Sada F. Kitely, who was in charge of the Crescent Heights branch library, was scouting for a new location. The Calgary Public Library's oldest branch was then located in the nearby Hicks Block, where it had opened in 1913. The city paid $7,500 cash for the restaurant building, and it housed the library branch for the next fifty years. The building was converted into a professional centre after the library closed in 1993.

In 1943, lettering on the distinctive round corner sign changed from "White Spot" to "Crescent Heights Public Library", and the Rainbow Room became a reading room. GLENBOW ARCHIVES PA-3487-9

Route: Continue north along Centre Street to 16th Avenue (the Trans-Canada Highway). North of 16th Avenue lies Tuxedo Park, once part of the village of Crescent Heights but later developed as a separate residential district. Cross both Centre Street and 16th Avenue, and proceed west along 16th Avenue.

W. A. Gough Violin Maker & Restorer

Address: 120–16th Avenue N.W.
Style: Converted bungalow with false front
Architect: Unknown
Date: 1912

This small building's false front conceals the pitched roof behind it. SHANNON LEE RAE

Anderson Plumbing, a Calgary firm established in 1912 by Millward Anderson and still owned by his descendants, originated in this small stucco building in 1912. By World War I, the company moved to another Crescent Heights address; the original shop remained vacant for years and then served as a residence in the 1920s and 1930s. Longtime businesses occupants later included Nat's Barber Shop (1941–55), owned by Nathaniel Marbach, followed by a series of barbershops until the 1970s. Since 1986, it had housed a violin sales and repair shop. Ower Al Gough, who made his first violin at the age of six, enjoys a continent-wide reputation as a violin restorer.

Route: Continue west on 16th Avenue, and cross 1st Street N.W.

Crescent Heights Methodist Church (Unitarian Church of Calgary)

Address: 204–16th Avenue N.W.
Style: Half-timbered detailing; no particular style
Architect: Unknown
Date: 1908 (additions 1909, 1923, 1958)

Although located across the street from Crescent Heights proper, this stucco church dates back to the district's days as a separate village and originally lay within its corporate boundaries. SHANNON LEE RAE

This stuccoed, wood-frame church was built in 1908, the same year Crescent Heights was incorporated as a village. It was originally Crescent Heights Methodist Church, which became Crescent Heights United after the 1925 union of Congregational, Methodist and Presbyterian churches in Canada. The congregation amalgamated with nearby North Hill United in 1968, forming Rosedale United Church (later renamed Wild Rose United Church). The old church was sold and became the Unitarian Church of Calgary.

Route: Turn right, and proceed north on 1st Street N.W.

Balmoral School and Balmoral Bungalow School

Address: 220–16th Avenue N.W.

Style: Free Classical (cottage school); Classical (sandstone school)

Architects: Hugh McClelland and William Branton (sandstone building)

Date: 1913 (bungalow school), 1914 (sandstone school)

Balmoral School. SHANNON LEE RAE

The last of Calgary's eighteen sandstone schools was also one of the finest. Balmoral School's full metal cornice, strong central arch, and dramatic clock tower create a monumental effect. The building has inspired two myths: that it was designed by Thomas Mawson, the English landscape architect hired in 1913 to develop a long-range plan for Calgary's future development; and that the clock was never installed in the tower because the mechanism went down on the *Titanic.*

Balmoral School was named for the former subdivision in which it was built, and which was long ago incorporated into the Tuxedo Park district. Balmoral Bungalow School, the wooden structure on the northeast corner of the schoolyard, was finished first. It was one of two such buildings constructed on this property in 1913.

Built for "emergency" educational needs, bungalow schools were intended for eventual sale and conversion into apartment buildings once they had been replaced by more substantial buildings. But the need remained, and bungalow schools like this one continued in use for generations. Its companion has since been demolished.

Like its contemporaries across the city, the wooden Balmoral Bungalow School was designed for temporary use and eventual sale as a residential building. Instead, it has served generations of students. SHANNON LEE RAE

The sandstone school was completed in 1914, and it doubled as Crescent Heights Collegiate (later renamed Crescent Heights High School) from 1915–29. Future premier William Aberhart was principal of Crescent Heights when it was housed here. The empty clock face was originally painted to appear as a clock, and, until it was later painted over, the time was perpetually 12:23.

Route: Continue north on 1st Street S.W.

Hicks Block

Address: 1804–1st Street N.W.
Style: Edwardian Commercial
Architect: Unknown
Date: 1912

This typical two-story Edwardian building, built for Calgary dentist Dr. William A. Hicks, has a place in history as the site of the city's first branch public library. The Crescent Heights Branch opened here in 1913 and remained for three decades before moving into its own building in 1943. It was easily accessible on the Tuxedo Park streetcar line and handy for students at Balmoral School directly across the street. (Balmoral students might appreciate knowing that Harold Potter operated a store and sub-post office in the Hicks Block from 1920–21, decades before novelist J. K. Rowling created her famous boy magician.) Within a year of its opening, the library expanded into a second storefront that became the boys' and girls' department. The building also housed a Methodist Sunday school in 1916. The storefronts were modified in 2003.

The most notable storefront tenant in the Hicks Block was the Crescent Heights Public Library, located here from 1913–43. SHANNON LEE RAE

Tour ends. Should you wish to celebrate with a drink, continue north to 17th Avenue N.W. and cross. Turn right (east), and continue east to the Regal Beagle (108–17th Avenue N.W.), built in 1932 as the home of Calgary Power accountant Fred Buchan and now a licensed pub.

Comment on Sources

Many written sources, both published and non-published, were useful in writing this book. For general history of Calgary, I rely on Max Foran's *Calgary: An Illustrated History* (Toronto: James Lorimer & Company, 1978) and Hugh Dempsey's *Calgary: Spirit of the West* (Calgary: Glenbow and Fifth House Publishers, 1994). Colin K. Hatcher's *Stampede City Streetcars: The Story of the Calgary Municipal Railway* (Montreal: Railfare Enterprises, 1975) is the best source for streetcar development and its impact on the city's growth. The works of Henry C. Klassen provide excellent background on business history. I look to the works of James H. Gray, Grant MacEwan, and Jack Peach for rich story material. The *Century Calgary* series of books, published in 1975 in commemoration of Fort Calgary's centennial, are also a valuable resource. Walking tours published by the city, the province, private individuals, and community organizations cover such areas as Bridgeland-Riverside, Cliff Bungalow-Mission, Connaught-Beltline, Elbow Park, Inglewood, Mount Royal, Rosedale, and Stephen Avenue and district. Themed tours include the Petroleum History Society's unpublished downtown petroleum history tour (2003) and my own *Calgary's Historic Union Cemetery: A Walking Guide* (Calgary: Fifth House Ltd., 2002).

For building materials and construction, see Richard Cunniffe's *Calgary in Sandstone* (Calgary: Historical Society of Alberta, Calgary Branch, 1969) and Jack M. Manson's *Bricks in Alberta* (Edmonton: John M. Manson, 1983). Cunniffe traces the city's sandstone industry back to 1886, when Wesley Fletcher Orr and Joseph Butlin opened their quarries; Manson outlines the history of the brick industry in the province, beginning in Calgary in 1886 with the establishment of Peel's brickyard in what is now the Roxboro district. "Sandstone City," a 1987 poster published by the City of Calgary Heritage Advisory Board, features a map with the locations of fifteen quarries, and it links select historic buildings to the quarries where their stone originated. For building types and styles, as well as historical architectural context, see Donald G. Wetherell and Irene R. A. Kmet,

Homes in Alberta: Building, Trends and Design, 1870–1967 (Edmonton: University of Alberta Press, Alberta Culture and Multiculturalism, Alberta Municipal Affairs, 1991); Leslie Maitland et al, *A Guide to Canadian Architectural Styles* (Peterborough, Ont.: Broadview Press, 1992); and Virginia McAlester, *A Field Guide to American Houses* (New York: Knopf, 1984).

There are many good sources about Calgary buildings, of which the following are only a few examples: Bryan Melnyk's *Calgary Builds: The Emergence of an Urban Landscape, 1905–1914* (Edmonton: Alberta Culture/Canadian Plains Research Center, 1985); Gregory P. Utas' 1975 Master of Environmental Design thesis, *Calgary Architecture, 1875–1915* (Calgary: University of Calgary, 1975); Janice Dicken McGinnis and Frank Donnelly's *Reports on Selected Buildings in Calgary, Alberta* (Ottawa: Parks Canada, 1976); *Calgary: A Decade of Heritage* (Calgary: Calgary: Heritage Advisory Board and the Planning and Building Dept. of the City of Calgary, 1988); L. M. Bragagnolo's "The Apartment in Calgary's Architectural Landscape, 1908-1930" (unpublished term paper prepared for Dr. M. McMordie, University of Calgary, 1993); and, for a later period, Trevor Boddy, *Modern Architecture in Alberta* (Regina: Alberta Culture and Multiculturalism and the Canadian Plains Research Center, 1987), Geoffrey Simmins, editor, *Calgary Modern, 1947–1967* (Calgary: Nickle Arts Museum, 2000), Pierre Serge Guimond and Brian R. Sinclair, *Calgary Architecture: The Boom Years 1972–1982* (Calgary: Detselig Enterprises, 1984). and Robert M. Stamp, *Suburban Modern: Postwar Dreams in Calgary* (Calgary: TouchWood Editions, 2004). Donald B. Smith's *Calgary's Grand Story*, forthcoming from the University of Calgary Press, takes the novel approach of interpreting the history of the city through the prism of a single building complex, the Lougheed Building/Grand Theatre. The City of Calgary's Inventory of Potential Heritage Sites includes vast files and numerous reports and studies documenting individual buildings throughout the city. There are also many published and unpublished histories of specific Calgary buildings, including schools and churches. For architects and their commissions, see Lorne G. Simpson and Marianne Fedori, *The Practice of Architecture and Construction in Calgary 1900–1940* (Calgary, 1995). Foran's *Calgary: An Illustrated History* and Donald B. Smith's *Centennial City: Calgary 1894–1994* (Calgary: University of Calgary, 1994) contain excellent bibliographies on Calgary, and the Glenbow and Calgary Public Library catalogues are available online. *This Old Calgary House: Resources for Researching the History of Your House*, a bibliography published by the Calgary Public Library in 2004, is also a useful resource.

Primary research:
Be your own History Detective

If you liked this book, and would like to do something similar about buildings or homes that interest you, all it takes is a willingness to do some research and a lot of persistence. *A Guide to Researching Building History* (Calgary: City of Calgary Archives and the Heritage Advisory Board, 2000) provides a useful methodology for reconstructing the history of an existing or demolished building. (This publication, as well as others relating to heritage and historic tours, can be downloaded from the "Heritage Planning" section on the city's official website.) Starting with a building's address, it is possible to create an historical profile of occupants from the annual *Henderson's Directory.* Voters' lists and telephone books are useful in verifying occupancy dates. *Henderson's* also lists people's occupations or businesses, and this valuable information can be used in further researching the personalities involved. Some individuals will have biographical clipping files at the Glenbow and Calgary Public libraries. In other cases, establishing a date of death (using cemetery records or online resources) can help in searching for obituary notices in microfilms of old newspapers. Obituaries often contain a capsule history of a person's life and could lead the researcher to living relatives who might have stories and photographs they are willing to share.

Records at the City Archives include building permit registers, tax rolls, and assessment history cards, and these can indicate date of construction or modification, ownership history, and even the name of the building contractor. Historic land title searches, a fee-based service, are available through the Southern Alberta Land Titles office and also yield names and dates for past owners of property.

Sadly, most of the City of Calgary's comprehensive set of architectural drawings, collected through the building permit process, was discarded in the late 1950s. A search for such documents is often a case of hit or miss. Those that exist can be found at the Canadian Architectural Archives, the Glenbow Archives, and the City Archives.

Similarly, not all buildings have historical photographs, but the Glenbow, Calgary Public Library and City Archives have extensive collections. More than 80,000 images are searchable online on the Glenbow's database (www.glenbow.org/lasearch/searmenu.htm). Fire insurance maps illustrate the footprint, or outline plan, of a building at a given date, and indicate the construction materials and number of floors. Each map usually covers several city blocks, offering an "at a glance" visual impression of entire streetscapes.

Journalists often declare their work to be the first draft of history, and examination of historic newspapers confirms this assessment. Then as now, reporters wrote to deadline without always having all the facts, and they often had their own biases or agendas. It sometimes takes more than a few grains of salt to digest a microfilm reel of the *Albertan*, the *Calgary Daily Herald*, or the *Calgary News-Telegram*. Still, newspapers are a crucial source for local history, offering perspectives and documentation that exist nowhere else. Unfortunately, none of these journals is indexed, but extensive clipping files at the Glenbow and the Calgary Public Library offer a good level of access.